What if you had a set of tools to help young people grow
and develop into resourceful, productive adults?

What would it look like if you were able to build high quality
connections at home, school or on the athletic field?

This book will show you how to make it all happen!

An Invitation, A Belief and A Promise...

When we change ourselves, we change how people see us and respond to us.
When we change ourselves, we change the world.
—Robert Quinn, *Building the Bridge As You Walk on It*

We believe that young people develop through the positive attention of parents, teachers and athletic coaches, to name a few. We believe that when adult mentors intentionally form strengths-based partnerships on behalf of the young people they serve that this provides a foundation for increased resilience, achievement, and well-being.

We invite you to discover (and rediscover) what's best about yourself and others through a lens that focuses on your strengths, your ability to be resilient, and your capacity to develop the power of high quality relationships.

We promise to provide you with practical research-based information, strategies, and activities that can benefit you and the young people you serve.

Praise for *SMART STRENGTHS*

SMART Strengths is a wonderful addition to the growing pantheon of works documenting the wisdom of the strengths-based approach in schools and the positive psychology upon which it is based. With both apt and often moving school-based illustrations and also tools to learn how to spot and build a student's strengths, the authors reveal that through healthy relationships with the key adults in their lives, students flourish with "growth mindsets" as opposed to stumbling because of preoccupation with deficiencies. A "must read" for all the important players (parents, teachers, coaches) in a student's life.

—PATRICK F. BASSETT, President, National Association of Independent Schools

I am excited about the possibilities *SMART Strengths* offers to the training of parents and educators. It represents a pathway to understanding dimensions of growth we have neglected for a long time. Strengths-based development is not merely a technical issue, but is at the very heart of the challenge of human development. *SMART Strengths* is practical in the best sense of that word. I plan on placing it directly into the hands of teachers, future and current school leaders, and above all, parents. I highly recommend this text to anyone interested in personal development, and especially for those who are charged with fostering and facilitating growth in others.

—TOM WARD, Director, Principal Leadership Academy of Nashville,
Vanderbilt University Peabody College of Education

SMART Strengths will change a long standing belief among coaches, parents, teachers and supervisors that one must identify an individual's weaknesses in an effort to help improve their performance. *SMART Strengths* provides a plan and roadmap for improving oneself first so we in turn may improve others. Identifying and reinforcing one's talents and strengths is the most effective way to improve the outcomes for children, students, athletes and employees. *SMART Strengths* can apply to any individual whose responsibility is to help others improve.

—TIM FLANNERY, National Federation of High Schools (NFHS) Assistant Director

This is an important book. I learned a lot from the powerful stories and practical methods for building on kids' strengths rather than pecking at their weaknesses. It can help any leader—whether on the playing field, the classroom, the home or the workplace—become a better developer of young people.

—JIM THOMPSON, Founder and Executive Director, Positive Coaching Alliance

Since graduating with the inaugural class of the Master of Applied Positive Psychology (MAPP) program at the University of Pennsylvania in 2006, the authors of *SMART Strengths* have been at the forefront of the application of positive psychology to education. Among their accomplishments is the transformation of Culver Academies into a strengths-based organization. This is the amazing story of their work, told so that others can follow in their footsteps. A must read for teachers, principals, superintendents, school board members, coaches, parents—anyone who believes that cultivating strengths and resilience is an important part of education.

—JAMES O. PAWELSKI, Director of Education and Senior Scholar
in the Positive Psychology Center at the University of Pennsylvania;
Executive Director of the International Positive Psychology Association

SMART Strengths provides powerful insight on the value and importance of building positive relationships by identifying and nurturing personal strengths. This book should be required reading for teachers and coaches committed to best positioning young people for success in the classroom and on the athletic field. The authors also provide parents with a dynamic and interactive experience that challenges more traditional motivational theory and offers greater perspective on the values and qualities they should demand from the children's teachers and coaches... and themselves.

—STEVE STENERSEN, President & CEO, US Lacrosse

John Yeager, Sherri Fisher, and David Shearon are to be commended for writing a truly informative, impressive book. They have skillfully synthesized a large body of research about a strength-based approach for nurturing responsibility, caring, and resilience in our youth. In a clearly written style they offer practical, realistic exercises and strategies that can be applied by educators, parents, coaches, and others who work with children and adolescents. I am certain that this book will serve as an invaluable resource to be read and re-read by any of us who have the privilege of influencing the life of children and adolescents. I recommend it highly.

—ROBERT BROOKS, Ph.D. Psychologist on the faculty of Harvard Medical School
and co-author, *Raising Resilient Children* and co-author, *The Power of Resilience: Achieving Balance, Confidence and Personal Strength in Your Life*

This book will immediately crystallize the importance of parents, teachers and coaches joining forces for the betterment of the young people they serve. *SMART Strengths* is a must read for adults who want practical strategies to help youth flourish. I highly recommend it!

—DAVID J. POLLAY, author, *The Law of the Garbage Truck: How to Respond to People Who Dump on You, and How to Stop Dumping on Others*. Ocean Ridge, Florida

By coupling years of rigorous research from the field of positive psychology with real-life stories from teachers, coaches and parents; John Yeager, Sherri Fisher and Dave Shearon offer us a practical handbook for building character strengths in ourselves and our youth. *SMART Strengths* teaches us first and foremost, that in order to become more effective teachers, coaches or parents, before we can develop the character strengths of our children, we must first apply the SMART model to our own lives. —DAN HAESLER, Teacher, Emanuel School, Sydney, Australia

SMART Strengths is an all-important step for bringing the essential truths of positive psychology into schools. Yeager, Fisher, and Shearon outline the conceptual basis for their work and then, more importantly, offer concrete, real life examples of how we can change young people's lives in significant ways. I hope this work will be followed by many others like it.

—DAVID STREIGHT, Executive Director, Center for Spiritual and Ethical Education

SMART Strengths provides a foundation for helping our teachers play to their strengths at Christel House Academy, Indianapolis. This affords them to bring out the best in our underserved student population, by helping students leverage their own strengths to become more self-sufficient, and self-confident contributing members of society. —CHRISTEL DEHAAN, President and Founder, Christel House International

As I read I was consistently impressed by the rigor and practical application of the learning we've had about strengths and positive psychology to the growth of kids to their full potential. We often take for granted that parenting, teaching or coaching kids is nurturing in itself. What I learned, and what warmed my heart, was to understand that there is a breakthrough level of nurture that can be reached by applying the *SMART Strengths* approach to how we parent, teach and coach. I'm convinced that applying the lessons from *SMART Strengths* to how we do our work will yield improved results and more positive, confident, happier people across the board. —DUKE GILLINGHAM, Culver Parent, Dayton, Ohio

SMART Strengths is a treasure chest of stories, research, and replicable strategies that can be used to empower your family and school community. Parents, students and teachers learn to develop high-quality connections and collaborative methods to bring out the best in one another, all leading to a whole that is greater than a sum of its parts. —ELIZABETH SMITH, Parent, Needham, MA

Wonderful stories and examples!
　　　·　　—NELL NODDINGS, Lee Jacks Professor of Education, Emerita, Stanford University

"An important book." *SMART Strengths* is an inventory of new ideas on how we as parents and teachers can help our children develop a strengths language which will assist them with navigating the challenges they face. Taking the focus away from what is wrong with an individual is the first step. After reading this book I am convinced it is a must read for parents and educators. It was tremendously informative and helpful.　　　　　　　　—UNA JACKMAN– Parent, Detroit Country Day School

SMART STRENGTHS

SMART STRENGTHS

A Parent-Teacher-Coach Guide to

Building Character, Resilience, and Relationships in Youth

John M. Yeager, Ed.D, MAPP
Sherri W. Fisher, M.Ed., MAPP
David N. Shearon, JD, MAPP

Kravis Publishing
Putnam Valley, New York

Published by Kravis Publishing
Division of The Whitson Group, Inc.
3 Miller Road, Putnam Valley, NY 10579
www.whitsongroup.com

Wishing, Willing, and Hope photographs on page 231 by Liisa Ogburn

Author John Yeager photograph on back cover by Gary Mills

Author Sherri Fisher photograph on back cover by Margaret Fisher

All excerpts from Character and Coaching, and The Character and Culture of Lacrosse on pages 119, 122, 125, 126, 128-135, 138, 139, 219, 229, 243, 244 with permission from Dude/National Professional Resources, Inc., 25 South Regent Street, Port Chester, NY 10573

The Pot-Shots cartoons on pages 33, 43, 70, 75, 77, 186, 212, 222 and 253 copyright Ashleigh Brilliant, www.ashleighbrilliant.com

Manufactured in the United States of America

First Edition

ISBN: 978-0-9834306-0-5

1 2 3 4 5 6 7 8 9 10 — 17 16 15 14 13 12 11

In memory of Reed Ollett, whose life inspired my passion to focus on strengths, and in appreciation of Nancy Robinson Grew, my third grade teacher and my first positive educator. —J.Y.

To my many students and their families who inspired me to learn more about strengths, resilience and relationships, and to Marty Seligman for making that opportunity possible through MAPP. —S.F.

Thanks to all the faithfully-serving school board members across the country who know that higher achievement must be accompanied by greater well-being, for students, teachers, administrators, and parents. —D.S.

Table of Contents

Foreword

In September 2005, a small group of adults ranging from newly-minted college graduates to international business whizzes gathered at the University of Pennsylvania for the first session of the Master of Applied Positive Psychology program. Because there were no precedents for how to use this unique degree in any profession, the class was composed of pioneering men and women who would be among the first to apply this education to their respective fields, thus creating a unique approach that might have the potential to alter their career and those of others.

Among this dynamic group was John Yeager, a focused and athletic man who was on a mission from the Culver Academies to come back with some new tools to help develop the character of the students and enhance their learning; Sherri Fisher, an education management consultant and coach energized by applying positive psychology science to her years of experience creating success strategies for students, families and schools; and Dave Shearon, executive director of continuing legal education for the state of Tennessee and a former school board member who was determined to help school boards and other education policy leaders find more positive, productive directions.

As the year unfolded, these three bonded personally and professionally while creating an extensive blueprint for injecting a strengths-based approach into K-12 schools. Beginning with faculty at Culver who voluntarily shortened their summer vacation to take part in the pilot of what became the SMART Strengths model, Yeager, Fisher and Shearon have refined their approach and helped other schools and school systems adopt a positive, strengths-based language and culture of learning.

In this book, the trio has laid out an easy to follow guide for impacting students, coaches, parents, and teachers to:

- Start with a personal understanding of their own strengths
- Show teachers, coaches, and parents how to create climates of acceptance, resilience and curiosity that accelerate growth and change
- Identify ways to collaborate with others so that strengths can complement each other

- Set goals more effectively
- Create optimism about one's future self
- Develop and refine an approach to life that is appreciative, gritty, and proactive

This book is the new gold standard in the field of positive education. It demonstrates how to change a school system, one person at a time, so that it's not just about bringing positive education to students; it's also about maximizing the strengths of the adults who interact with them in every environment that fosters character. This unique program has already been successfully tested in a number of independent and public schools, so this book is sprinkled with the personal stories of those who have worked with John, Sherri, and Dave and benefitted from their thoughtful reworking of traditional teaching methods.

This book is a must-have resource not only because it carefully lays out the genesis of Positive Education, but also because it is a step-by-step guide to cultivating buy-in at any school and patiently nurturing the change, one person at a time, until the environment has become contagiously positive. The back of the book has resources, checklists, and worksheets that address every aspect of positive education and how to make it happen in your own family and community.

One of the blessings of graduating from the first MAPP class is that we have already seen the fruits of our work while blazing new paths for others to follow. But it is also bittersweet because there are so many things we might have done differently had the knowledge about character strengths, resilience, positivity, and savoring been available earlier in our lives. I experienced those pangs as I read this book and thought about the countless missed opportunities for positive education in my own children's lives. What if they had gotten a strengths assessment instead of just educational test results? And what if every coach they've ever worked with, starting at early ages, had used green light responding or optimistic explanatory tools to help them reframe a negative mood?

I hope that everyone who has a child or works with a child, reads this book and studies it for the important takeaways on every page. If you apply this knowledge in your own life, you will undoubtedly impact those around you, and if you intentionally share it with others in a systematic way, you will be part of the positive education revolution that John, Sherri, and Dave have initiated.

With all positive thoughts of success,
CAROLINE ADAMS MILLER, MAPP

Introduction

You cannot be anything you want to be—
but you can be a LOT more of who you already are.

—Tom Rath, *StrengthsFinder 2.0*

"You can be just like me," entices the professional athlete or astrophysicist invited to speak at the school. No, you can't. You can't be anything you want to be. That's one of the great myths in education. But when you know and live from your strengths, the things you are good at, you can improve the way you do almost everything—including the way you learn, teach, parent, and coach. Two compelling examples come to mind.

During his first years of teaching, Ed Kelley, a 10th grade humanities teacher and athletic coach at the Culver Academies, an independent school in Indiana, was sure that a hard-as-nails approach was the way to motivate and develop adolescents. He was certain that if he wanted students and athletes to work hard and respond to him, he had to light a fire under them. Over time, he realized that this style didn't really work well for him or his students. Ed learned that by tapping into his own and his students' strengths, everyone could win by being more engaged and productive. In the classroom as well, Ed has created an environment that allows students to play to their strengths when sharing their perspectives on literature and history. His classroom functions as a team that helps each student learn and grow. They learn just as much from each other's viewpoints as they learn directly from him. Similarly, on the football field and basketball court, Ed's engaging and empathic style provides his players with a sense of confidence to be the best they can be individually, and collectively this means better teamwork for all.

Halfway across the United States in Boston, Lauren Wilson, a parent of two children, originally believed her role as a parent was to protect her kids from their innate weaknesses so that they could be competitive among their classmates. She was unwittingly aligned with negative messages that she perceived she was getting from school, such as getting her kids to "measure up." These concerns combined with rising expectations for higher grades and test scores, long-term achievement, while expecting healthy attitudes and behaviors, created anxiety at school and at home. By focusing on her strengths and the strengths of the teachers at school, Lauren has developed realistic optimism that has become contagious with her children. They now have a common language to talk with Lauren about their strengths, and they use these for improved achievement, development of positive habits and choices, and building high quality relationships. Recently her son, who was a below average student when he began high school, graduated among the top ten students in his class and will be attending a very selective college.

Although Lauren and Ed live in different parts of the country, they have a lot in common. They realize that creating healthy partnerships—developed on building strengths, resilience, and relationships—can help young people improve academic achievement, overall well-being, and satisfaction and enjoyment at home and at school.

Through Lauren and Ed's experiences and the stories of many others, we have witnessed first-hand how playing to strengths, developing the ability to bounce back by using resilience skills, and cultivating healthy relationships can help students build successful lives. Our fascination with this different way of educating parents, teachers, and students ultimately led to our crossing paths.

Building Strengths: John's Story

When I was in third grade, my teacher Miss Robinson greeted us daily at the classroom doorway. She always had something nice to say to each one of us and she always tried to bring out the best in us. I remember the time she was out sick for a day, and my concern that life would never be the same if she didn't come back. Miss Robinson's classroom was a comfortable place, and she was a welcome change from my first and second grade teachers. My first grade teacher wouldn't let me use the bathroom one day, because I didn't have to go when the rest of the class had gone. Well, I showed her! Unfortunately, the shame of a yellow puddle under my desk wasn't the way I wanted it to go. Being called a "doormat" by my second grade teacher didn't help me, either. Fortunately, Miss Robinson changed the cycle for me. She treated me as if I were on top of the world. She played to my strengths and didn't ruminate about my weaknesses. She was demanding at times and held us accountable, but was always fair. It is quite interesting that I remember so much that happened over 46 years ago. Miss Robinson's actions became my mantra and helped inspire me to become a teacher, a calling that I have embraced for the past thirty-four years.

After many years of teaching at the secondary school and university level in the Boston area, my family and I picked up roots in 2000 and left for Culver Academies, an independent, Grades 9-12 boarding school in north central Indiana. Several years into my position as the school's Director of Character Excellence, one of my students was killed in an automobile accident. I was devastated. Reed was loved by all who knew him in our school community. He was a Renaissance man of many talents, and parents, teachers, girls and boys alike were attracted to his charisma.

Reed's parents asked me to say a few words at his memorial service. As I anxiously prepared my remarks, I referred to the strengths activities we had done in class and found it easy to expound on his kindness and generosity, playfulness and humor, and his appreciation of beauty and excellence. As a further testimonial to this exceptional young man—and to help the students in my class heal—we created a booklet reflecting on Reed's strengths. Each member of the class chose a strength that they believed really showed in Reed. We presented the booklet to his parents at the end of the term. It was quite an amazing experience.

Reed's passing nudged me to take very seriously the power of strengths within all of us. I began to read everything I could about strengths, resilience, and relationships and how they influence behavior. In the spring of 2005, I was fortunate enough to be admitted to the inaugural class of the Master of Applied Positive Psychology at the University of Pennsylvania, the first program of its kind in the world, where I had the opportunity to learn from the top scholars in Positive Psychology. It was also there that I met and began collaborating with Sherri Fisher and Dave Shearon who were also on the strengths, resilience, and relationships journey.

Building Relationships: Sherri's Story

My entrée to the Positive Psychology program also came from an epiphany. I awoke one morning to the troubling realization that I did not want to go to work at the school where I had been a private-pay educational consultant for six years. It wasn't one of those "maybe-I-need-a mental-health-day" feelings. My work frustration increased as some children I serviced continued to struggle in this particular school despite significant and increasing help. My professional recommendation was to begin searching for more appropriate educational placements that would be a better fit with the students' strengths. Parents were intrigued with this approach. But the school's suggestion was that the children were depressed, and that they and their families needed therapy. I realized that one unintended and unfortunate result of the deficit model approach was that because the students had been labeled with emotional and learning problems, some of the teachers understood the children or the families as the problem and, as a result, made even fewer classroom accommodations.

After seeking out a career coach, I made lists of dream careers and explored a vision and purpose for my professional life. As a result of this coaching program, I found, among other things, that I had driving needs to learn, counsel, problem solve, and teach. Since I had done those things in over twenty years of work, this information came as an affirmation, a surprise, and quite honestly, somewhat of a disappointment. I did not understand how I could be so unhappy at work if I was in the right field!

Working with a coach myself was completely unlike anything I had experienced in any other sort of counseling or professional development. It was forward-looking and focused on identifying what I was consistently and naturally good at—teaching and coaching. It did not ignore the shadow side of my strengths, but instead looked at how weaknesses might in fact be strengths if used in a different way or in a different system. Discovering that there was an actual field of study called Positive Psychology was the key to reframing my "old-as-new" career as a learning specialist.

As a coach and consultant who blends research-based approaches from Positive Psychology with many other skills, I now had work that was more than a vocation to me and I believed that I had found a deep well of gladness within myself. I also knew a group of people with a great need—educational leaders, including administrators, teacher-leaders, parents, students, and communities, who also needed the paradigm shift that focuses on strengths and the positive, on the value of people, and on guiding all members of learning communities toward developing what is already wonderful about them.

My coaching and consulting experiences, combined with Dave's work with school administrators, prompted our UPenn capstone work: researching a large school district to begin developing a foundation of research for Positive Psychology in education.

Building Resilience: Dave's Story

My interest in the Positive Psychology program originally came from the work I had done in twenty-five years in law and education, including winning a seat on the Nashville, Tennessee public school board. Serving 70,000 students in 137 schools,

I was very interested in teaching pedagogy in school organizations and how to get improved performance. I also came to realize that healthy relationships were a key to teacher satisfaction and subsequent student success in the classroom. I continued to read and study education and assessment policy, leadership issues, and in these readings kept coming up with references to Martin Seligman's book *Learned Optimism*. I was captivated by the topic of explanatory styles—how people either positively or negatively respond to challenging events.

It was, however, through an experience with one of my sons that the light went on for me. Tyler played baseball for 14 years, and I worked with him on some of the mental aspects of the game. I was intrigued by how some players dealt with adversity on the playing field. They could strike out or make an error and be able to come back and perform well in the next inning or next game. When Tyler was 12, he was playing in the field, and the ball was hit to him and bounced off his glove, giving him an error, and the hitter was now on base. After the game, I asked him, "What about that ball in the fourth inning?" Tyler's response was that the ball had taken a "bad hop." I wondered, did he really see it that way or was he not taking responsibility for his mistake? My attorney training clicked in, and I wasn't satisfied and continued my line of questioning. "Now, Tyler. You just missed that ball, didn't you?" My son once again responded, "It took a bad hop." On the third time that I started my question with, "Now, Tyler," he literally turned around and walked away from me. In one of my better parenting moments, I let him go.

Even at that moment, I was starting to recognize that though I thought my son wasn't taking responsibility for an error, that thinking didn't match with his demonstrated willingness to step up and his ability to bounce back. Some time later, I read Seligman's *Learned Optimism* and suddenly understood my older son. He's an optimist with a natural and strong positive explanatory style. That was a powerful epiphany for me, especially when I realized I was a pessimist. I began to understand a thinking process that is a fundamental component of Positive Psychology.

Positive Psychology in Education

Over the past two decades, a number of brilliant, dedicated researchers have turned their attention to our inner universe, and especially to the patterns of thinking, feeling, and relating that create human success. These researchers in the field now known as Positive Psychology have discovered some of the fundamental processes that enable human success, and they have further developed ways to help each of us better understand and adopt these patterns of thinking, feeling, and relating.

Schools today face unprecedented challenges. More of the same, even done more efficiently and effectively, will not meet the challenge. Schools are called to create human success at levels never before achieved. To meet this high and noble challenge, they will need the assistance of what Positive Psychology has discovered about strengths, resilience, and relationships.

Positive Education is the incorporation of the science of Positive Psychology into the life and work of schools. While it may sound daunting to educators to hear of something else that schools should be doing, further investigation suggests that Positive Education first benefits teachers personally and then benefits them again by making it easier to get students to engage with and persist in the work they need to master academic material. Finally, Positive Education inevitably works to create a school culture that supports the caring, trusting relationships that distinguish excellent schools from their poor and mediocre peers. This can help decrease the influence of stereotypically negative educators or *keepers of the nightmare*, a term coined by Terrence Deal, co-author of *Shaping School Culture*.

Educators and educational leaders hold the same sacred mission that teachers and wise elders have always held: to assist the next generation as they seek to learn the knowledge and skills they will need to achieve acceptance, respect, and success in shaping a good life in the world in which they live. To achieve these goals, today's students will need intellectual resources superior to those of any generation that has ever lived. However, intellectual resources will not be enough; they will also need substantial resources of optimism, collaboration, creativity, emotional intelligence, motivation, and relational skills.

Strengths and Positive Education

We need a psychology of rising to the occasion,
because that is the missing piece in the jigsaw
puzzle of predicting human behavior.
—Martin Seligman

Led by the pioneering research of psychologist Martin Seligman, from the University of Pennsylvania, many scholars have turned their attention to looking at patterns of thinking, feeling, and relating that facilitate human success. Seligman originally studied depression, and he came to believe that psychology was what he called "half-baked," with its focus on fixing people instead of looking at strengths as well as deficiencies. Seligman and other researchers discovered some of the fundamental processes that enable human success, and they have further developed ways to help each of us better understand and adopt these patterns of thinking, feeling, and relating.

Positive Education isn't a "head in the sand" approach, where parents, teachers, coaches and students go around with big smiles on their faces and face each day with unrealistic optimism. Positive Education is about identifying, developing, and using one's strengths to offer the first pathway toward greater engagement, greater achievement, and greater well-being. Just naming the strengths of a parent, teacher or student can be an uplifting experience, and focusing on strengths helps colleagues of many years find new ways to relate to each other in positive, productive ways.

Our Work

After completing the University of Pennsylvania Master of Applied Positive Psychology program, the three of us began to test out the waters of building strengths, resilience, and relationships in schools. Sherri and Dave made repeated trips to Culver to work with John. Over a four-year span, we trained a majority of the teachers in the school and implemented a systems approach to encompass the whole school community. This strengths-based approach integrates academic, wellness, athletic, fine arts, and leadership programs.

From our work at Culver, we started replicating aspects of the model at different schools throughout the country. We have now seen how this process works in rural and urban schools where there are depleted resources and challenging socioeconomic issues. This provided us with the motivation to write *SMART Strengths*. We have written *SMART Strengths* to help you replicate our success in your school, family, and athletic team.

How to Use This Book

As with many books, this book makes most sense when read beginning to end. But we recognize that not everyone reads a book in that way. In case you want to skip to parts that most interest you, here is more information on how we've structured the book. *SMART Strengths* is divided into two parts.

Part One: Building Strengths. In this section of the book we show how parents, teachers, and athletic coaches can identify and activate their own strengths to help young people capitalize on their assets in school. We share how strengths offer the first pathway to greater engagement, achievement, and well-being.

Part One uses the acronym S-M-A-R-T to structure the learning format. These five steps will be introduced in sequence, and as you become more comfortable with the model you'll find it possible and even desirable to think of S-M-A-R-T like a cycle where you may enter or exit at any stage.

S-M-A-R-T Model

Spotting	When you know your own strengths, you are a better observer of strengths in others and are more attentive to spotting what is good instead of trying to find fault.
Managing	Your strengths are a family of traits that can be combined, tapped and promoted for bringing out the best in you and others.
Advocating	Learning to advocate with your strengths will help you build a bridge from yourself out to others. When you put your learning into your own words and actions, you can effectively convey both your strengths and your needs.
Relating	Good relationships are about using strengths while connecting with and appealing to others. Sometimes strength buttons get pushed when other people's strengths are in conflict with your own.
Training	Once you have tools, approaches, exercises and techniques to use in helping you spot, manage, advocate and relate your strengths individually and in relationships, you will want to use them to develop these skills in others.

Part Two: Building Resilience and Relationships. This section shows how resilience is more than just the ability to bounce back from adversity; it is also the capacity to bounce forward in the presence of opportunity. We focus on developing clear-eyed, positive mindsets, and springy resilience in parents, teachers, coaches, and young people. Also, we bridge the connection between strengths, resilience, and relationships. We provide tools to develop healthy relationships for mobilizing and building the high quality interpersonal connections among adults and students that support engagement and accomplishment.

Chapter Structure

Each chapter includes stories, research, and practical exercises intended to help you see parenting, teaching, and coaching though a different lens—one that promotes strengths, resilience, and relationships—so our children can live flourishing lives. Here are some tips on how to interact with each chapter feature:

- **Stories.** Read each parent, teacher, coach and student story closely to see how you identify with it. We have changed some of the names in the stories. We also vary gender descriptions when there is no name provided. Can you predict what can change as you become better at identifying and using your own and others' strengths?

- **Practical strategies.** To make the most of your S-M-A-R-T learning, we have included opportunities for you to deepen your understanding of your own strengths, resilient thinking and behavior, and your relationships with others.

- **Research.** Many strategies and tools are connected to Positive Psychology research. Looking for research-supported approaches? You will be able to find the original studies by using our detailed references in the notes pages at the end of the book. Also there are research-tested and applied activities throughout the book and in Appendix B.

- **Mindful Moments.** You can record what you learn in each chapter by jotting your in-the-moment thinking in a guided mini-journal format. Research shows that this thinking is often changed or lost even over a small period of time, so we'll help you keep track of your "Aha" moments in the *Mindful Moments* Journal. Within each section of the book, there are numerous activities that accompany the reading. In the *Mindful Moments* Journal you'll document discoveries and reflect on what you have learned so far as you move along your journey parenting, teaching and coaching. The information you have been learning all of your life makes it possible to make connections among old and new learning. By the time you have finished reading the book, you will have written a personal strengths-focused guide.

- **Positive Education at Culver — A Case Study.** We will provide you with the various initiatives that we have developed at Culver. We will show you the nuances of establishing a strengths-based school community.

- **Student Activity Guide.** Towards the end of the book, there will be a compilation of Positive Psychology applications and scripted activities that you can apply for the young people you connect to at home, in the classroom, or on the athletic field.

- **Resource Directory.** A list of resources and references helps you to choose follow up reading, explore additional topics in Positive Psychology and education, and connects you to groups employing strengths approaches in schools.

Seeking Something Better

Despite book or workshop titles that make change look easy, there are no simple "just add water" methods to help build strengths, resilience, and relationships. Learning is a process, a journey, and, once achieved, a confirmation. Nel Noddings, a noted scholar on relational ethics and caring in education, explains that confirmation happens when "we help steer a person to his or her better self, and that person says, 'Here is someone who sees something better in me.'" This is a powerful motivator for young people.

When parents, teachers, and coaches provide students with ways of identifying their own strengths and how and when these strengths come alive, adults offer youth the opportunity to see the best in themselves and others. One parent who is also a teacher we work with says it this way: "Regarding character strengths, I feel like I no longer have to apologize for being too nice and too happy. I now feel like I have ownership of my strengths." A workshop participant remarked, "I now think differently about how I teach." We hope that *SMART Strengths* confirms the best in you and in the youth you serve!

JOHN YEAGER
SHERRI FISHER
DAVE SHEARON

PART ONE

Building Strengths

Chapter One

Developing a Common Language

*Being able to put a name to what one does well is intriguing
and even empowering.*
—Nansook Park and Chris Peterson

Over our many years of work with schools and families, we have seen amazing transformations in adults and youth who have shifted from concentrating on improving weaknesses to focusing on assets. Importantly, we have found that parents, teachers, and coaches who know and understand more about themselves and about what they do well—knowing and using their strengths—have completed the first step in making strengths come alive for young people, too.

So to be really conversant with their students' strengths, parents, teachers, and coaches need to do strengths work in their own lives. Only when parents, teachers, and coaches have spent time in their new "strengths shoes" are they most fit and ready to appeal to young people's strengths. Another way of thinking about this is there is no, "Do as I say, not as I do" in developing and applying strengths at home, in school, or on the athletic field. We all do the work and we all benefit!

What Are Strengths?

A strength is a natural ability or asset. It may seem to go without saying, but there are no bad strengths. By definition, they are all good. Strengths are a family of individual differences: distinct characteristics that people possess to varying degrees. They are shown in thoughts, feelings, and actions, and are malleable (some more than others, as we'll see), measurable (there are psychometrically validated tests for both children and adults), and they are subject to numerous influences, both proximal (within and close to you) and distal (outside and far from you). As a result, you can build—and build on—strengths.

Throughout this book, we will be referring to strengths in different ways and showing you through Positive Psychology research and your own action research how strengths are active in your life and the lives of the students for whom you are responsible.

Know Your Strengths

Many parents, educators and coaches are very good at teaching young people what their deficiencies are—both intentionally and unintentionally. For example, a teacher or parent might convey that unless you have an A+, you are deficient to some extent. If you do not win the game, you are a loser, no matter how well you may have played. However, as adult mentors, if we can discover talents that are already within us, we are more prepared to help young people realize their assets and add them to their tool kit of life skills. This measures us against ourselves and, as long as we are using our strengths powers for good, we are more than our performances. We are not suggesting that adults ignore weaknesses, but if you want to build strengths, that needs to happen on a strengths foundation. Consider what Tom Rath, the author of *StrengthsFinder 2.0*, and his colleagues at the Gallup Organization have found in research with adults: "The most successful people start with a dominant talent—then add skills, knowledge and practice to the mix. When they do this, the raw talent serves as a multiplier. Talent multiplied by Investment equals Strength."

Why Strengths for Parents, Teachers, and Coaches?

Many parents, teachers, and coaches of Pre-K–12th grade children in our nation's schools have much in common. They value success, achievement, and cooperation but may struggle with how to bring out the best in themselves and youth. It is easy to teach the way we were taught, despite research that shows the need to teach in ways that further engage students, causes them to persist through difficulties, and works to create active knowledge that's available to tap and apply in new, non-classroom situations.

Parents

Most parents want to develop and hone their skills in order to raise successful children. When parents know and practice their strengths they can:

- help their children develop positive habits and choices

- build high quality relationships at home
- adjust their level of involvement with their children to provide the right environment for developing independence
- enhance their children's overall well-being—physical, emotional, mental, social and moral

Teachers

We have found that playing to strengths re-energizes the teachers we have worked with, in public and private schools, and in affluent and low-income ones. When teachers know and practice their strengths they:

- magnify student strengths to increase achievement and satisfaction
- decrease classroom management issues
- improve relationships with parents
- motivate young people

Athletic Coaches

There are over 40 million youth who participate in organized sports teams in our country, and there are over four million coaches. When coaches know and practice their strengths they can:

- bring out true enjoyment, satisfaction, and excellence in youth
- increase performance on the athletic field

Why Care About Strengths?

Why do we care so much about strengths? Strengths research shows us that people who use their strengths are more engaged in their life and work, are happier, and are more productive. Repeated experiences of engagement build an investment account of well-being to be debited during difficult times. We willingly push ourselves harder when we find engagement and meaning in our work, learning, and play. We also know that some strengths are correlated with life satisfaction (your happiness), that others predict school success, and others still are connected to work happiness. Importantly, we know what predicts success as an adult, and that many of these same strengths do not predict student school success. In Dave and Sherri's research while at the University of Pennsylvania, they discovered that an individual school district even has its own unique strengths pattern. This, you will see, can have implications for identifying the strengths that lead to success.

Why should you care about strengths? Strengths language can help keep both you and your student focused on the "good" of a person—what works—even when things are not necessarily going well. It is so easy to focus on what is wrong, but using strengths can help you take a step back from a conflict situation and get a new view. This can help you and your student understand challenges through a newer, more practical lens that makes it easier to develop strategies that work with what a person already has, rather than what they need. You can appreciate why you feel so strongly about some things but do not care so much about others. Finally, you can find new ways to connect and build the high quality relationships with colleagues, partners, and students that will extend your collective strengths.

Values

Strengths have a lot to do with what we value. Often times what is most important to you is something you take for granted, like breathing. It's only when you're gasping for breath that you realize just how important it is! Look at the list of fill-in-the-blank statements below. Quickly complete them. Don't overthink your answers, because your top of mind responses will contain the important information you'll need.

Mindful Moment: Values

I would never _____

I hate it when _____

I would be so relieved if _____

I don't know why they make me _____

I deserve _____

It would always be better if _____

The best way to do things is _____

In our workshops with both students and adults, we have found that the answers to these questions give important clues to our strengths. Be honest and don't change your answers! We will revisit this activity later in the chapter.

Ancient Wisdom Meets Modern Science

Strengths are our values translated to behavior. They are firmly documented in every literate culture of the last 3000 years. While the science of Positive Psychology is relatively new, the strengths we act on are not. As well, focusing on strengths instead of weaknesses is nothing new and is founded in the timeless and enduring virtues that the Greek philosopher, Aristotle, spoke and wrote of nearly 2400 years ago. He claimed that a major purpose in life was to experience happiness through living a virtuous life. One way we do this is to experience "excellence of activity." When you know how to do something well and act on this, it can bring pleasure, engagement, and meaning in your life, and help you accomplish more. The more things you know how to do well, the more avenues you will have for enjoyment and positive growth.

Developing strengths to live a good life requires time and experience. The strengths we talk of are predicated on six virtues, including the formation of four cardinal virtues of wisdom, courage, moderation, and justice. Aristotle claimed that a virtue or strength is developed through action: "Brave people became brave by doing brave things." He said there were six states of character development: brutishness, self-indulgence, weakness of will or caving into temptation, strength of will or acting or mastering temptation, character excellence, and heroic excellence (See figure on page 34). According to this model, all humans are born brutish in nature, subjects of our own little world, crying for food and attention, then moving through a time of self-indulgence, hopefully leading to character excellence.

We see character turning points in schools with children and adolescents when they navigate their journey from self-indulgence to weakness of will, and eventually, to strength of will. We believe this is where teachers, parents, and sport coaches can best work together to support students. Many young people have the best of intentions, but they may still be weak of will and cave into temptation. Students who still can't seem to change their behavior usually know intellectually that they should do so and how they should respond. But they don't always do this, of course. Even as adults we still struggle in areas and fall prey to temptation. Understanding alone, without emotional development and skills to reject the allure of choosing pleasure over responsibility, is not enough.

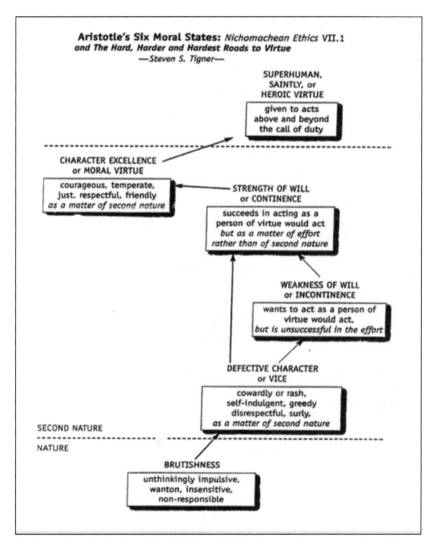

Aristotle's Six Moral States: *Nichomachean Ethics* VII.1
and The Hard, Harder and Hardest Roads to Virtue
—Steven S. Tigner—

SUPERHUMAN, SAINTLY, or HEROIC VIRTUE
given to acts above and beyond the call of duty

CHARACTER EXCELLENCE or MORAL VIRTUE
courageous, temperate, just, respectful, friendly *as a matter of second nature*

STRENGTH OF WILL or CONTINENCE
succeeds in acting as a person of virtue would act *but as a matter of effort rather than of second nature*

WEAKNESS OF WILL or INCONTINENCE
wants to act as a person of virtue would act, *but is unsuccessful in the effort*

DEFECTIVE CHARACTER or VICE
cowardly or rash, self-indulgent, greedy disrespectful, surly, *as a matter of second nature*

SECOND NATURE

NATURE

BRUTISHNESS
unthinkingly impulsive, wanton, insensitive, non-responsible

Six Ways to Eat a Potato Chip

The narrative, "Six Ways to Eat a Potato Chip," is one way to educate young people and parents, teachers, and coaches about strengths and states of character. Boston University School of Education professor Steven Tigner created this instructive story. The purpose of the story is about developing self-regulation, and its lessons can be applied to situations at home, schoolwork, athletics, and friendships. This is how we adapt it for parents, teachers, and students. You can substitute any behavior for the chips.

Six Ways to Eat a Potato Chip — A Journey to Self-Regulation

Take 1: Brutishness. I bring a bag of chips into class as a prop. First, I grab a handful of chips and start stuffing them into my mouth, with the same grace seen in my dog when he is given the dinner plate to clean off. The audience is at first taken aback by my behavior, and must think that it is pretty disgusting.

Take 2: Self-indulgence. As I start eating the chips with a purpose, and savoring each delectable morsel, I start making the "yum" sound to the point of having a serious relationship with the chips. Don't even think that I might share; the chips are for me, not you!

Take 3: Weakness of Will. I begin eating the chips, and after a while I realize that I have had enough and begin to the put the bag down. My hand and arm begin to shake uncontrollably as I am trying not to cave into temptation, but my will isn't strong enough, and ultimately another handful of chips goes into my mouth. When I then try to put the chips down, my hand goes back into the bag. I may feel badly about my choice, but that is not enough to change it.

Take 4: Strength of Will. I eat from the bag again, and decide I have eaten enough. This is no easy task, as my hand and arm shake, but I eventually return the bag to the pantry. My "will" eventually takes over, and knowing I shouldn't eat any more, I act on this. Although I am exhausted from the struggle to master temptation, I am successful in the effort to self-regulate.

Take 5: Character Excellence. I eat a moderate amount of chips and put them down. I feel no desire to eat more, and I am not emotionally drawn to eating more.

Take 6: Heroic Excellence. No such thing as a heroic eating of chips. Have an apple instead!

Here is another example of what can happen when we fail to act in the way we would if we had better strengths awareness and strength of will. It is midnight, and Anna is texting her BFF (best friend forever) about the events of the day, knowing full well that she hasn't studied for the science test she'll be expected to take in the morning. She is in the zone with the electronic conversation, even though she knows in the back of her mind the importance of doing well on the test. But the allure of the social connection is getting the best of her. Through this kind of struggle, however, she may learn about managing the urge to persist and eventually reject the pull of temptation. Next time she will be better able to manage her will whether the challenge is cheating on an exam, taunting a fellow player on the athletic field, or not practicing diligently to reach her full potential.

After struggling with temptation, a person's will may become stronger. Although Anna may still have a desire to act in a certain way, she does not need to be controlled by it and can master temptation. This takes effort, and possibly much trial and error during childhood and adolescence, but the outcomes are good for healthy human development even though this process seems exasperatingly slow for parents and teachers who may forget that they were once so challenged.

Parents, teachers, and coaches play a big role, intentionally or not, in the development of children's character through helping them identify and build their strengths. After a person masters temptation, he or she may aspire to the next stage of character excellence. This is achieved through diligent ritual and rehearsal until parent, teacher, and student eventually don't feel desire so much and instead act rationally, without needing to repress emotion. Potato chips, anyone?

Measuring, Appreciating, and Building Positive Traits

Because of Positive Psychology and its research applications, we can now do things that Aristotle never even dreamed of to help people assess, identify, and build strengths. Martin Seligman, of the University of Pennsylvania, teamed with Chris Peterson, from the University of Michigan, to rigorously research Aristotelian and other Greek thought, various philosophies and religions from ancient to modern, as well as non-religious wisdom traditions. They eventually distilled 24 "strengths of being" that have been valued by all literate ancient and modern cultures around the world for 3,000 years.

The practical result of this research is the VIA Signature Strengths Survey (VIA-IS). Directions for you to take this follow later in this chapter. This 240-item psychometrically validated test identifies one's strengths in six virtue categories mentioned earlier: wisdom, courage, temperance/moderation, justice, humanity, and transcendence. Each category includes a variety of associated strengths. (See figure below)

VIA Classification of Strengths	
Virtue	**Character Strengths**
Wisdom and Knowledge — cognitive strengths that entail the acquisition and use of knowledge	• *Creativity:* thinking of novel ways to do things • *Curiosity:* taking an interest in all ongoing experience • *Open-mindedness:* thinking things through and examining them from all sides • *Love of learning:* mastering new skills, topics, and bodies of knowledge • *Perspective:* being able to provide wise counsel to others
Courage — emotional strengths that involve exercise of will to accomplish goals in the face of opposition either external or internal	• *Honesty/authenticity:* speaking the truth and presenting oneself in a genuine way • *Bravery:* not shrinking from threat, challenge, difficulty, or pain • *Perseverance:* finishing what one starts • *Zest:* approaching life with excitement and energy
Humanity — interpersonal strengths that entail "tending and befriending" others	• *Kindness:* doing favors and good deeds for others • *Love:* valuing close relationships • *Social intelligence:* being aware of the motives and feelings of self and others
Justice — civic strengths that underlie healthy community life	• *Fairness:* treating all people the same according to notions of fairness and justice • *Leadership:* organizing group activities and seeing that they happen • *Teamwork:* working well as a member of a group or team

VIA Classification of Strengths (continued)	
Virtue	**Character Strengths**
Temperance — strengths that protect against excess	• *Forgiveness:* forgiving those who have done wrong • *Modesty:* letting one's accomplishments speak for themselves • *Prudence:* being careful about one's choices; not saying or doing things that might later be regretted • *Self-regulation:* regulating what one feels and does
Transcendence — strengths that build connections to the larger universe and provide meaning	• *Appreciation of beauty:* noticing and appreciating beauty, excellence, and/or skilled performance in all domains of life • *Gratitude:* being aware of and thankful for the good things that happen • *Hope:* Expecting the best in the future and working to achieve it; believing that a good future is something that can be brought about • *Humor:* liking to laugh and joke; bringing smiles to other people • *Spirituality/religiousness:* having coherent beliefs about higher purpose and meaning in life

(Peterson and Seligman, 2004). By permission Oxford University Press, Inc. ©Classification of Character Strengths, Chapter 1.1 Introduction to a "Manual of the Sanities" from "Character Strengths and Virtues"

After completing the VIA research, Peterson collaborated with Nansook Park, then at the University of Rhode Island, now at the University of Michigan, to develop the VIA-Youth, a 198-item questionnaire that addresses strengths in children between the ages of 10-17. More information for accessing this test will follow later in the chapter.

As a means of evaluating personal strengths as they add up to the traits of character, the VIA assesses what we value culturally, translated into what we value about ourselves. While all of the character strengths surveyed in the VIA are present in everyone, the top five are strengths that an individual endorses as their main means of positively interacting with the world. However, top five strengths are not magical. It is possible, for example, that your 6th or 8th strength may have the same raw score as the ones the test will provide as your top five. In workshops and coaching we ask, "Which of these strengths sound like you?" You should feel perfectly comfortable looking into other strengths you endorsed that may not be at the top of the list.

You might have looked at the earlier chart enumerating the VIA's strengths and virtues and right away connected with some of them. For example, if creativity is a top strength, you would probably be able to identify several areas in life where the strength is evident. If teamwork is very important to you, you would probably have noticed that strength. Of course the actual test has been constructed to do more than just let you pick from a list. Parents, teachers and athletic coaches will find this to be a particularly useful exercise as they identify themselves through strengths.

Because the VIA uses a classification of strengths and virtues present in each individual, it avoids introducing a deficit model that defines some individuals as having good character strengths while others have bad character strengths. We remind you that this is an asset-based model that focuses on what is the best in people. Strengths that appear at the bottom of the list are not weaknesses. Instead, strengths language provides an avenue for parents, teachers, coaches and students to see themselves at their best, in ways they might otherwise not have considered. Importantly, when groups of people are aware of their own and others' strengths, it provides a strengths vocabulary common to all.

Strengths work is most effective in parents, teachers, coaches and high school students when we draw from an additional strengths framework. For this, we turn to the strengths-at-work set of 34 themes of strength (also referred to as talents) from the *Clifton StrengthsFinder*. The assessment can be found in the book, *StrengthsFinder 2.0*, written by Tom Rath, Gallup Organization's Global Practice Leader and our classmate from the University of Pennsylvania/MAPP program. The book includes a code and access information for taking this test. While some of the *Clifton StrengthsFinder* strengths measure something unique to that test, you'll see that there is some crossover with the VIA strengths. The late Philip Stone, a Harvard psychology professor and Gallup Organization scientist, found that the results of each inventory "complement each other and add richness to a student's understanding."

Talent Strengths — Clifton *StrengthsFinder*	
Achiever	A constant need for achievement
Activator	Eager for action; only action can make things happen
Adaptability	Flexible; live in the moment; productive
Analytical	Objective; you like data; you search for patterns and connections
Arranger	Conductor; like to figure out the best way; enjoy managing all the variables
Belief	Core values that are enduring; tend to revolve around family; altruism; spirituality; ethics
Command	You take charge; need to share your opinion; not afraid of confrontation
Communication	You like to explain; describe; host; speak in public; write.
Competition	You compare; look at what others are doing; their performance is the ultimate yardstick
Connectedness	You are considerate; caring and kind; a bridge builder for people of different cultures
Consistency	Balance is important; you see the need to treat people the same; consistent application
Context	You look back for answers to understand future; look for blueprints and structures
Deliberative	You are careful; vigilant; a private person; you know the world is unpredictable and risky
Developer	You see the potential in others; you interact with others to help them be successful
Discipline	Your world needs to be predictable, ordered and planned; you set up routines
Empathy	You sense the emotions of those around you as though their feelings are your own
Focus	You need a clear destination; you seek to answer the question, "Where am I headed?"

Futuristic	You see in detail what the future might hold; this picture pulls you forward
Harmony	You look for agreement; you seek common ground and steer others a way from confrontation
Ideation	Fascinated by ideas; you delight in discovering why things are the way they are
Includer	You want to include people; make them feel apart of the group; you avoid groups that exclude
Individualization	You are intrigued by the unique qualities of each person; a keen observer of others' strengths
Input	You are inquisitive; you collect things from words and facts, or tangible objects
Intellection	You like to think; you enjoy your time alone for musing and reflection
Learner	You love to learn; the process more than the content or the result, especially excites you
Maximizer	Excellence, not average, is your measure; transforming something strong to superb is thrilling
Positivity	You are generous with praise; quick to smile; always on the lookout for the positive
Relator	You are pulled toward others you already know; you derive pleasure/strength from close friends
Responsibility	You take psychological ownership of anything you commit to, large or small; very conscientious
Restorative	You love to solve problems; you are energized by it and enjoy bringing things back to life
Self-Assurance	You have faith in your strengths; you know you are able— able to risk and deliver
Significance	You want to be significant in the eyes of others; you want to be recognized and heard.
Strategic	You sort through the clutter and find the best route; you see patterns where others see complexity
Woo	You enjoy the challenge of meeting new people and getting them to like you; you are drawn to strangers

Adapted from *StrengthsFinder 2.0* by Tom Rath. Copyright, 2007 GALLUP PRESS, 1251 Avenue of the Americas, 23rd Floor New York, NY 10020

SMART Strengths

So how do you build your strengths? Throughout this book, we will use the *SMART* approach to help you learn and apply each concept for yourself and with your children, students, or athletes. The *SMART* approach starts with you and then moves out to others.

S-M-A-R-T Model	
Spotting	When you know your own strengths, you are a better observer of strengths in your student athletes and are more attentive to spotting what is good instead of trying to find fault.
Managing	Your strengths are a family of traits that can be combined, tapped and promoted for bringing out the best in you and your student-athletes.
Advocating	Learning to advocate with your strengths will help you build a bridge from yourself out to others. When you put your learning into your own words and actions, you can effectively convey both your strengths and your needs.
Relating	Good relationships are about using strengths while connecting with and appealing to others. Sometimes strength buttons get pushed when other people's strengths are in conflict with your own.
Training	Once you have tools, approaches, exercises and techniques to use in helping you spot, manage, advocate and relate your strengths individually and in relationships, you will want to use them to develop these skills in others.

Spotting Strengths

The better that you are able to recognize strengths within yourself, the more aware you will become at distinguishing, acknowledging, and appreciating strengths in others. Determining your strengths answers the age-old question asked by philosophers, sages, as well as today's Positive Psychology researchers, "What is the good of a person?"

The first strengths you will learn about are your "being" strengths. To begin working with them, you will take the Values in Action (VIA Signature Strengths Test) mentioned earlier in this chapter. To take this test, go to www.authentichappiness.com and register. Adults register with a username and password. You will need to answer a few questions, the answers to which are kept anonymously, after which you will be able to take any of the assessments on this site. The test for youth aged

10 to 17 years of age is also accessed at the site. Later in the book we will ask you to have a student in your life take the test. For this, an adult will need to access the youth test through their adult account. The VIA has been taken 1.3 million times and as of this writing is free. (For a fee, you can receive a more detailed report from https://www.viacharacter.org/Reports/MyReports.aspx)

There are 240 questions on the adult test, and 198 on the youth version. Either one takes about 20-25 minutes to complete. When you have completed all of the questions, click to receive your top five "Signature Strengths" and then scroll to the bottom and click again to get all 24 strengths. Be sure to put these in the journal section of this book marked "VIA Strengths," as you will be referring to these strengths often.

Strengths spotting FAQs. We are asked many questions about strengths. After taking the VIA, you will be able to answer some of the frequently asked questions. Below are some that will be answered in this book:

- Can you have too much of a strength?
- Can I get more of strengths that are not my Signature Strengths?
- Are strengths fixed, or can you build up a strength that is not represented in your top 5?
- Can certain strengths team up in less desirable ways? If so, how do we deal with that? If not, how can we change?
- Which of your strengths correlate with well-being?
- How does this connect to other ideas in education like Multiple Intelligences and Differentiated Learning?
- Be sure to make a list of your own questions in the *Mindful Moments* Journal and note the places where you find your answers.

Managing Strengths

Once you are able to know your strengths then you can best manage them to find ways to spot them in yourself and appreciate positive traits in others. By managing and capitalizing on your strengths, you "use your powers for good" to see the big picture and stay focused as you manage a jigsaw puzzle of responsibilities in serving your children and students.

A family of strengths. Imagine having a list of the best things about you! Imagine further that by learning about these strengths, you can engage them for good in yourself and in the world. When you completed the VIA, you were provided with a set of top strengths. On the VIA, remember, you can also see all 24 of your strengths. Did you get them? The top five are just a starting point. Try to think of your signature traits as a family. No one strength acts alone, and in fact, they are of most value when they can be seen in relationship to each other or working in teams.

How can you tell if you have a certain strength? Say you looked at the chart earlier in this chapter, and right away thought that you have the strength of teamwork. This is confirmed when you hear later from a co-worker that you are a great team player. You aren't surprised to see the strength of humor in your top five, either, since laughter is important to you. Having other people laugh energizes you, too.

Remember the *Mindful Moment: Values* exercise? See if you can connect your top-of-mind answers to your strengths. For instance, if you completed "I hate it when…" with "I have to return my car to the shop because it was not repaired correctly," you might ask what strength underlies that. It might be "appreciation of beauty and excellence." A little more thinking about that strength might make you realize how much you enjoy an exquisite performance or that just yesterday you felt a sense of awe and wonder while you watched an incredible save at a soccer game. For "I don't know why they make me…" you may have written "apologize to people when I have not done something wrong" and you might connect that to your "honesty" strength. Think a bit more about how honesty is important to you and you might find other connections, too.

Trait and state strengths. Some character traits are similar to personality traits. University of Michigan psychology professor Chris Peterson calls these tonic strengths and uses examples such as curiosity, modesty, and zest. We call them persistent or *trait* strengths. Students who are curious nearly always tend to find ways to make course work more interesting through exploration and discovery. Teachers who exhibit zest and enthusiasm in the classroom tend to make material come alive for the students and may have a higher noise and activity tolerance than teachers without that strength. Parents who endorse creativity may find they enjoy supporting their student through projects and challenges.

Chris Peterson calls *phasic* assets those strengths that appear only in certain situations such as teamwork, bravery, and open-mindedness. We call these transient or *state* strengths, since they tend to present themselves when called upon, as if they are workers who have been transferred to a new office. Although there are times for individual work in the classroom, students may exhibit their collaborative or teamwork strengths only within a group, and maybe not at all, their parents may think, when they are home. Not all events or situations warrant the exhibition of bravery, since this happens when a threat or challenge appears, such as a student standing up for another student without regard to the unpopularity or emotions involved in the action.

Remember Aristotle's mantra from earlier in the chapter: "Brave people become brave by doing brave things." When young people practice this transient strength, though, they begin to own it, and know when to use it. There are certain situations when a teacher, parent, or student's open-mindedness is essential to weighing evidence and making clear judgments about course material and assignments.

Best supporting strengths. When people ask us about the value of strengths 6-10, Sherri explains that she calls them your "best supporting strengths." They may not be used all the time, but can help to support your signature traits. For instance, you may have a signature strength of forgiveness, but your best supporting strength of perspective will help you know when to use it or not. You may have the signature strength of curiosity, but your best supporting strength of social intelligence may keep you from being too nosy. Similarly, you may have the signature strength of honesty and find it bolstered by your best supporting strength of kindness. In the *Mindful Moment* on the next page reflect on how and when your best supporting strengths are present.

Mindful Moment: *Strengths Families — Knowing and Using Your Strengths*

What are your strengths? What do they look like in action? _____

_____

_____

_____

How often and under what circumstances do you get to do activities that engage your strengths? _____

_____

How can you increase opportunities to use and develop these strengths in everyday life and work? _____

_____

What are your most powerful strengths combinations? How can you tell?

_____

_____

_____

How can you use these strengths teams more often? _____

_____

What are your best supporting strengths? How and when do you use them?

_____

_____

_____

The lesser strengths. There is a tendency for people to be oblivious to their strengths. Once you know something you do well, you tend to look at what you don't do well. We have worked with many adults and children who glance over their top five strengths and immediately look to their 20-24th strengths to find out what they are and why they are there. We can learn that lesser-endorsed traits can also have value by having us pay attention to how they are expressed in our lives.

For example, John's 24th strength was "appreciation of beauty and excellence." There is a beautiful lake that laps up to Culver's campus, and he remarked that from August to May every year, the lake disappeared. John was so focused on his work at school in developing teams (teamwork is his first strength) that the natural beauty of the lake didn't seem as important. After realizing this, he began to adjust. "Appreciation of beauty" wasn't one of John's weaknesses; he just hadn't spent the time developing it.

Strengths and life satisfaction. Some strengths are significantly related to over-all life satisfaction. Hope, zest, curiosity, love, and gratitude are examples. When we mention these strengths to parents, teachers, coaches, and students at our seminars, we see smiles come to the faces of those who highly endorse these strengths. We are particularly interested in how gratitude can transform families and schools. Young people tend to be self-absorbed. It is a natural part of the brain-development process. We have found when children and adolescents frequently share gratitude with others, they are more engaged in school.

Robert Emmons, the leading researcher in the science of gratitude and author of *Thanks!: How the Science of Gratitude Can Make You Happier*, says that gratitude is "good medicine, and its side effects are few…. Gratitude, we have found, maximizes the enjoyment of the good—our enjoyment of others, of God, of our lives. Happiness is facilitated when we enjoy what we have been given, when we 'want what we have.'"

In Appendix B, you will have a chance to try out Positive Psychology research-validated gratitude interventions with young people. Gratitude is the strength that benefits the giver and the receiver making both of them happier. When you thank someone, even someone who may be uncomfortably modest, they are grateful for your gratitude. You can use gratitude in the service of other strengths. In the earlier example about John finding that "appreciation of beauty and excellence" was his 24th strength, he was very grateful for the opportunity to live in such a lovely place, and this became a "Best Supporting Strength" for him. What are you grateful for? Refer to your *Mindful Moment* on the previous page and explore.

Shadow Traits: The dark side of strengths. Have you ever been to a high school reunion thinking you knew all about your classmates only to find out that people you expected to find in the FBI's "most wanted" list are now—gasp—fine upstanding members of the community? How does that happen? Strengths needed for school success, like love of learning for its own sake, general curiosity, self-regulation, and diligence, do not necessarily get parceled out to all of us equally. As a result, some students who were bright, skilled, and motivated did not do well at "school" but made excellent entrepreneurs or artists. Bill Gates and Steve Jobs come to mind.

Earlier when we introduced strengths, we said that there were no bad strengths, and this is true. There are, however, bad uses of strengths. When parents, teachers, coaches, and students use their strengths to excess, problems can arise. For instance a student's perseverance can get him in trouble because his late-night commitment to his schoolwork has him working on five hours of sleep during the school week. This is a real challenge. He doesn't know how to act differently. In this case, most of the negative effects are ones that the student must deal with, such as illness from being run down, more difficulty with attention because he is tired, and poorer quality learning as a result. He may even blame others for his problems, or behave in ways that make it even harder to get his work done. The shadow side of a strength is at work, and the student will continue to act in the same way until he understands and can manage his strengths.

A strengths story. Sometimes the shadow side of strengths is working behind even more inappropriate behavior. Several years ago, one of John's student-athletes, Glen, was dismissed from the varsity lacrosse team for disrespecting other players and the head coach. Glen was very upset with the coach's decision and asked if he could speak with John, who was hoping that the young man wasn't coming to see him for a "get out of jail free card"—for John to advocate for him to be reinstated to the team. What Glen had done was insensitive and selfish, and John had to think about a way of making the meeting as positive and productive as possible, knowing that the consequences fit the nature of the crime. When Glen came to John's office the next day, John decided to take the high road and ask what Glen's top VIA strengths were. His top strengths were humor and playfulness, and leadership. The remaining three were hope and optimism, honesty and authenticity, and social intelligence.

John knew this about Glen, and he also was aware of feedback from other students that highly correlated with this. Glen was generally well-respected by his peers for these strengths. He was very likable and his sense of humor was contagious.

When properly motivated he was an exceptional leader. However, in the recent athletic situation, his humor went to the dark side, and his leadership detracted from other players' abilities to fulfill the team mission. Even the capable coach could not accept this kind of behavior.

A smile came to Glen's face when John asked about how his leadership comes alive at school—in the dorm, in the classroom, and on the football and lacrosse fields. He then grinned ear to ear in mentioning that he is "a funny guy," and others are attracted to his playfulness. Then John paused, and with a very serious look on his face, asked, "Glen, why are we here right now having this conversation? What happened?" There was another pause, and Glen, with tears coming to his eyes, meekly said that he took both his leadership and his humor to excess, to the dark side. At that moment, Glen realized that he was in control of his actions, of how he saw himself, and how others saw him. John and Glen spoke about how much enjoyment he derives when he focuses on these strengths in service to others. He began to realize that the players look up to him and that by cueing into his strengths more, he would be happier and provide better service as a leader. After reflecting for a while longer, he went to the head coach of the team and apologized and explained how his strengths had "gone south." The coach allowed him back on the team.

The conversation between John and Glen lasted only 20 minutes. Glen realized that he had control of his strengths and now knew how to balance them. Like Glen, we all have a shadow side to our strengths. Shadow strengths are even more powerful when teamed with other strengths, as Glen's example shows. It is important to know situations in which they come out, so we can help ourselves and our students monitor and balance them. When we do that, we have the best chance to be "in the zone" in our interactions with others. How would you handle a difficult student? Would you see the strengths in someone like Glen when he wanted another chance? Glen used his best supporting strength of hope and optimism when he decided to apologize to the coach. He was genuinely sorry and believed that he would have a good outcome from saying so. That the coach let him back on the team was unexpected, but it reinforced his sense that the coach was fair, another best supporting strength for Glen, who turned out to be the unofficial leader on the squad for the remainder of the season.

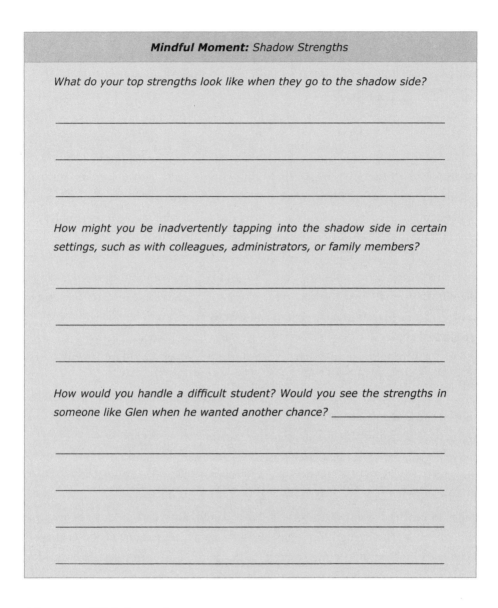

Mindful Moment: *Shadow Strengths*

What do your top strengths look like when they go to the shadow side?

_____

_____

_____

How might you be inadvertently tapping into the shadow side in certain settings, such as with colleagues, administrators, or family members?

_____

_____

_____

How would you handle a difficult student? Would you see the strengths in someone like Glen when he wanted another chance? _____

_____

_____

_____

_____

Advocating With Strengths

Advocating with strengths involves using the language of strengths and initiating conversations with your children, students and athletes around their strengths, knowing how those strengths manifest in different activities and situations, and managing any shadow sides of their strengths. This is your bridge from yourself out to others. In the story about Glen above, John helped Glen see that he was not using his strengths powers for good. Glen was easily able to agree with John about this and to use his strengths language when he went to apologize to the lacrosse coach. Imagine if someone came to you with a sincere apology that revealed self-reflection, which included their contribution to the problem as well as a solution for preventing such behavior in the future. You start by talking about strengths and their role in your life and the role you see them playing in your students. In Chapters Two, Three and Four we will suggest activities that will add depth to the strengths conversations.

Relating with Strengths

Good relationships are about connecting with and appealing to others. One way to help young people be more engaged in school is for parents and teachers to match up their own strengths with their respective children/students. Our strengths buttons get pushed when other people's strengths are in conflict with our own. In fact, one way to know you have a strength is when you are annoyed.

Pushing strengths buttons. We all have strengths buttons, and they are the proof that we own our strengths. If you wince when your four-year-old proudly proclaims to her grandmother, "I know how you made my dad," your modesty and self-regulation buttons may be being pushed. If your blood boils during a call to the cable company when the on-hold message repeatedly plays, "Your call is important to us," your honesty button is being pushed.

Think about strengths you wish your students had more of, and they are probably ones that you have and value—for yourself. They just might not be the other person's strengths. Go back to the *Mindful Moment: Values* exercise presented earlier. Remember that your values hint at your strengths. The next time that you are tempted to say, "Well, when I was a kid," realize that you are tapping into values that you developed in the time period and context when you were growing up, and that you may be remembering the good old days and your feelings about them selectively. In fact, many strengths change across the lifespan.

Carlene worked in a residential school for girls. She believed that it was her responsibility to "write up" and discipline any girl who tested, let alone broke, any rule. Carlene's top strength was fairness, and she exercised this by meting out punishments with equal harshness to all students. Simply revealing to her that strengths change across the lifespan helped Carlene use her strength of perspective and gave her permission to work more appreciatively, to see what was working. The result was not only a happier group of students, but ones who wanted to please Carlene, something that she had never experienced in many years of youth work.

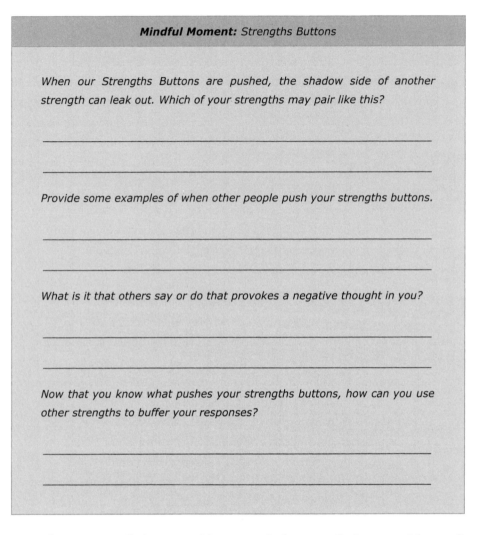

Mindful Moment: *Strengths Buttons*

When our Strengths Buttons are pushed, the shadow side of another strength can leak out. Which of your strengths may pair like this?

_____

_____

Provide some examples of when other people push your strengths buttons.

_____

_____

What is it that others say or do that provokes a negative thought in you?

_____

_____

Now that you know what pushes your strengths buttons, how can you use other strengths to buffer your responses?

_____

_____

By being aware of what pressed her strengths buttons, Carlene was able to call upon one of her other strengths, perspective, to help match up with the girls and enhance her overall relationships with them. When parents, teachers, and coaches know how to strengths match in this way, they can enhance their respective relationships with children/students and help them learn how to match their positive traits up with their peers. Strengths matching is not an attempt to match people with the same strengths but instead is about knowing and using your strengths to help appeal to the strengths of others. By appealing to others we see their strengths in what they do and can offer an attractive or interesting way to bring out the best in them and ourselves. When parents, teachers and coaches match strengths they can:

- Identify and capitalize on their own and others strengths to bring out the best in each other
- Mobilize and build high-quality social connections in class, at home, and on the athletic field to appeal to and empathize with others through writing and speaking
- Recognize strengths in others in their writing and in their speaking
- Learn how to tell anecdotes in the form of strengths stories that help bring out the best in others
- Provide constructive feedback using strengths language
- Persuade effectively

One way to help young people be more engaged in school is for parents, teachers, and coaches to match their own strengths up with their respective students' traits. We will discuss this in greater depth in Chapter Two. Remember Carlene? She is not unique in her strengths pattern. Adult strengths tend toward kindness, authenticity/integrity, fairness, and open-mindedness. (See figure below). Researchers Nansook Park and Chris Peterson found there are common traits among adolescents as well, such as gratitude, humor, and love, while prudence, forgiveness, spirituality, and self-regulation were less common.

Parenting and teaching is challenging work, because our students are not "fully cooked" with their strengths—and we may need to appeal to their strengths in light of our own.

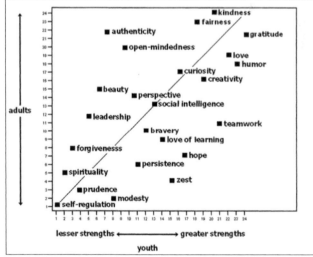

By permission Oxford University Press, Inc. ©Page 154, Figure 6.23 – Strengths Profiles for Youth (N=250) Versus Adults (N=83,576) in the United States from "A Primer in Positive Psychology" by Peterson, Christopher (2006).

We have found in working together that it has been essential to know each other's strengths and try to connect them. All three of us have "strategic" as a high trait from the *Clifton StrengthsFinder*. So we each have a tendency to want to strategize in our own ways. That can get a bit messy and confusing when it comes to a project such as writing a book together! We were, however, aware of this earlier on, and by going to our other strengths, we were able to match up nicely. A comparison of our top VIA traits from the first time we worked together looked like this: (See figure below)

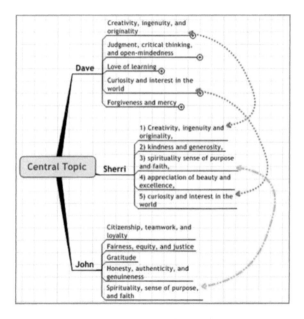

Dave uses his creativity and curiosity to look at new ways of thinking. Sherri is also very creative and curious, and her gratitude and appreciation of beauty and excellence helps to bring out the best in all of us. John, on the other hand, is the consummate team player and keeps us on the same page and moving ahead together through inevitable times when it might seem simpler to do things alone. In our seminars, participants work in groups to imagine and produce a way of modeling their joint strengths, being mindful of the ways in which a group or family may occasionally have too much or not enough of needed strengths.

Mindful Moment: *Strengths Matching*
Compare your strengths with another person you know well.

Are they similar? Do they differ? _____

_____

_____

_____

_____

_____

How do you use your strengths for good when you both interact? _____

_____

_____

In a bigger group, such as a family, team or faculty, how can strengths matching help to substitute for strengths that are not well represented at the top of the VIA list? _____

_____

_____

_____

_____

_____

Training — Making *SMART Strengths* Stick in Schools: The Culver Story

Culver educates its students for leadership and responsible citizenship in society by developing and nurturing the whole individual—mind, spirit, and body—through integrated programs that emphasize the cultivation of character.

— Culver Academies Mission

In 2006, we began working on institutionalizing a strengths-based approach at the Culver Academies—a rigorous co-educational, college-preparatory boarding schools in Indiana, where John is the Director of the Center for Character Excellence. There are approximately 780 high school students at Culver. The school is unique in that classes are co-educational, but the boys' and girls' leadership systems are different. John had primed the pump to integrate strengths.

With the blessing from Culver's administration team and its Board of Trustees, we ventured into a multi-year process to train administrators, teachers, staff, students, coaches, and parents with sustainable strengths-based strategies to support Culver's mission. Sherri and Dave were right alongside John in designing and implementing the process.

First, we began a "soft sell" approach that helped neutralize the traditional tension with a faculty when they see changes and maybe new responsibilities on the horizon. It was essential to build high quality social emotional connections with faculty members. We invited teachers to participate in the first strengths seminar, a three-day intensive program, held a week after school ended in early June. With a small professional development stipend on the side as added motivation, twenty-two teachers volunteered to 1) spend three days of their vacation with John, Sherri and Dave, and 2) write a five-page action plan reflecting on what they learned and how they could implement it at Culver. These plans were to be actively and voluntarily pursued by teachers on their summer vacation.

We were quite surprised with the active participation and dialogue from the teachers over the three days. For the first time, we had teachers saying, "This is the most meaningful professional development I have experienced in my teaching career." Another said, "I now think differently about how I teach." And one teacher remarked, "The idea of playing to strengths is powerful and simple. I don't need to beat myself up over who I am not."

The epiphanies were real and the strengths message started sticking. Teachers embraced an understandable, meaningful and effective alternative to "fixing" for developing young people and each other. Even some of our resident *keepers of the nightmare*, those teachers who are consistently negative, made the shift to a more student-centered approach to learning.

Over the past several years, the strengths language at Culver has become viral and contagious as many faculty, staff, administrators, and students now share the common language and skills. We have continued to work with faculty during the school year and each summer to develop our site team. The site team is comprised of leaders who have emerged from within the school community and among the faculty and who have fully embraced the Positive Education practice. As teachers have become competent in a new language, we've created a second-level seminar that focuses on building strengths into the academic curriculum and an additional customized coaching program for site team members as well as faculty and staff who are considering new challenges at the school. Also, many non-teaching staff members have become intrigued by the program and asked our Dean of Faculty if they could participate in similar professional development. The site team now coordinates ongoing application and training work with various staff support departments throughout the school.

Now new students arriving each August have completed the on-line VIA-Youth. Later, students will take the *Clifton StrengthsFinder* (CSF) during their junior year as part of Culver's formal leadership programs. We have found that putting a name to a character strength and knowing what particular traits look like in action has been instructive and informative for many students as they navigate their pathways to growth in the classroom, leadership in the living unit, in the athletic arena, and on the stage.

Strengths research at Culver. In 2006, we conducted formal research at Culver to see if certain character strengths were indicators of academic achievement, leadership, and overall health. We found there is consonance of character strengths among freshman and senior participants. Kindness, humor, love, and integrity were all within the mean top five of both cohorts. Female participants strengths tended to be higher than males in the VIA humanity and transcendence virtue categories, while male strengths were higher in the courage category.

Unsurprisingly, students who scored higher on persistence and love of learning had higher grade point averages. Our findings about leadership were consistent with the conclusions of researchers who have investigated the relationship between strengths and leadership. Although fairness was significant across both freshmen and senior cohorts, the strengths of open mindedness and leadership, and trends towards prudence, forgiveness, perseverance, and spirituality, were more meaningful at the senior level. Perhaps these are developmental, and they may also be an outcome of our leadership programs. We also studied the areas of sleep, nutrition, and physical activity or exercise. Self-regulation and prudence were meaningful indicators for sleep, nutrition, and physical activity or exercise. More research is indicated as we continue to develop Positive Education programming at Culver.

We have added an important stakeholder in the education process: parents. With over 90% of Culver's students boarding, contact with parents is typically limited to phone, email, sporting events, and two parent weekends during the school year. We have now helped to complete the circle by having parents begin to match their strengths with their children and teachers through our *Parents Strengths Initiative* (PSI). (See Appendix A)

Culver has been transformed in thought, word, and deed by a school-wide approach. As we are beginning with you, it is important to remember that the immediate value of identifying, understanding, and acting on strengths originates with the individual parent, teacher, coach, and student. Strengths become more valuable and their power multiplies when integrated in partnerships, small groups, and families. Their consummate value comes when they are implemented in our schools.

This chapter examined how adult mentors can better understand and apply their strengths through learning the *SMART Strengths* Model. In Chapters Two, Three, and Four, you will learn how teachers, parents, and coaches can play to their own strengths to help young people leverage their strengths in school, at home, and on the athletic field.

Chapter Two

Strengths in School

When we seek to discover the best in others,
we somehow bring out the best in ourselves.
—William Arthur Ward

W as there a teacher who really made a difference in your life? For John, it was his third grade teacher, Miss Robinson. He vividly remembers one moment when she greeted him at the classroom doorway. She always had something nice to say to John, but that day was special. He doesn't recall the words she said, but he can still remember the feeling, and smiling from ear to ear.

During the early stages of writing this book, John contacted Miss Robinson, now retired from both teaching and as a elementary school principal, and told her how important that moment in the doorway was to him, and how much he still valued the memory after almost 46 years. Her strong, low pitched voice echoed with gratitude. At age 77, she hadn't lost the spark in her voice, and it triggered another memory in John. It transported him back to third grade and a time she held him responsible for some "off task" behavior in class. She was tough at times, holding all students accountable, but she was always fair. Because he was important to her then (and still is to this day), the bond that happened in the doorway opened other doors for John. Her strengths of kindness, fairness, gratitude, and love evidently appealed to John, and he has modeled that behavior with his students, too. While Miss Robinson didn't have the benefit of empirically based strengths assessments, she intuitively knew what worked for her and her students, and in retrospect she clearly had strengths that were so durable that neither she nor John ever forgot each other, even though he was only eight years old when they met. This chapter will show how teachers and students can be partners in learning by using the common strengths language that creates a classroom climate where students and teachers flourish.

What Teachers Need to Know About Strengths

There is fierce debate about what makes for a great teacher. Millions of hours of video, for example, show what teachers do and compare that to students' "knowing" strengths in the form of high-stakes testing results, but what about other aspects of teacher greatness? How do students' strengths team up to play into their teachers' greatness? As you have seen, when teachers know and understand their own and their students' strengths and how they are compatible with each other, they provide the best opportunity for greater student satisfaction and academic achievement.

There is, however, a leaky bucket of teacher retention in the United States today. Unfortunately, nearly 50% of teachers do not stay in the profession for even five years, citing difficulty with lack of planning time, workload, classroom management issues, and poor relationships with parents and administrators as some of the their many sources of dissatisfaction. Turnover accounted for by retirement is relatively small compared to teacher job dissatisfaction and teachers pursuing other jobs. In the climate of accountability fueled by national initiatives such as No Child Left Behind (NCLB), teacher emotions already affected by the perception of overwork and undervalue are vulnerable to the challenges of reform agendas. We have found that playing to strengths significantly re-energizes the teachers we have worked with in both public and private schools.

What Students Need from Teachers

Quite simply, students need to matter to their teachers. When young people feel and think they matter to others, they tend to be more positive and are more motivated to succeed. School success matters, too, and is considered to be one of the leading developmental assets among middle and high school students as compiled by Peter Scales and his colleagues at the Search Institute.

Bill Milliken, the author of the *Last Dropout*, and a high school dropout himself, agrees with the Search Institute's assertion that there are five predictors of young people's success in school. The first is to have a personal relationship with a caring adult in your life. The second predictor is having a safe place to go to. Thirdly, success is also determined by getting a healthy start as a young child. The fourth predictor of success is the development of marketable skills. Finally, giving back something about yourself as a person that is valued by your community lets you be part of something bigger than yourself. In some schools this is called community service, but a more apt term may be "servant leader." Milliken goes even further to say, "Programs don't change people. Relationships do." You'll read more about this in Part Two of the book.

The Strength of Natural Caring

Mattering is synonymous with caring and shares the sense that other people are important and that we should be concerned with their well-being. Miss Robinson cared about her students. Parents and teachers can be demanding and have high expectations, but still show their concern for young people. Adults can't fake a caring attitude, though. Young people can smell phony behavior a mile away. They know when a parent or teacher is not authentic and genuine.

Karen Reivich, co-director of the Penn Resiliency Project, says: "Students know the teachers who are and who aren't authentic. That is the first thing the students read. This person is showing me themselves or this person is putting on a show!" Nel Noddings, the author of *Happiness and Education*, emphasizes that caring for young people and being cared for as a teacher should not be considered to be mutually exclusive. In student-teacher relationships, we continually change places whether it be in a brief encounter, an episode, or a chain of experiences. The process of caring is a two-way street.

Teachers who naturally care for their students are attentive to and understand the strengths cues of young people in their charge. This attention is accompanied by a feeling. Many teachers have a sense of motivational displacement, when the child's motives become their motives. Noddings provides a fitting example: A teacher watches a young child learn to tie her shoes and actually imagines tying them for her.

When we provide students with ways of identifying their strengths and how and when they come alive, we offer them the opportunity to see the best in themselves. To that end, Noddings has made an interesting distinction between natural caring and ethical caring. The ethical model is, "What would I do if I was at my caring best?" This provides pause to think about the ethical implications of what a decision to act might be.

Natural caring is more about caring as an end in itself—where caring has been developed to the point that is now a habit you don't even need to think about. Natural caring has its greatest chance of appearing when healthy relationships have already been forged. (We'll cover more on relationship building in Part Two of this book.) It is more likely, then, that the call to action to care will happen around people you already know. Noddings predicts that teachers who are with students for a longer period of time may have more influence, since this can provide the environment to say, "I want to respond to you in a caring way even when I don't feel like it." As a result, good teachers establish conditions where natural caring flourishes. Further, Noddings reminds us that, "institutions can provide the conditions for caring, *but* it is human beings that can provide the care."

Unfortunately, the dark side may appear in misguided caring. A principal may say, "I am hard on my teachers, because I care about the students." One morning we conducted a brief "Building Strengths and Positive Emotions" workshop at an elementary school where teachers reviewed their top strengths and how they can be used in the classroom. The teachers were clearly energized by the activity and we sensed that the teachers felt cared for during that time. Later we were told by a disgruntled teacher that the school principal started off the afternoon session by telling the teachers that they were not doing a very good job preparing their respective students for the state standardized tests—that it was their fault that test scores were not up to expectations. His one-minute admonishment effectively negated the previous three hours of caring.

Strengths for Academic Success

Emerging research indicates there is a positive relationship between academic success and certain character strengths. Nansook Park, the co-author of the Values in Action Inventory for Children, has found that the cluster of strengths in temperance/moderation of the VIA (forgiveness and mercy; humility and modesty; prudence; and self-regulation) tends to predict academic grades. Self-regulation or the ability to be disciplined is a very powerful behavior modifier. However, self-regulation is not well represented among signature strengths of children and adolescents. In a study we conducted with high school students, participants who scored higher on persistence and love of learning had higher grade point averages, which is itself a strong predictor of academic success. Also, the relational strengths of fairness, gratitude, honesty, and hope, and the performance trait of perspective contribute to doing well in school.

Cherry Picking Strengths

Teachers have asked us if there are certain strengths that their students should have in order to be more successful in school. While there is a positive relationship between academic success and character strengths, as we mentioned earlier, self-regulation has numerous benefits across the lifespan. While strengths research has shown that the cluster of strengths in temperance and moderation tend to predict good academic grades, there is research that considers pro-social behavior a predictor of academic achievement. The Search Institute asserts that, "young people who care deeply about how they do in school have accepted the challenge to confront increasingly difficult subject matter as they move through their school experience." The developmental assets of achievement, motivation, and school engagement contribute significantly to school success. Angela Duckworth, of the University of Pennsylvania, has even shown that self-discipline is a stronger predictor of grades than IQ. After studying 8th graders she concluded that young people with "grit" or a strong "stick-to-itiveness" were able to endure their commitment to persevering in the classroom and this predicted higher GPA.

So the real answer is that yes, some strengths make the road through school easier to navigate, both for kids and the adults who care for them. But this does not mean that we should focus on developing those traits to the exclusion of the ones that are a student's signature traits. Instead, we need to learn how to use our powers and strengths for good.

Using Strengths for Good

As part of the Positive Psychology for Youth Project, 9th grade students at Strath Haven High School in Wallingford, PA, participated in a strengths-based Language Arts curriculum. Compared to their strengths measured before participation, after twenty-five 80-minute lessons, the students' learning/performance strengths such curiosity and love of learning increased significantly. Research showed that this also carried over to subsequent academic achievement in language arts when the students were in 10th and 11th grades.

Strengths that Predict Academic Success

- Diligence/perseverance
- Self-discipline—Self-regulation
- Prudence
- Love of Learning
- Creativity
- Open-mindedness
- Curiosity
- Perspective

Looking ahead to the university level, persistence, self-regulation, and love of learning were found to be predictors of both student satisfaction and grade point average. Having learned these strengths in their early schooling bodes well for young people's future learning.

However, having other signature strengths does not preclude success. Christine Duvivier, CEO of *Positive Leaders*, researched identified strengths and gifts in secondary school students who were not in the top 20% of their classes. She called these students "The Bottom 80™" and examined them in the context of education objectives and future prospects. Knowing and spotting their strengths makes all the difference.

In Her Own Words: Christine Duvivier, *Positive Leaders,* Wellesley, MA

Although students in what I call "The Bottom 80™" are often told they have learning disabilities or lack motivation, I found that they learn and are highly motivated when the situation suits their interests and their gifts. A number of the students have great intellectual, social, creative, manual, spatial, or athletic abilities. They enjoy learning in non-traditional ways, such as self-teaching, physically interacting with the subject, story-telling or watching video, for example. Some of the students have high levels of initiative and self-motivation, preferring to learn by exploring on their own, and they actively resist being shown how to do something.

A common theme among the "Bottom 80™" group was tenacity and diligence when a topic interests them. Then they become completely absorbed in learning, and dive in head first. These students have gifts that are well-suited to successful lives, but often these abilities are not amplified and enhanced in school. Instead, we may think that these students are not capable because their gifts do not match what we look for in school when the real-world evidence is that creativity and out-of-the-box thinking are incredibly valuable.

SMART Strengths for Success in School

Since students' subjective well-being (longer-term overall happiness), a key component of school success, increases when they perceive teachers to be supportive of them, teachers can help improve student success when they relate to students emotionally, display fairness, encourage student questioning, and recognize students' academic success by tying it to strengths. There will be more on how to do this both later in this chapter and in Chapter Eight. When students trust their teachers, they tend to more enthusiastically participate in academic assignments and other undertakings.

There are no simple "just add water" programs for academic achievement. Success is a combination of teachers and students playing to their respective strengths to develop trust and enhance the classroom partnership. With trust and caring on board, teachers can help young people aspire to their strengths, in both performance and relational matters at school.

By developing a common strengths language in the classroom, teachers and students become partners in the learning process that creates a climate for increased learning, achievement and overall satisfaction. Let's follow the *SMART* investment process to make this a reality. In this chapter you will practice by…

S-M-A-R-T Model

Spotting	When you know your own strengths, you are a better observer of strengths in others and are more attentive to spotting what is good instead of trying to find fault.
Managing	Your family of strengths can be promoted for bringing out the best in you and others. In the classroom this improves student engagement and achievement.
Advocating	Learning to advocate with your strengths will help you build a bridge from yourself out to others. When you put your learning into your own words and actions, you can effectively convey both your strengths and your needs.
Relating	Good student-teacher and student-student relationships are about using strengths while connecting with and appealing to others.
Training	Once you have tools you will want to use them to develop these skills in your students.

Spotting Strengths

*Teachers and students learn a common strengths language
in classrooms and schools and clearly identify their respective strengths.*

Identifying Student Strengths

Jeremy Riffle, the principal of Triton Elementary School in Bourbon, Indiana, has made the commitment for his 5th and 6th grade teachers to learn the strengths of every one of their students. To accomplish his school-wide strengths mission, all Triton's teachers have taken the VIA, and the VIA-Youth has been administered to

all 5th and 6th graders, in groups at the school's computer lab. To show his enthusiasm and to be sure that every student understood every question, Jeremy read the
test to all students. Now each of those students has a strengths profile that includes
the VIA-Youth language.

Activity: Have Students Take the VIA-Youth

- To access the VIA-Youth you can use the account you made in Chapter
  One when you took the adult version of the VIA at www.authentichappi-
  ness.com. Those under 18 years old cannot register themselves.
- Log in and scroll to the part of the website which lets you register a child
  for the VIA-Youth.
- There are 198 questions. Reading them while students answer should
  take about 30 minutes. Do not help students answer the questions or
  hint at what you think an answer might be. Just as when you took the
  test, each student responds for himself or herself.
- Be sure to scroll to the bottom of the page that has the top five strengths
  and click on the button to access all 24 strengths.
- You may want to print or save a document with each student's strengths.
  The results for each student are stored on the website.

Group administration for children has several benefits. Besides being sure that
all students understand the questions and how to answer them, when a whole school
community participates in and supports the strengths mission, it is much more
likely to bear fruit.

Building and Exercising Strengths Muscles

One way for character strengths to be fully utilized at an elementary level is to
provide students with activities that help them create mental models of strengths.
Here is one way to do that.

Activity: Mental Models of Strengths

Defining a strength, writing it in a sentence, and sketching a drawing of it can help form a bridge for understanding what a strength looks like and how it comes alive in the student's life.

Name of the Strength _____

Definition of the Strength _____

_____

_____

_____

_____

_____

Write about the strength in a sentence _____

_____

_____

_____

_____

_____

_____

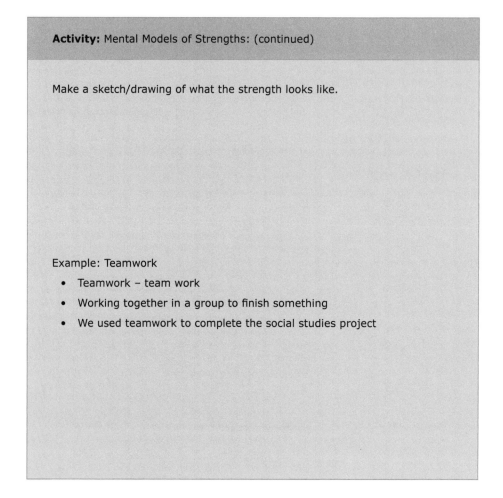

Activity: Mental Models of Strengths: (continued)

Make a sketch/drawing of what the strength looks like.

Example: Teamwork

- Teamwork – team work
- Working together in a group to finish something
- We used teamwork to complete the social studies project

This process helps students understand their strengths in action, and it is especially important prior to 5th grade, an appropriate time for students to begin taking the VIA-Youth. When mental models of strengths are integrated with a story, a sketch or drawing, an analogy or a body or physical movement, each student makes a concrete, personal connection to strengths language. For younger students, some of the language, of course, may need explanations from a teacher. For example, it will likely be important to teach what "temperance" is, with examples, so when students come across the word, they will be able to comprehend the meaning on a deeper level. When 5th graders take the VIA-Youth, the foundation will have been laid for building upon strengths and learning how to use them to achieve school-related and personal goals. This will also aid students before their transition into middle school and continued work in Positive Education.

In Her Own Words: Dana Vellios, Guidance Counselor at Glenwood Elementary School, Media, Pennsylvania

I work with students individually, in small groups, and in whole group settings. My initial goal was to develop a strengths curriculum that was as rich as possible. I gave the VIA to a couple of fifth graders, and noticed that the outcome wasn't as rich as I hoped it would be. Realizing that the VIA is developmentally appropriate for students to take who are around ten years old or older, I spent a lot of time going over the vocabulary of the different strengths, and it made me start thinking that if I had started conversations with children at younger ages to learn about this, then I could prepare them better.

I used my basic knowledge of students through trial and error to find out what they knew and what was working for them. For instance, I went into a kindergarten class and discussed what a strength was. I pointed to my biceps muscle and tried to get the young children to understand what strength meant—to see if it was something that they could grasp. It worked! I was able to have them concretely see the function of the muscle, and to make a subtle shift over to other types of muscles. I told them, "We all have strengths. They are like muscles, like the muscle in our arm. We also have strengths inside of us, like things we are good at." As students continue to grow in different areas, lessons in strengths can continue to be given at the appropriate developmental level, which will enable the VIA-Youth to be as useful as possible for 5th grade students.

I always start my groups off with, "Tell me something good that is going on with you. Why is it going well for you right now?" Even at a young age, I want my students to have a connection back to strengths, just like our muscles. I also ask, "Who can tell me about a time at home where they see Mom, Dad, or a grandma or grandpa make their muscles strong? Can we make our muscles stronger by lifting weights? It's the same thing when making yourself stronger at something you are good at." One student said, "I am good at playing soccer." And I asked, "How could you get even better playing soccer?" The student immediately responded: "Well, I practice and try really hard." Just think how much more valuable that effort will be when he can choose the strengths that will help most!

The reinforcement of strengths muscles by teachers is an important step in helping young people develop a common language, as students navigate their journeys through the elementary years.

Managing Strengths

In the classroom, managing strengths improves
student engagement and achievement.

Strength Managing in the Classroom: A How-to

John appeals to his student's strengths by first spotting his own VIA signature strengths: citizenship/teamwork, love of learning, gratitude, fairness, and zest. He is a true believer that the whole is greater than the sum of its parts. He strives to set up a team-learning environment in the classroom. Students learn from each other in class by collaborating. Most everything about how he operates in the classroom is about teaming to get the students to work with each other in the learning process. John is also a consummate life-long learner. His bookshelf is full of texts, and he does not tire of learning new information or ways to do things that can help him be a more effective teacher. Also, students can always count on a thank you as they leave class for having shared with him their thoughts and ideas. Every student matters to John, and he has the energy to stick close to the expectations of everyone in class.

To help bring his classroom to life, John practices strengths-matching with his students. Let's first take a look at the signature strengths of three of John's students—Jack, Shantelle, and Margaret (See figure on next page). Notice how well they are able to provide examples of how each strength manifests for them.

Student 1 – Jack

Creativity. Creativity is my strongest attribute and is most evident in my ability to look at a situation and almost immediately process three or more probable ways of approaching it. Even when given instructions to follow, I constantly find myself processing them and looking to find different means of going about a certain situation.

Perseverance. My perseverance is evident in almost every aspect of my life. My friends continue to call me an over-achiever. Not only do I plan on accomplishing the goals I set for myself, I plan on accomplishing them efficiently and beyond expectations of everyone else.

Perspective. Other students will often come to me for guidance on schoolwork, whether it be a senior service project, mathematics, or even French. I always seem to be answering questions for my classmates when they find themselves confused, which I owe to my success within the classroom.

Authenticity. I have always been a person of integrity because one who questions their ability to be truthful to others, questions their ability to be truthful to themselves. I will always be honest with those around me, because only then will I know I am being honest with myself.

Leadership. I use my leadership to help other people. Sometimes, people need reassurance that they are doing a good job, or feel the need to be punished for doing something wrong, and I feel I have the leadership skills to take control over others and over a certain situation where I would be able to successfully get my point across or succeed in a positive way.

Student 2 – Shantelle

Fairness, equity, justice. I have been told numerous times by friends and family that I am "too fair" sometimes, letting others take advantage of me. I disagree that I can be "too fair" to others; I only treat others with such manners because I hope to be treated in that same way. No matter the situation I am put into, I treat everyone as equally and fairly as I would like to be treated.

Hope and optimism. My mother always taught me to look at my glass as half full instead of half empty. When my friends are going through rough patches in life I am always by their side reminding them that even though it may not be easy right now, in the end something good will come out of it because "When one door closes another door opens."

Bravery and valor. When friends get criticized by others, I stand up for them, reminding them that they are not alone. Experiencing divorce at a young age was not easy, but part of me is thankful for this because it has not only helped me to appreciate what I do have, but it has also made me a stronger person. My family has taught me to not only stand up for what is right, but also for what I believe. Now I am not afraid to speak my mind, standing up for myself while at the same time respecting others' opinions.

Spirituality, sense of purpose, meaning. At times, we may feel unloved, betrayed, or as if we do not belong or deserve to live. When someone tells me that they are feeling unloved or left out, I remind them how much they mean to not only me, but also how much their family and friends appreciate them. My second character strength, "Hope and Optimism" helps me with these types of situations because I am able to see the best in any one situation and remind someone how important they are to others and to finding their own purpose in life.

Modesty and humility. If I receive an award or certificate, I am not the type of person to scream with joy or even wave the certificate in the air. I tend to keep accomplishments to myself and instead focus on other's accomplishments and good deeds. It's not that I am not proud of myself for accomplishing something, but I do not "seek the spotlight". I would rather take my time and effort to congratulate others on their achievements than seek recognition for myself.

Curiosity. Curiosity is probably one of the best words that has ever described me. I love to learn and honestly wish I had more time in a day to take more classes and have the opportunity to learn more about my interests.

Social Intelligence. In my teen years, I have been told repeatedly how well I listen to and understand other people's problems. Because I hate to see my family and friends upset, I am constantly trying to make them feel better when things go wrong within their lives. I have always been a very talkative and social person, which has given me a lot of practice in understanding the feelings of other people.

Gratitude. I have always felt blessed for the different things given to me throughout my life. Whether it was an experience, a gift, or kind words, I have always been thankful for receiving them. I refuse to take my blessings for granted because as easily as I received them, they can also be taken way. I believe that if I am grateful for things I have, I can never be accused of being greedy or unappreciative.

Creativity. There is never a single explanation for something or just one solution to a problem. I try to creatively analyze every aspect of a situation before making my choice on that specific situation. Creativity allows me to be able to not fit the human stereotype across the world of being uniform. A person's own originality makes them unique to the world and I know that I have a specific creative manner about myself that allows me to successfully analyze the world in my own way. I could care less what people think of my ideas or solutions because most of the time my explanation ends up being the most thought-out and thorough solution.

Hope and Optimism. No one has the ability to control my life and my future except for me. By having this right I will continue to make sure my future is bright and constantly moving in the right direction. I am very confident about what my life will be like in the future because of my refusal to fail. I am very open to new things and plan on taking advantage of every opportunity that comes my way.

Because he knows that Jack is a leader in the classroom, John can count on him to try out new things with other students, opening up his creative side. Being both a self-starter and a leader, Jack is a role model in the classroom. Other students listen to him because he is consistent and honest.

Shantelle has a strong sense of fairness and is attentive to any inconsistency or hypocrisy among teachers and other students. She stands up for what she believes is right and won't back down. However, she sees the best in other students. Shantelle is also very humble and has a strong sense of purpose. John plays to her strength of fairness in his teaming approach with the class. He can always expect the best from her when she works in small groups with other students.

Margaret tends to procrastinate on assignments and, if the subject matter isn't interesting to her, she will make it known through rolling her eyes and trying to get the attention of others in the classroom. This can be a huge distraction for John and really pushes his diligence and teamwork strengths buttons. Margaret is fairly self-absorbed and resists any teaming activities. Because John has known Margaret for several years, he realizes this is a good opportunity to re-connect through her strengths. John knows that she is creative, and if he can figure a way to kindle her curiosity, then he may able to give her some latitude in working through the assignment. This is not to say that he has to change the assignment for Margaret. But instead, he offers her the opportunity to look at the material in a different way that appeals to her.

John is also aware of his and his students' shadow strengths. His interest in classroom teamwork may be exaggerated when he doesn't connect with students who favor working more independently. Jack's perseverance gets him in trouble when his commitment to his schoolwork causes sleep deprivation. A typical strength used to excess is "perseverance" observed in maximizing students who are driven to excel in everything. We might think this is a gift and extrapolate it to imagine All-American athletes on Rhodes Scholarships, but managing the shadow side of a strength like perseverance can be a real challenge.

Shantelle is sometimes perceived as being too optimistic, when her hopefulness may not be realistic, and Margaret's curiosity and creativity can get the best of her, when there is an assignment due with no wiggle room. Teachers and students who know the shadow sides of their strengths can learn to set boundaries to prevent themselves from going to the dark side.

When teachers appeal to the strengths of their students, it allows students to consciously and sub-consciously know that they are being cared for—that "my teacher is seeing the best in me."

Managing Strengths in the Curriculum

Reading stories in the primary grades and studying history, literature, and social studies in middle and high school provide natural homes for examining the character strengths and motivations of individuals and groups, both fictional and non-fictional. The classroom comes alive when students compare their individual strengths with traits with those of characters in literature and history. Students can identify with and understand characters through a different lens.

Jane Gillham, co-director of the University of Pennsylvania's Penn Resiliency Project, and a faculty member at Swarthmore College, reminds us that teachers and counselors need to understand curriculum at an adult level, to make it a part of their daily life. Any teacher can hold fast to a curriculum script, a type of blind adherence, but to be competent with any program is to think through the model and to apply the wisdom of that model. There needs to be a fit and readiness, so that the teacher's strengths come alive in appealing to student strengths. Ted Sizer, the author of

Horace's School, says, "Having the skills today is a small part of the whole. Being committed to using them consistently tomorrow is the crux of it . . . Habit, obviously, relates to disposition." School staff will have to want to apply strengths skills with students; to be effective, adults must have internalized strengths' utility and reasonableness.

In Her Own Words: Christine Cook, Reading First Cognitive Coach; Instructional Coach/Data Assessment Coordinator. Triton Elementary, Bourbon, IN

The more that a common language is used about strengths, the more we can pinpoint strengths in each other, and the more we can show kids. I really think it is not just taking an inventory that will help young students truly understand, "Oh yeah, I am really good at that." Sometimes it is easier to see strengths in others. So therefore, since we want something to really be part of our culture, and academics are where we spend the majority of our time, we need to teach strengths in conjunction with our regular curriculum. This is an important part of lessons that integrate how we already teach characterization. What is the motivation for characters to do certain things? What strengths may have led to the choices historical personalities made? Some people need to see the link or have it spelled out. When teachers see that strengths are connected to the other things we are doing and to our vision for students, the value of this approach is so clear.

Mark Linkins, curriculum director for the Wallingford-Swarthmore School District, PA, would agree. He has seen the return on investment in the language arts classroom at Strath Haven High School. Ninth grade students read the classic, *The Odyssey*, where the rich text is used for identifying signature strengths. Students see dynamic character transformations in the book—very clearly. For example, humility and perspective are developed over time. Curiosity and self-regulation are seen as shadow strengths. These are certainly areas that connect with 14 and 15 year-old students. Similarly, Brad Trevathan's ninth grade humanities classes at Culver Academies study *The Odyssey*. He has his students reflect on their own character strengths and shadow strengths (those used in excess) and compare them to the major characters in the classic, while understanding the tension between weakness of will and strength of will that they encounter in their own lives.

Strengths Around the Harkness Table

Culver Academies teacher Ed Kelley uses Harkness methodology, developed at Phillips Exeter Academy in New Hampshire, in his 10th grade Humanities class. This approach is employed by many secondary schools today. Students sit around an oval table and interact through discussion. They are encouraged to contribute their own ideas and learn good discussion skills within the group. This is a student-centered approach to bringing out the best in students by having them reason among each other, not following the teacher's lead, whose role is to listen, take notes, and help guide the discussion when necessary.

Ed's classroom focus is on skills development, one of which is effective communication. This requires students to open up to the group. Ed assesses their ability to analyze a number of literary and historical pieces and share them articulately

with the group. That can be very difficult for the freshmen and sophomores he teaches, because they are also concerned about how they look, how they sound, and what they are saying. They may be afraid to be wrong in front of their peers. Ed promotes strong empathy skills in the classroom. Students need to empathize with the student who is speaking, who might be nervous. Ed says, "I use strategies in the areas of praise, motivation, optimism, and resilience. They are essential. I remain positive as I challenge students." When they are concerned and feel that they can't perform a task within the group, he reminds them that they already have specific characteristics that enable them to be successful overcoming these challenges.

In His Own Words: Ed Kelley, Humanities Teacher, Culver Academies, Culver IN

I look at their character strengths. It might be a student who is somewhat reserved but is very creative—that is one of her top strengths. So, I need to find a way where I can utilize the creativity in a discussion where she will feel comfortable. We were recently discussing "romantic art." There is a girl in class who loves studying art and loves the romantics. I am going to feed on that and encourage her to share her love of art with the class. When we have a class discussion, I am going to prod her a little bit and say, "This is where you are strong. Let's see it come out. Tomorrow, we are going to be talking about Joseph Turner, one of your favorite romantic painters." Just in that email, I will get a response that says, "You know what, I am really excited about tomorrow's class. I am usually reserved with discussion, but because I realize that I am creative, and I love art, I will feel more comfortable participating in the discussion." I will give her an opportunity to speak first. I will say, "In an effort to initiate the conversation, let's have Barbara speak first about her interest in art." That's one way to get a student to communicate with the group when they are usually reserved but now feel more comfortable.

Another would be a student who is somewhat reserved or concerned about how they are being perceived by their peers. His or her top strength, however, is humor and playfulness. When we study *Gulliver's Travels* and Voltaire's *Candide* satire can be quite funny. It is not always humorous, but it is often through parody implying humor. So I approach the student. "You are funny. Your peers think you are very funny. You are often reserved, because maybe you are afraid to be the academic in the class discussion. Can we utilize your humor when we are talking about parody or satire? Can you think of any films that you love because they are funny and that maybe you can share with the group?" And that student was more than happy to say, "You know, I love these films. Let's talk about them in discussion tomorrow." I said, "Sure, you lead the discussion." I am approaching students and their reservations and focusing on their character strengths to bring out a skill that needs to be developed further.

Mindful Moment: *Classroom Strengths Management*

What are your students' strengths? _____

_____

_____

_____

_____

_____

How do you support and appeal to different strengths in different students?

_____

_____

_____

_____

When do your strengths get in the way of bringing out the best in your students? _____

_____

_____

_____

_____

_____

Advocating Strengths

After understanding how to identify and exercise strengths,
teachers and students can communicate in different ways
about their respective strengths.

Strengths 360° — Student to Student

Many young people are self-conscious about how they see themselves in the world and are concerned about how their peers see them. Some students tend to either exaggerate or understate their signature strengths. By asking students to share what strengths they see in each other, students can compare the way others see his or her strengths. The feedback from external observers, both students and teachers, can help provide checks-and-balances to participants' choices on their respective strengths profiles.

At one high school, junior girls were invited to share what they thought to be the strengths of their fellow students. Each girl was provided with a copy of the 24 VIA strengths and definitions. Then, in small groups of approximately six students each, the girls shared what they thought to be the signature strengths of each other. One girl observed that the majority of people in her group suggested that creativity was one of her strengths. She said, "No way!" and claimed that this trait was far from being a signature strength as observed from her individual VIA score. But each girl shared an example of her *being* creative—her strength in action. The value of the "Strengths 360" provided her with multiple observations of being creative. Because her peers see her strength of creativity, she sees herself differently. She now owns this strength.

Activity: The 360° Feedback Gallery

These activities provide a graphic understanding of how other students see each other.

- Based on reviewing the 24 strengths of the VIA, have students choose what they believe to be another student's signature strengths.
- With large newsprint, have each student write their name on the top of a sheet.
- Tape each sheet to the wall and have the student stand next their corresponding sheet.
- Give each student a marker.
- Going either clockwise or counterclockwise, have each student rotate to the next sheet and write down the strengths they observe in each corresponding student.
- If there are multiple endorsements for a certain strength, then the student will place a check-mark next to the strength.
- After completing this portion of the activity, have the students circle around one of the completed sheets. The teacher asks the students to provide one or two examples of how they see this strength come alive in the chosen student.
- Then the chosen student will share how their VIA strengths match up with what his or her peers perceive as strengths.
- Rotate to each student in the class.

Activity: The 360° Feedback Strength Cloud

Here is an additional way of accessing the 360° approach that can be used to represent the top strengths of individuals or the entire group.

- Go to www.wordle.net to create "Strength Clouds."

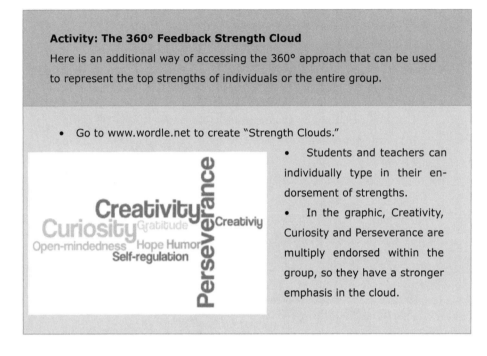

- Students and teachers can individually type in their endorsement of strengths.
- In the graphic, Creativity, Curiosity and Perseverance are multiply endorsed within the group, so they have a stronger emphasis in the cloud.

Teachers Magnifying Other Teachers' Strengths: The Positive Introduction

Appealing to strengths can make for a more vibrant classroom for both teachers and students. Here is another interactive activity. For this you will need a partner. If you are using this book as part of a group or a class, we suggest that you pick someone that you do not know too well, such as a colleague from another department. If you are reading this book alone, find a trusted friend who will play along and be honest.

You are going to introduce yourself by telling a story about when you were at your best. You may write this story before you share with your partner and read it aloud, or you may just tell it. Here is an example of what a positive introduction might sound like:

> I had been warned about 13-year-old Phillip by several people, a few of whom he had scared off—including his teachers, his principal, and his mother. "That boy is a piece of work," was the general consensus. When Phillip and his mother arrived in my office, his face was red and his eyes swollen. His mother announced, "I wish you good luck. It was all I could do to get him into the building.
>
> As she departed, I introduced myself to Phillip and attempted to build some rapport. I anticipated a challenge. "I know I'm not the first coach you have had,"

I helpfully pointed out, "so I'd like to know what your goals are for our sessions together so that we can be sure to incorporate them into the meetings." Phillip did not wait to formulate his answer. It spilled out of him. "My goal is to never see your face again!" he spat angrily, narrowing his eyes to thin slits and turning away from me with his arms tightly crossed. I was briefly shocked; it was the first time I had ever been told this by any student. I tried not to react too quickly lest I respond with anger at a boy who had merely answered my question quite honestly, and the thought of what to say came to me surprisingly easily, despite never having had his particular answer offered to that question.

"Phillip, I think that's a wonderful goal," I said with real enthusiasm and a lack of sarcasm that astonished even me. He turned to me looking quite stunned, anger at least temporarily defused, and listened as I continued. "I only work with people until they don't need me anymore, so I will do everything that I can to make it possible for you not to need to see me again. I can't promise when that will be, but I will promise to honor your request." By now Phillip was quite confused, but he wasn't as angry, and I wasn't feeling threatened by his very straight-forward comment. And he did need me; he needed to learn to use his powers for good.

During subsequent meetings, there was sometimes tension. He complained to his mother that I was positively the most stubborn person he had ever met, but he never refused to attend a session. (Perhaps he meant that I was stubbornly the most positive person he had ever met. It can be frustrating to work with someone who is sure there are solutions to problems!) There was also lots of growth, and one day I knew that Phillip was ready to use his toolbox of strategies and self-knowledge independently. I reminded him of my promise when we had first met, prefacing what I was about to tell him—that his goal had been met and he didn't need to see me anymore—by reading Phillip the notes about our first conversation. "Wasn't I just awful?" he remarked with embarrassment. "Well, were you happy then?" I asked. "Were you being your best self?"

It's not just that Phillip learned skills like reading and writing, and learned content like Biology and Algebra. He developed self-efficacy, that he had the power to produce results.

While this story is about a student, remember that your story *does not* have to be about work. In fact, you might have had a "me at my best" moment at any time in your life. It could even have been a time when you were a child. What matters is that you were using your strengths so automatically that it was just like breathing.

Afterwards, you did not necessarily think anything special had happened, but now looking back you realize that your strengths were teamed in just the right balance for you to be at your best.

In the example on the previous page, the storyteller showed great social intelligence and self-regulation when she did not react to being both yelled at and spat upon. Further she showed creativity as she admits to having an in-the-moment solution to a situation that she had never experienced before. What other strengths do you see in action?

Activity: Positive Introduction: Me at My Best

- Choose a partner. Decide who will share first.
- You will each have 3-5 minutes to share with this partner. Keep your story to this time frame. Tell your "Me at My Best" story straight through: a beginning will set the scene, the middle will expand and add details for the listener, and the end will wrap things up.
- Your partner will *listen for the strengths you used* during this best moment and *tell you what she or he heard.*
- You will return the favor.

When we conduct this part of the workshop, teachers often remark that they weren't aware of some of the strengths that their respective partners revealed in them. This is a key to knowing that they are strengths. Just as we are unaware most of the time that we are breathing, our strengths are there all of the time, even when we are not paying attention to them. Some people have even shared in journal entries with us that they discovered something to like and even admire about someone they previously disliked. With this in mind, our teachers then were prepared to develop some strengths-based approaches for the classroom.

Mindful Moment: *Expressing Strengths*

What did you most admire in your partner's story? What strengths were evident? _____

_____

_____

How did you tell your partner this, if you did? _____

_____

_____

What surprises were there, if any, in what you learned about your partner?

_____

_____

_____

How did the storyteller feel about having their strengths highlighted?

_____

_____

_____

How did the listener feel about the storyteller? _____

_____

_____

_____

Relating Strengths

*Teachers and students matter! When you are more aware of each other's assets,
you can better relate to each other, and in turn, use strengths
to great benefit in the classroom.*

Strengths Buttons and Shadow Sides in Classroom Relationships

April and Fina are friends. The adults at their middle school wonder if the two girls might be better off in separate classes. Teachers say that Fina is too impulsive, too energetic, and disruptive in the classroom, too likely to engage in risky behavior, and too likely to make a joke at someone else's expense. Her grades are suffering. The natural consequences system the school uses is not working, and both the teachers and the school psychologist are looking for some new tools to help. April, on the other hand, is often too nice, too tolerant, too likely to be hurt over and over, and too likely to have broken wing friends. She is easily led and has recently been caught for cheating in her science class when she let Fina look at her answers to a test.

What should be done about the girls? Of course, your strengths will play a role in how you understand the situation. What are your immediate reactions to the girls? What strengths buttons may have been pushed?

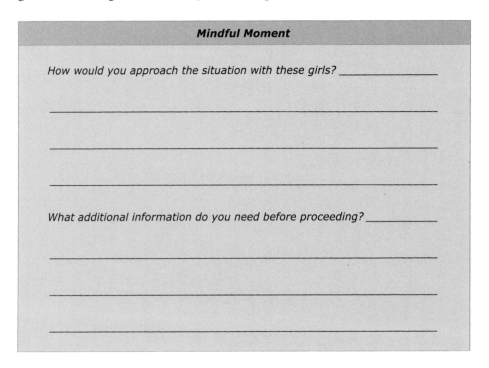

Mindful Moment

How would you approach the situation with these girls? _____

_____

_____

_____

What additional information do you need before proceeding? _____

_____

_____

_____

Who would need to be involved in your plan? What strengths would they bring to the situation? _____

_____

_____

_____

_____

Now we'd like you to reconsider your top-of-mind answers by including some information about the girls, thinking about how they might not be using their powers for good, and imagining how you could change this situation. How might knowing this information give you new insights into an action plan?

Fina's signature strengths are:

- Humor
- Zest
- Honesty
- Bravery
- Social intelligence

April's signature strengths are:

- Love
- Forgiveness
- Hope
- Perspective
- Kindness

Knowing what you do about the shadow sides of strengths, how could you suggest ways to help? For more on this topic, refer back to the story about Glen in Chapter One.

In Her Own Words: Joan Young, former kindergarten teacher, now 4th grade teacher and educational coach/tutor in Menlo Park CA

I work with "Ted", a 14-year old boy who has Asperger's Syndrome. He loves to get off topic and tell me a story about school or the latest political faux-pas or something not related to our study. He has a great sense of humor, and I can always count on some big laughs when I share stories about my day in kindergarten. One of the favorite stories that he references regularly is one when I had a student who put a red-hot candy up his nose. Of course, "Ted" finds this story much funnier than I do, but the point is that he likes to be a part of something that happens to me outside of our session. And he knows that I enjoy his stories, no matter how off the wall (which they sometimes are!). In order to fuel our work together, we schedule about 2 or 3 mini "humor breaks" during the session so that he can be off task and know that it's time limited, but also so he can benefit from the laughter that quells his anxiety when working on difficult assignments. Humor is definitely a powerful strength of his and helps motivate him to get through his work so that he can share or hear a story. This structure helps him from going to the shadow side of his humor.

Student Strength Teams and Natural Caring

One way to look at April's behavior (from the last several pages) was to see her as being generous to a friend and hopeful that it would not be a problem. When students know their strengths, they have more information to make better choices. Here is what else can happen when students care for one another. Each year at Culver, John has the opportunity to work with a group of twelve exceptionally bright and socially intelligent middle-school students who vie for four full-scholarships to the school. They are competing against other students who also possess strong grades, laudable community service, and a strong breadth of other activities.

Prior to the interviews, each candidate completes the online VIA-Youth inventory. Then they participate in a collaborative activity that has candidates work together for a common goal. The final activity has the candidates divided into three groups of four. The explicit goal of the activity is for each group to internally share their character strengths and then create a graphic representation of how the individual strengths support the group. Of course, group facilitators look for more information than that. This is the same approach as the teacher activity you read about earlier in this chapter. The question is: "If you were to work together as a team for the upcoming year, how would convey to others your group's strengths?"

Students worked diligently in their three small groups and put together strengths profiles and constructed three original and instructive "strength graphics" using markers on newsprint paper. The students compared their signature strengths, then used different markers and a theme to portray their group traits. Each group then presented how they created and developed their respective strength approach. What was most exciting was how these 8th graders immediately took to each other, wanting to know more about each other. They were actually forming small teams. Gone from the surface was the individual competitive anxiety and social comparisons.

Instead, these students had a chance to meet each other and get to know others as fellow human beings who had great strengths of character that could shape a successful team. Their shared identity came from being in search of a scholarship opportunity. This was genuine. The bottom line was this: When we get young people together, and help them to know and understand each other, and encourage them to know their respective strengths, it can be, as VIA researchers Nansook Park and Chris Peterson say, "intriguing and even empowering." As a result of last year's program, ten of the twelve finalists decided to come to Culver. They credited the development of relationships and the knowing others through their strengths as reasons for their choice.

Teacher Collective Efficacy

Imagine that you have two sets of talented faculty with comparable students develop a similar new curriculum initiative. Where one program may flourish in one school, it might flounder in another. The difference is usually mediated by the relationships developed within each respective faculty. Developed by Texas A&M's

Roger Goddard and his colleagues, *collective efficacy* is the belief of teachers that the faculty as a group can execute the positive courses of action required to successfully educate students. It is a confidence in the ability of a group of teachers to reach a shared goal through having common expectations for action. This helps teachers with creative problem solving to reach goals and to willingly collaborate with challenges faced at school.

More importantly, educator collective efficacy is significantly related to both math and reading achievement at the elementary level and to cross-curricular achievement at the high school level, even when controlling for measures such as socioeconomic status, minority enrollment, urban/suburban/rural location, size, and prior student achievement. In other words, it is not about how many physical resources are available. Instead, it is about the people. Faculty collective efficacy significantly influences not only the ways in which teachers approach their work; it also has a direct impact on high school students' verbal, math, and science achievement. Knowing the strengths of a faculty is foundational to working as an effective team.

More Than the Sum of Your Parts: Mapping Strengths Teams

In one of our summer seminars, we had a mix of teachers from two different high schools. In one group there were five teachers who had the opportunity to demonstrate how their VIA strengths could influence their collective efficacy. Gary, a history teacher; Dave, an English teacher; Joan, a school counselor; Linda a school librarian; and Nancy, a school language teacher were grouped together.

If you look at the thematic representation in the figure to the right you will notice that Joan became the center of the group. From there, the group began to make connections as they gathered their strengths in relation to hers. For example, Joan and Gary shared fairness and open-minded- 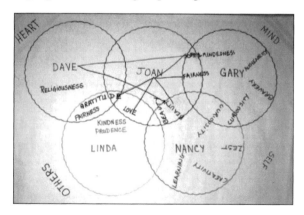 ness, Nancy and Joan shared beauty, Linda and Joan shared love, gratitude, and fairness. So they found that they connected in a kind of Venn diagram that looked like the Olympic rings.

Nancy drew the circles, using her creativity. Linda was the one who did all the writing. A former elementary teacher, her beauty and excellence showed in her penmanship. Depending on the task the group is assigned, they now know where to lean or lend themselves based on each individual's strengths and the needs of the task. There were no weak links in their chain—they were tied together.

Gary, one of the members of the group, mentioned, "In general, any time one does a survey of this nature, there is a tendency to project oneself to others. I think human nature can drive us to be cautious of exposing who we really are. This activity proved to us that we could feel comfortable in our own skin with our strengths."

We have found that teachers are more caring and trusting of each other after spending time connecting their strengths. This bodes well for their respective school and students. One Culver teacher said this:

I have thought about leaving the field many times, but since our school has been building strengths, optimism, resilience, and relationship skills among our faculty, I see my work in a different light. I really was born to be a teacher.

Mindful Moment: Strengths Mapping

What are the strengths of your fellow staff members and of your students?

_____

_____

How can you help bring out the best in them?_____

_____

_____

What strengths do you have in abundance? How can you foresee using these?_____

_____

_____

What strengths might you need to borrow for more effectiveness? Do you know where to find these in your school? _____

_____

_____

Training Strengths — Building *SMART* Students

Strengths improve with deliberate practice. Spot, manage, advocate,
and relate your strengths individually and in your relationships,
and you will be able to use them to develop these skills in your students.

Jeremy Riffle, the principal of Triton Elementary, serves a student body of whom about 50% are growing up in generational poverty. Riffle and Triton teachers have focused on strategies to "help erase some of the back story" to bring out their student's strengths and provide them with a "future story."

Jeremy has personally mentored a student, Daniel. To begin with, Jeremy reviewed Daniel's top VIA strengths with him. Through conversation with Daniel, he found the boy's signature *trait* strengths to be curiosity, gratitude, appreciation of beauty and excellence, love of learning, while a signature *state* strength was bravery. Daniel's curiosity had tended to be a shadow strength when it came to trying new things.

One day, Jeremy simply asked him: "What do you have a passion for?" Daniel responded as follows:

> **Daniel:** I have a passion for cooking, and I want to be a chef, and I want to be in a band.
> **Jeremy:** What are you doing on a daily basis to become a better chef?
> **Daniel:** Well, we don't have a lot of food in our house.
> **Jeremy:** Okay. What do you do to become a better band member?
> **Daniel:** Well, I really like to play the guitar, but several of my guitar strings are broke.
> (Jeremy provided guitar strings to help that student with his future story. Now there is also a high school student who is giving Daniel guitar lessons during his "specials" class time. After a series of lessons, Daniel met with Jeremy again.)
> **Daniel:** You know, I learned a song, and I want to play it for the teacher and students in the music class.
> (Daniel went to his music teacher and told her, "You know guitar lessons are so much cooler than music class." The teacher didn't take offense to what Daniel said and replied: "You know what? I agree with you, Daniel. And I am so excited to have you come and play." Daniel ended up playing for her music class!)

Daniel needed to have resources to achieve his goals and to put his strengths of curiosity, appreciation of beauty and excellence, and love of learning into action, but so many students don't have the resources to build a future story. Jeremy Riffle has encouraged every one of his teachers to pick one child, just to be an extra resource. It may just mean stopping by to say, "How's it going? What are your strengths?" This is the first step toward getting students to play to their strengths.

Activity: Prompts for Creating a SMART Future Story

- What is something you really enjoy and would love to do more of?
- What are you doing to help this happen? How do your strengths help?
- Can you use your strengths in new ways so that you can enjoy this thing more often?
- What else do you need? Who can help you?
- Who is somebody you look up to? What is it that you admire about this person?
- What are his or her strengths? What do they do well?
- What are some things in this person that you also see in yourself?

Student Strengths: Students Training Students

Gabe Paoletti is a program director in a parochial high school. He facilitates strengths-based retreats for students at his school and has his older students help teach younger students how to use their strengths.

In His Own Words: Gabe Paoletti, MAPP, MA: Campus Minister for Retreats & Spiritual Development, Camden Catholic High School, Cherry Hill NJ

As part of the school's retreat program, I work with sophomores, and we focus on developing an inherent sense of purpose and meaning through engaging service. First, I have students identify their own strengths before having them teach sixth grade students what their strengths are. I found that the tenth graders were best able to understand what their gifts were through helping others—when they see the results on someone else's face, right away they can see the inherent meaning. You really learn something when you teach it.

The process started in Health Class, where I presented sophomores with three lessons on the strengths. As an introduction to the strengths, we had them do positive introductions and then code each other's for strengths by reviewing the list of the 24 VIA strengths. From the list of the 24 VIA strengths, the students find at least eight strengths that they heard in each respective student's positive introductions. I wanted students to be creative in finding them, because the goal with bringing in the sophomores was to have each of them help show the sixth graders what their strengths were and how they used them throughout the retreat. Some of the stories were a stretch for finding strengths, and the sophomores really had to work to identify others' positive traits.

Although it would be more conventional to first have students learn about the strengths and then share a story where they show their strengths, I decided to take another route and have students first write a story about a time when they were at their best before they learned about the strengths. Then they took the VIA, and after this another student coded the story as a way to verify and build the students' self-efficacy around their strengths. I really wanted the students to be able to search for strengths in their stories, even if it was a stretch.

In His Own Words: Gabe Paoletti (continued)

During the retreat, the sixth graders participated in a "strengths obstacle course" where students had an opportunity to show different strengths. Afterwards, they participated in a trivia activity where students identified random strengths that would help them get to an answer.

A key thing was, as students were creating the retreat in class, I constantly made them aware of what strengths they were using with their ideas. When students came up with certain ideas, I would say "that was a very creative idea," or "you are showing a lot of social intelligence there for noticing that, whereas some students might feel uncomfortable doing that."

SMART Strengths for the Future

Whether or not a student comes from a privileged or impoverished background, the hope is that young people's strengths will come alive throughout their K-12 school careers and help them past graduation—whether it be getting into college or entering the job market. When students have the opportunity to play to their strengths over time, they will easily be able to have stories about how they have spotted and managed their own strengths. They have learned how to advocate their strengths to appeal to others in forging healthy relationships, and they can now train others to use their strengths for good. We want our graduating students to say: "These are my strengths. This is how they come alive. This is what I do better than anybody else."

When students participate in college interviews, typical responses to "what do you want to do or be questions" revolve around: "Well, I work hard, show up on time, and you can count on me, sir." We believe that students need more than that, that they need to be able to convince someone why they should be admitted to a school or considered as a viable candidate for a job. The way to do that is through having students understand their character strengths. By learning how the strengths work well together, and explaining and demonstrating to future universities or employers "this is why you want me—this is what makes me different from everybody else."

In His Own Words: David Bonner, Director of College Counseling, The King Low-Heywood Thomas School, Stamford CT

Using the VIA as a facilitation tool, my twenty-minute introductory conversations with students reveal the kind of authentic information (hopes, dreams, desires, wants, needs, interests, and passions) that may have taken two or three hours of meetings to reveal in the past. What is more, they warm to their topics, and their connection is more relevant and personal. As I review their meeting notes in preparation for writing a recommendation, I am struck by how well they reflect their individuality through their personal stories: the authentic anecdotes that provide so much value in our recommendations and in building relationships.

Armed with some very simple questions, I debrief students after collecting or confirming some of the basic information they need to cover at the start of their meeting (for example, "Where are you in the process?" "Have you signed up for the SAT?" and "Have you visited any colleges?") The surprise was that I only really needed one or two questions, "How do you feel about the VIA?" and "Can you tell me about a time one of these strengths has served you well?" Each of these was consistently met with a very positive response. As an educator who is interested in getting to know these students as well as possible, I have found that the VIA has provided a very powerful, efficient, and effective tool for getting to hear our students' stories.

While there have been very few, sometimes a tough issue comes up. These have been addressed in a very affirming way through respectful listening by the counselor, repetition of the feelings the student is sharing, and, as appropriate, words of support. While expected, conversations with students have led many to realize that their strengths will be useful in writing their essays. So, one set of activities will be designed to help them write authentic essays. For those who have written essays, we work with them to look for strengths (VIA and others) within their writing.

This chapter examined how teachers and students can be partners in the learning process by developing a common strengths language that creates a climate for increased learning and achievement. Teachers can also be strengths partners with the parents of their students. In Chapter Three, we will show how parents can be good mentors, modelers, and managers by shaping young people's behavior through their ideals, words, and actions and will show how parents can best match their strengths to their child's behavior.

Chapter Three

Strengths at Home

The best way to make children good is to make them happy.
—Oscar Wilde

What's Good about Your Child?

Try to remember what your child was like when he or she was little. Was she constantly getting into things? Was she confident as she learned to walk? Did she laugh at herself when she fell down? When you sent her to time-out, did she happily occupy herself by singing at the top of her voice while stomping her feet in rhythm? Perhaps instead he seemed very shy and said very little. As a result, he didn't love his busy and stimulating preschool and going new places in the car was sometimes traumatizing for you, too, as he wailed in fright for fear of losing you. He never needed to go to timeout, because he was so eager to please, and as a result you expected him to do well when he started school.

Fast-forward to your first parent teacher conference in kindergarten. The child who stomped her feet and sang in timeout is now described by her teacher as "still learning to wait her turn" during circle time, and the boy who was so eager to please is "not regularly completing his work," even though you've been told what a hard worker he is. It's easy to start playing the fix-it game early on with kids, since so much of school is about measuring.

Many of the things that school measures are loosely included under the term progress. There are progress reports at every grade level several times a year and, in the culture of accountability ushered in with high-stakes testing, it can become easy to blame someone in the parent-child-teacher triangle when progress does not occur as expected. When children are young, uneven progress may be attributed to developmental issues. As they get older, there are hundreds of possible labels, diagnoses, and explanations for lack of expected growth. Many of these real issues can be easily confused with lack of apparent effort or poor preparation. Also, it can be easy to see strengths very specifically, in terms of academic success and classroom-friendly behavioral expectations, rather than to look at strengths more broadly. Now that you know more about strengths, though, we hope you will look at your strengths and those of your child a bit differently.

When our children are young and each day is full of new words and skills to practice and master, both children and time spent with them can be delightful. You might even take offense when others don't seem to notice your baby's or toddler's strengths. After all, who can resist the charms of a child, with chubby cheeks and gap-toothed smile, with happy, silly playfulness and earnest determination? Once children reach school age, however, it often does not take long for both children and their parents to discover that school is not always as new or exciting or joyful as being little. While screaming tantrums may have been replaced with strident conversation, squeals of delight may sometimes seem a thing of the past. Where, you may ask, are the strengths in that?

Parents share the desire with one another that their children grow up to be happy, productive, and self-sufficient members of society. Beyond that, our desires for our children are inevitably affected by our own "values in action." These strengths, as you recall, are the good of a person. They are also part of the values lens through which we view our children, their teachers, and our relationships with both of them. If you have the strengths of love of learning and self-regulation but those are your child's lesser strengths, it can be difficult to understand why he or she does not "just do it" when it comes to school work even though you are certain that school (and your home life) would be so much better (there's a value-laden word) if that happened. Imagine the life of a teacher who has not only his own strengths to spot and manage but also those of an entire classroom of students, including yours. How do they do that?

Differentiated Learning and Strengths

In Positive Psychology we talk about whether the outcomes of research should be *descriptive* or *prescriptive*. When you are thinking about your child, we encourage you to think descriptively. We believe it is important to begin by describing student behaviors, both current observed ones and future desired ones, before making prescriptions about how students should be taught. When you took the VIA Signature Strengths test, you endorsed behaviors (actions) you regularly engage in. This helped identify your strengths. Separated from these behaviors, strengths language can be merely another way of labeling and that language is only helpful if it is connected to behaviors, experiences, and values.

To practice thinking descriptively about strengths, you will also need to begin to separate your opinions and attributions about *why* your child behaves the way they do from what they do—the way they actually behave. For example, when a child's progress report says that more effort is needed to improve grades, that is an opinion. If instead the teacher says, "Matthew has not handed in four homework assignments this term. His grade would have been higher if he had turned in this work," this is descriptive, because it has identified a behavior that can be changed. Identifying behaviors can help guide the process of differentiating for learning. Sometimes the strengths we spot in ourselves and others aid this process, and sometimes, remember, they blind us and need to be managed to get us more of what we really want.

One way that schools have differentiated for learning is by identifying somebody as a visual learner, an auditory learner, a kinesthetic learner, a multi-sensory learner, a tactile learner, or perhaps an experiential or even multisensory learner. Neuroscience has shown us through brain imaging that behaviors alone cannot always provide a clear diagnostic picture of a struggling learner. Certain types of tasks are going to lean on some skills and abilities more than others and, of course, not everything is testable. Beyond that, brains develop over time and what seemed to be someone's style as an elementary school student may be different by high school. Despite this, it is very tempting to label the way a child learns instead of making note of what *helps* the child learn. Whether a student quickly imagines from a teacher's words what an assignment should look like, or whether instead the student benefits from having a model, that is just the beginning of how we can differentiate or individualize when we teach children at home and at school.

Spotting Strengths

Lindy is a fifth-grader in a very competitive school district, as measured by state-mandated testing scores, SAT scores, graduation rates, and students' very selective college acceptances. The district's push for excellence appealed to her parents who chose the district for its reputation. Now each weeknight Lindy can spend several hours working on homework and her parents dutifully sit with her at the kitchen table until the work is completed. Often this leaves both child and adults exhausted and sometimes teary, but it is viewed as the price for excellence. Lindy's parents applaud both her and their own diligence.

A few weeks into the school year, Mr. Dawson, Lindy's teacher, has noticed the girl's fatigue. In his class journal, he makes a note: "seems tired." He is not too concerned, though, since Lindy turns in her work and meets standards on assessments. Many of his students play at least one team sport and take dance, music, or karate lessons in addition to having busy social schedules. "Tiredness is the currency of excellence," he tells parents at Parent Information night, who nod at each other with affirmation. When the first progress report goes home, Mr. Dawson has recognized Lindy's diligence. "With more effort," Mr. Dawson writes, "Lindy can move from 'meets expectations' to 'exceeding them.'"

By November, Lindy is no longer completing assignments in class and is giving her parents much more push-back at home. She complains about feeling ill in the morning and, when her parents send her to school anyway, she asks to visit the school nurse. The hip-hop dance group class she loves has been taken off her schedule, and her mother has not signed Lindy up for the next term. Weekends are now devoted to catching up on the folder of unfinished work that Mr. Dawson has willingly sent home on Fridays by parent request. Even over the Thanksgiving break, Lindy plays at catch up instead of hanging out with her friends and sister.

By the beginning of December, it is time for Lindy's parent-teacher conference. Mr. Dawson has a fat portfolio of Lindy's work to show her parents. He describes his attempts to get Lindy to complete her work and compliments her parents on their commitment to her homework. "Can you tell me how much time she spends on school work?" he asks, unaware that his assignments take up the bulk of her non-school time. Once it is clear that the workload and performance are inconsistent with the amount of time spent, Mr. Dawson and Lindy's parents have some choices to make.

Often times, this is the point at which parents become angry, either at one another for not having prevented things from getting this far, or at the teacher, for failing to communicate sooner about the child's difficulties. They may refer a child for testing or start polling their friends who up until now have heard little about concerns for the child's academic performance, lest Lindy look embarrassingly as if she does not measure up. Let's look at this story in the framework of the *SMART* model and see how to prevent problems through strengths spotting, managing, advocating, relating, and training.

Mismanaging Strengths

At the beginning of this story, Lindy, with her parents' help, is already working very hard and long to complete her homework. Her parents sit with her, guiding her through assignments that often take hours. They recognize that their daughter is willing to expend much effort. They value hard work, too. In addition, Lindy's parents do not want her to struggle unnecessarily, and out of their love for her, they take turns being her support system.

Oftentimes parents begin helping out and are not sure when their student should be able to work solo. Other times, children really are struggling and appear to give up easily rather than persisting at a challenging task. In either case, it is easy to believe that trying harder and perhaps longer will lead to success. One obvious and unanswered question is whether Lindy has the skills necessary and is able to work independently.

Sometimes parents have been sitting alongside their children since kindergarten when they practiced reading together and simply have not moved on to having their student work alone. Other times students really do need the nudging of someone else—parent, teacher, tutor, classmate. When this happens, especially kids who have the strength of "teamwork" may find that they like feeling supported by buddying with someone. Sometimes parents who believe they have been gifted with a child may have a strong "sense of purpose" strength connected to their child-rearing approaches. In addition, if they are confident that they are doing the right thing, Lindy's parents may not ask for confirmation about their approach from her teacher.

Mr. Dawson, with 30 years experience behind him, may have a well-developed strength of "perspective," placing Lindy's performance within her class as a whole rather than seeing her individually. Until she struggles in his classroom, this open-mindedness will probably lead him to believe that Lindy is doing fine in fifth grade, even if she is not. In this way, the strengths of everyone involved in the life of a child can make it difficult to see the child's "forest" for the strengths "trees."

Managing Strengths

Here are the Signature Strengths of Lindy's parents, teacher, and herself.

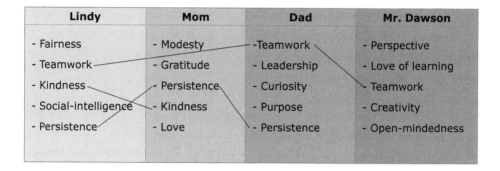

Lindy	Mom	Dad	Mr. Dawson
- Fairness	- Modesty	-Teamwork	- Perspective
- Teamwork	- Gratitude	- Leadership	- Love of learning
- Kindness	- Persistence	- Curiosity	- Teamwork
- Social-intelligence	- Kindness	- Purpose	- Creativity
- Persistence	- Love	- Persistence	- Open-mindedness

Note that in this group, everybody shares at least one strength with someone else. This is important, because Lindy, her family, and her teacher will need to work as members of a team, even if teamwork is not a strength for all of them. Since her parents will be taking on a communication role on behalf of Lindy, they will need to be aware of ways they can strengths-match to help get more of what everyone wants for Lindy. Remember that working through your strengths is more effective than directly trying to fix weaknesses, and that people who use their strengths in everyday life and work were found to be lastingly happier. This kind of happiness— well-being—leads to success. Of course a weakness is the target here, and using strengths is the most effective way to hit the bull's-eye. When a person's strengths are mindfully used in the service of challenging and meaningful goals, exciting changes and shifts can take place.

Sometimes the strengths that make us very good at what we do in one role need to be tweaked. Mr. Dawson, for example, has the strength "love of learning." He's been a teacher for 30 years, and certainly this has helped buoy him through some challenging times. He is able to take the long view of things using his strength of perspective, can use his creativity strength to develop alternative approaches for teaching children who may struggle, and he is open-minded about new possibilities that he might not yet have considered. In some ways this makes him an ideal teacher for Lindy, who needs a flexible teacher who will team with her.

Lindy and her parents share the strength of persistence. What challenges might they face? At first glance, Lindy and her parents are matching and using their strengths well. However, it is possible to stick to a task or use an approach long after it is not really working and think that doing more of the same will result in a different outcome. When it comes to behavior, staying on the same path—the "go with what got you this far" approach—can be difficult to abandon. While Lindy was able to maintain her grades, her parents' approach was actually getting everybody less of what they really wanted. Lindy needed a social life, to be part of a team such as the dance group, and to feel independent. Her parents needed to see Lindy as capable rather than needy.

After Mr. Dawson discovered how much time Lindy (and her parents) were spending on school work, he reconsidered what work she actually needed to finish and quickly created new pathways to support her task completion. For example, he partnered Lindy with another student who also benefited from being part of a team. He put less emphasis on completing every bit of work, since Lindy's "persistence" approach was getting in the way of her learning and well-being, and he shifted to more focused, shorter assignments that Lindy could complete independently. He was sensitive to Lindy's perception (social intelligence) that she be treated like everyone else (fairness) by speaking respectfully and directly about his goals for her. Once Lindy, her parents and Mr. Dawson were able to **spot** their strengths, they could change the way they used them to improve her productivity and recalibrate the balance in her life. At home, Lindy was better able to manage the intensity of her strengths as well as to use her strengths to advocate for her needs.

The Strength of Self-control: The Grit Challenge

In our fast-paced world it can be difficult to delay gratification. Classic studies by Walter Mischel in the 1970s found that the ability to delay gratification as a young child was linked to future outcomes. Compared to more impulsive children, those who can resist an immediate temptation go on to be more socially and academically competent as adolescents, can cope more effectively with stress, suffer less depression, and have higher grades. A study of 32 different personality variables including measures of self-control found that by college, only self-control predicted grades. One measure of this ability to delay gratification and stick with a task over time is called grit. Angela Duckworth, at the University of Pennsylvania, has found that grit, defined as "perseverance and passion for long-term goals," predicts success over and beyond IQ and conscientiousness. She reminds us that no one, no matter how talented, can be successful without hard work.

Grit is more than hard work directed toward achieving difficult goals. It is the sustained and focused application of one's talent over time—often a very long time indeed. Consider the 2010 Vancouver Winter Olympics, where a figure skating team who were in their 30s, Shen Xue and Zhao Hongbo of China, took the pairs gold medal. They had been skating together for 18 years and came out of retirement, winning their sport's top prize with a record high score after three previous attempts had left them disappointed but clearly not discouraged. Grit is so important that without it, talent alone will not result in high achievement. Sustaining one's focus and ambition over time takes both commitment and stamina. Parents, of course, can reinforce both of these behaviors by working with their children's interests.

Earlier in this chapter we talked about "descriptive" versus "prescriptive" behaviors. We can prescribe self-regulation and grit, but parents need to be able to describe it—to know it when they see it. Developing an internal self-monitoring and self-control system is not easy for everyone, and it is a developmental skill in children. Self-regulation also tends to be a culture dependent strength. In some cultures where this is highly valued, people are much more likely to have self-regulation as a strength. This is the case in many Eastern cultures, whereas in Western cultures, self-regulation tends to be a lesser strength.

According to research done by the University of Michigan's Nansook Park and Chris Peterson, self-regulation is even less likely to be represented among top strengths in children than adults, since it is a strength in development. While cultural norms may explain in part the exemplary grit of Shen Xue and Zhao Hongbo, consider Ben Carson, who grew up in Detroit's inner city poverty, the son of a single mother with a third grade education. He dreamed of being a physician and today is not only a renowned Johns Hopkins pediatric neurosurgeon having, for example, successfully performed the most delicate operations to separate conjoined twins, but he is also a professor in four different disciplines in the JHU medical school, the recipient of over 50 honorary degrees and numerous other awards, and was awarded the Presidential Medal of Freedom, the highest civilian award in the U.S. And this is just the short list.

Again we remind you that what makes people successful is not only that they have talents, but that they develop them.

Peer Pressure for Parents

Like many adults you probably think that you have outgrown peer pressure. Interestingly, social comparison is at work throughout your life, so before you say, "Oh, I'm not like that," consider the ways you are affected by what *you* think *other* people think of you. Many parents engage in daily homework battles with their children. Like Lindy's parents, they view the production of homework, high test scores, and solid grades as an extension of their parenting skills. In our communities, it is a closely-held myth that a student's performance is the responsibility of his or her parents. After all, kids need parents and other adults to set standards and rules, right?

A common term for this from the school's perspective is "parent-school partnership." By this the school generally means that parents will support the learning mission of the school and provide a home life that facilitates learning as a priority. In theory this is a great idea. In practice, families may find that this feels like parent homework instead of the student's. It also gets parents very involved in supporting "the homework business." For each student and family, the homework business is a growing concern! The more you help, the more help can be expected and needed to get the work completed. Also, students don't get to practice three important parts of learning to work smarter: being more **self-regulated**, more **self-efficacious**, and more **self-determined**.

Self-regulation, the ability to both plan before doing, as well as to do according to plan, is like a muscle, according to Florida State's Roy Baumeister. When subjected to overuse, the ability to self-regulate is depleted and therefore does not work so very well. Exercising one's self-regulation muscle consistently—such as keeping an accurate and up-to-date calendar of responsibilities—has important strengthening effects on other areas. Baumeister has found that people with a high level of self-regulation are more successful and more popular. Self-regulation failure, on the other hand, is at the heart of most personal and social problems in individuals and their societies. Self-regulation and the subsequent choices and decisions it influences must be developed within the individual student.

Self-efficacy, the belief that one has the capabilities to execute the necessary courses of action required to reach a goal, develops as the student works through both independent and directed trial and error. Albert Bandura of Stanford University says, "The most effective way of creating a strong sense of efficacy is through mastery experiences... If people experience only easy successes they come to expect quick results and are easily discouraged by failure. A resilient sense of self-efficacy requires experience in overcoming obstacles through perseverant effort." At home, adults are often faced with time limits and deadlines that conspire against having students independently learn the ways in which they are capable of planning and carrying out steps for projects, studying effectively for tests, and completing daily homework. Teachers often expect that parents will help at home, and no well-meaning adult intentionally leaves a child to struggle. At the same time, students need to learn where they have the ability to do their own work so that they gain realistic confidence in applying their *SMART Strengths*.

Self-determination, a psychological theory of Richard Ryan and Edward Deci, is concerned with motivation—how people move themselves or others to act. Ryan and Deci have noted, "People are often moved to act by external factors such as reward systems, grades, evaluations, or the opinions they fear others might have of them. Yet just as frequently, people are motivated from within, by interests, curiosity, care or abiding values. These intrinsic motivations are not necessarily externally rewarded or supported, but nonetheless they can sustain passions, creativity, and sustained efforts." School and home environments that impose external demands on students without taking into any consideration the needs of the child to be self-determined may find that the child requires significant and increasing amounts of external motivation to initiate behavior, and that this erodes the independence that parents and teachers hope to see developing over time. Finding a child's areas of passion and competence can help support self-determination.

The Three Ps of Performance

Priming: This term refers to the ways that certain parts of the brain are activated just before carrying out a task. Though it often occurs unconsciously, priming gets us ready to notice certain things and to feel and act in certain ways.

- Positive emotions broaden the possible scope of action and enhance creativity. Prime happiness by doing homework after a chat about what went well (more on this in Chapter Six). Resist the urge to be drawn into your child's complaints about school, if any. Don't give advice or tell the child what he or she should have done—just listen. Then handle those problems with an adult at school.
- Have a small healthy snack during the chat. Whenever possible, control that adrenaline surge and don't rush to get to the next activity. Your behavior,

remember, shows your children what you value. Your strengths are your "Values in Action" (VIA).

- Grouchy parents who hate homework battles need to self-regulate, too.

Practicing: This is just what it sounds like, repeating a desired behavior until it is a habit. In addition, you will want to:

- Record what works and do it again. This is at the heart of self-efficacy. While a certain amount of change in routine can be interesting and may liven things up and even improve performance, building automatic basic skills provides a platform for more complex learning.
- Make work first, play later the habit. After all, you don't get paid for avoiding focus on work or being distracted, do you? (Adults, too, so model the behavior you want—the child is the job, so no Blackberries while talking with your child or at dinner.)
- Avoid social comparison. At its worst, social comparison can lead to negative emotions such as sadness, anger, or disgust. Beware overscheduling kids in an effort to develop them into value-added but sad college applicants.

Persisting: Stick with it!

- **Take the long view.** By the time they reached middle age (the age most parents of high school students are themselves), the majority of "troubled" teenagers in a 40-year study were in stable marriages and jobs, were satisfied with their relationships with their spouses and children, and were responsible citizens in their community.
- **Expect high schoolers to do their homework.** Various homework research of U.S. 9th to 12th graders over 60 years shows percentile gains of between 10 to 30 points on standardized tests when students consistently do their work. Most teachers give credit for homework, too. Not doing homework can mean the difference between passing and failing.
- **Learn what interests your child and let them take the lead.** An interest might be a sport, an instrument or a subject area that they love. But maybe it is social contact, humor, drama, earning and spending money, the great outdoors, or novel problem-solving. This is at the heart of self-determination, the theory that we all require competence, relatedness and autonomy as we pursue goals for their own sake.
- **Learn to know when you are winning the battle but losing the war.** Most teachers offer after school extra help and schools have students who offer community service hours in the form of free tutoring.

Extending self-control beyond moment-to-moment behaviors is part of the "grit" challenge. Do you remember that Lindy's parents had her give up her friends and her dance group in favor of completing unfinished schoolwork? What else could they have done?

Mindful Moment: *SMART Strengths for Parenting*

Brainstorm a list of solutions that you think Lindy's parents did not consider when trying to get her to complete her homework. _____

_____

_____

_____

Since you know the strengths of Lindy, her parents, and her teacher, make a plan that will help everyone involved get more of what they want. Remember that her parents want to feel that they are doing the best job they can, her teacher wants to feel that he's being successful, and Lindy wants to be able to complete her work but not at the expense of having friends and extracurricular activities. _____

_____

_____

_____

_____

When Families Struggle

The quality of parents' relationships with one another has a lot to do with the adjustment of children. Everything from having a new sibling to maintaining poise after a disappointing arts or athletic performance can be affected by the consistency with which parents handle their children. According to distinguished child and family researchers and clinicians Philip Cowan and Carolyn Pape Cowan, co-parenting problems disrupt children's development, potentially resulting in undesirable outcomes such as externalized and internalized behavior problems, as well as less-developed skills related to school readiness, including academic and peer skills.

The challenges of parenting, including sleepless nights and little free time, do not always lend themselves to fun and intimacy. But in the context of completing one's education, furthering one's career, keeping social connections, acquiring a home, or dealing with extended family, co-parenting a child can be exceptionally meaningful and provide "We did it!" growth opportunities for parents. It is important for parents to see themselves as a strengths team working on behalf of the child, even if they are divorced, never married, or otherwise not living together with the child.

Stan and Gracie married while they were still both in college. He marveled at her ability to hold down a full-time job and a full-time college schedule. He called her his "can-do" girl and felt very blessed to be her husband. Gracie loved Stan's easy-going manner and found time with him to be relaxing and spontaneous—two things she was not. Their friends called them the perfect couple. They had two children, a girl and a boy in quick succession, both of whom developed behavior and learning issues. There was criticism from grandparents ("That sort of thing is not in our gene pool.") and their friends ("Your kids are so high maintenance."). By the time their children, Eliza and Jack, were school-aged, stresses of homework, sports, and music lessons soured Gracie and Stan's relationship, and their family life suffered. Jack in particular struggled in school and unlike Lindy, who you read about earlier in the chapter, he did not try to keep up with homework and his mother felt she had to become the "homework police" in an attempt to keep him from failing.

Family Strengths Graph

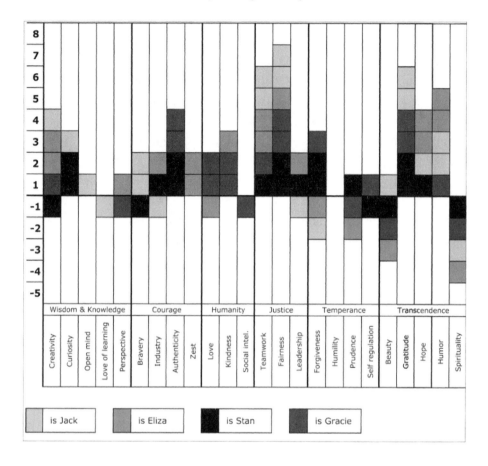

During a family coaching session, this family (not their real names, of course, but a real family's graph) created their own novel representation of their strengths (see figure above). Across the bottom are the 24 VIA strengths in their virtue categories. Up the left side are positive and negative numbers. In this model, everyone received 2 boxes above zero (+1 and up on the graph) for a Signature (top five) strength, 1 box for a top ten strength (also +1 and up), and one box below the line (-1 and down) for a bottom five strength. Each of the four family members is represented by a different shade. (Strengths between 11 and 19 are not represented in this family's model. That was their choice.)

When the last box was colored in, Eliza, who was often critical of her brother, spoke up. "Look at how many strengths we share, Jack! There's teamwork, fairness, hope, creativity, and humor." As you look at the graph, notice the abundance of strengths evident. Everyone—not just the kids—shares teamwork and fairness, and three of the four share creativity, gratitude, and humor. Because everyone is shown as a different shade, their combined strengths power, as well as their individual contributions, remain clear.

How do this family's shadow strengths come alive on their graph, too? Jack noticed, "I need to borrow some humanity and temperance. Is that why I don't do my homework? Can any other strengths stand in for those?" "Stan," Gracie mused, "we know we are so different from each other, and on the graph I can really see where you have strengths that I don't. Even when I am frustrated with you and the kids, I still love all of you and am grateful for tomorrow to keep trying to make things better. There it is, right on the graph!"

Let's fast forward to a few months later. Jack is now doing most of his homework, Gracie has retired from the homework police, Stan has used his curiosity strength to learn new ways to use his other strengths, Eliza and Jack are laughing *with* rather than at each other, and the whole family understands that when everyone wants the team to work a certain way that their fairness buttons may get pushed. This family—a real one—is *SMART*.

Strengths and Learning Disabilities

In the *Family Strengths Graph* on previous page, it is easy to see what's good. The current legal approach to special education, however, mandates a deficit model that focuses on what is wrong with a student. While diagnosing problems can help get the services that make a difference, the results are often not so positive: students see themselves as disabled and often become angry, disengaged, and depressed. Parents can feel entitled to services for their child who suffers in school, even when more services may not create more successes, and teachers may be put in the position of fixing what is wrong, even if it does not suit the educator's strengths. Here's where you ask around your parent network for help: Do they have insider info about teachers who are a good fit for challenging kids? Do they have a tutor who is magic with students? Even if you think you cannot afford the person, call anyway. You might get a referral or other helpful information for the time it takes to call.

While your child might need to be tested to rule out something more serious than lack of engagement (check with the student services department or your student's guidance counselor), if the school just says more effort is needed, you may need an outside expert who can identify the "trees" in your "forest." A meeting to discuss your child's school problems can be very contentious. By using a quasi-Appreciative

Inquiry approach, developed by Case Western University's David Cooperrider, and Diana Whitney, President of the Corporation for Positive Change, you can use the structure of the IEP/TEAM Meeting to both collaborate and lead on behalf of your child. (There is more on Appreciative Inquiry in Chapter Ten).

- Discover. Explicitly identify *what the teachers are already doing that works.* Share this aloud. Include the when, where, and how of it. Use strengths language to identify this and document it in meeting notes.

- Dream. What would it be like to have more of that? Feel the energy in the room change when the TEAM *explores possibility instead of limitations.* If the student is 14 or older, do include him or her at the meeting. It's the law, and it's their dream, too.

- Design. *Focus on getting more of what works*—more hands-on work, written directions, visual models, presentation in chunks, more time, fewer transitions…and ask for these in terms of what is already working.

- Destiny. How will the student be able to achieve the new goals? (There is more on goal setting in Chapter Nine.) Set regular check in times with the TEAM, and keep relationship building with the teachers.

In His Own Words: Buck Weaver, Ph.D. Clinical Neuropsychologist. Wayland, MA

The intelligent conclusion when a child fails at everything kids are supposed to do is not that he has a bright future ahead of him. My difficulties were in learning to read, write, pay attention, and be organized in school. Not only did I have these very significant struggles, I also had the social problems of loneliness combined with conduct problems in my home, school, and community. No doubt about it, my parents were often discouraged, and I came to believe that it was easier to be bad than to be stupid.

Quite frankly, I was good at being bad, and while my parents were often embarrassed by me, my father had a knack for reframing this ability as social intelligence that needed redirection. He taught me that I might not be able to control my grades but I could control other people's perception of my willingness to work. It was a pretty sneaky approach on his part, both because it taught me how to get along with people who were judging my work, and it also helped me develop my presentation of a positive attitude. I kept track of how many times I'd raise my hand and asked for extra help. I began to connect this with actually asking for help and advocating for myself. My high school teachers, though, were completely unsuspecting of my ultimate academic and professional accomplishments.

I graduated from high school in the bottom 5th of my class of 1969, with SAT scores (untimed) in the low 600's (combined). But my parents, tutors, and teachers made it possible for me to graduate with reasonable self-esteem. Though I did wonder why I should bother, I applied to and attended college, even though I had strong ambivalence about why I would be volunteering for another four years of what I hated. "Just try it," my parents said. And I did.

At college I discovered that girlfriends are great, that I was interesting, interested, and motivated. I figured out that my issues were not going away, and began to see myself more through my father's eyes. He believed in me no matter what, and he knew I had strengths. He pushed me to participate in anything that I could do well and value it. He de-emphasized what I did not do well, he was understanding rather than reactive, and he ignored lots of professional advice, especially the kind that encouraged him to take on lots of responsibility for my bad behavior. In other words, he did not believe that because of me he was a bad parent.

My parents worked to understand me rather than to punish me, and for this I am exceptionally grateful. My parents recognized that I had strengths, and that sometimes these strengths were liabilities. But they also had a knack for helping me when I needed it, getting other people to help me so that they would be able to retain their relationship with me, and as a result I mostly felt loved rather than criticized by them.

No one truly knows either the limits or potential of any child. I eventually graduated from Bowdoin College, followed by Memorial University of Newfoundland (MSc), the California School of Professional Psychology (Ph.D.) and received a Harvard Medical School Neuropsychological Fellowship at Children's Hospital Medical Center-Boston.

Mindful Moment: View the "Buck" story through the SMART model.

- *Spot*
- *Manage*
- *Advocate*
- *Relate*
- *Train*

Parent-Child Strengths Teams:

What strengths do you think Buck had as a child? As an adult? What behaviors suggest these strengths? _____

_____

What strengths did his parents seem to have? _____

_____

_____

How did they use those strengths in ways that helped Buck? _____

_____

_____

Which strengths did his parents, especially his father, help him to develop?

_____

_____

What were some of the short-term outcomes? The longer term ones? _____

_____

_____

What future would you have predicted for Buck? _____

_____

_____

The 3XG Journal: Tell Me Something Good

Relationship experts John and Julie Gottman remind us about what predicts relationship failure. The Four Horsemen of the Apocalypse are these powerful negatives:

Criticism — faultfinding
Defensiveness — it's all personal
Stonewalling — the cold shoulder
Contempt — verbal and nonverbal condemnation (disgust)

Instead train your strengths—the whole family of them—by shifting to the positive. One of the simplest things that you can do at home is to become more focused on what works, as you have read throughout this chapter. You can create a positive family ritual around this by keeping a "Three Times Good" or 3XG Journal. Here are the questions you ask and why. The questions are answered one time through for each of three good events.

Here is an example of a single event:
- What happened? (Just the simple facts.)
  » *I finished all of my homework.*
- What was good about it? (A peek into their values.)
  » *I had time for hanging out before bed.*
- Why did it happen? (Did I have anything to do with it? Or was it just random?)
  » *I used my arguing energy for doing the work.*

Do you want to know where students think they have control over good things in their lives? If good things are all apparently random occurrences, can you help students set goals for using strengths to get more of what they want? Are shadow sides getting in the way? You'll find out whether your student is using their strengths to get more of what they want at school and life. You will also find out amazing amounts of information, will help your children and co-parent feel more valued, and build the foundation of positive emotion for your ongoing relationship.

This chapter discussed how parents can help identify their own strengths and help their children spot, manage, advocate, and better relate with their strengths. We also examined the power of parental peer pressure, strengths, and differentiated learning, and the development of grit in young people. Chapter Four will address how sports coaches can apply their strengths with their varied coaching styles to best relate to their players.

Chapter Four

Strengths in Sports

Make sure that team members know they are working with you, not for you.
—John Wooden, Legendary Hall of Fame Basketball Coach

Several years ago, a clip shared on YouTube captured a high moment in school sports. It shows Jason McElwain, a high-functioning young man with autism and manager of a high school basketball team in upstate New York. Jason's coach allows him to dress for the last game of the season, without any promises of actually playing. In the video, the coach stands up with several minutes left in the contest and motions for Jason to go into the game. The deafening roar of the crowd cheers in anticipation as Jason steps onto the court. His first two shots miss, but his third shot is charmed as well as the rest of his baskets, which include six 3-pointers! The excitement of the crowd explodes each time, coming to a crescendo as the final buzzer sounds and players and the spectators mob a beaming Jason.

Jason's story is one way that sports can be a vehicle for happiness. When we demonstrate our best effort as a coach, similar to what Jason's mentor did, we can help our student-athletes become fully engaged in the game and have the greatest opportunity to enjoy the process. As human beings, we have many aspirations, motives, and desires that drive our participation in sport, either from the field, sidelines, or stands. This motivation can't be totally deciphered or illustrated in a brief bio sketch in the team program, by blowing the whistle, or cheering from the third row. Understanding motivation can come from the rich stories of sport participation that have inspired belief and a sense of purpose in many of us. As we listen to the cues that uncover the beliefs and meaning, we are more able to empathize with the joys, elations, and even the frustrations of playing, coaching or being a spectator.

The Purposes of Sports

Although the purposes of sports are varied and mean different things to different people, many would agree that organized sport participation can be intrinsically valuable and may bring great pleasure, engagement, meaning, and achievement to a wide range of participants. When sports are done right, we can learn the joy of movement and the challenge of taking risks. We can learn something about our strengths as well as our limitations. We can learn to work cooperatively toward a common goal. We can learn the importance of teamwork. We can build our communication skills. We can develop or reinforce confidence, trust, and humility. And if we weren't confident, trustworthy, and humble before we started playing or coaching, maybe we can learn a little about those qualities on the field.

Most coaches do not realize the scope of influence that they have on the athletes they serve, nor do many adults understand the reasons they became coaches. Parents may coach for the benefit of their children. Some secondary school teachers bring their craft to the playing field, while others merely fulfill their school contractual responsibilities. Nevertheless, all coaches are strengths educators and through their actions or omissions, have an effect—be it positive or negative—on the athletes they serve. Coaches who really make a positive difference are the individuals who guide with principles that not only make better athletes, but more importantly, help their athletes form a sense of who they are and what is important in life. They provide an opportunity for athletes to grow and challenge themselves.

It is also important to mention that there are coaches who believe that their responsibilities differ from what has been previously mentioned. Some coaches believe that performance-only climates matter most. They know the "Xs and Os," and they truly believe they are good coaches, but they sometimes fail to embrace their opportunities to expand the scope of an athlete's enjoyment and satisfaction that accompanies striving to perform well. However, most of what these coaches do is not outright malice. Rather, they may lack awareness of other approaches or forget with whom they work. Although these coaching blind spots are not easily erased, coaches may overcome them by learning more about their own strengths to become strengths-focused adult mentors.

Organized sports are a natural home for observing *SMART Strengths* in action. By learning about character strengths and ways to build and apply them, coaches help guide students to acknowledge, own, and apply their own strengths, to value their authentic selves, and to increase both their collective and self-efficacy in light of their performances. Kevin Hicks, Associate Head of School and Dean of Faculty at The Hotchkiss School in Lakeville, CT and a coach for many years, says that when athletes are willing to take some responsibility for their triumphs and setbacks, they tend to be more solution-focused when making change.

In His Own Words: Kevin Hicks, Associate Head of School and Dean of Faculty, The Hotchkiss School, Lakeville CT

Developing authentic character is a matter of co-creation. For thousands of years, the process has depended on being mindful of our relationship to others, and in many cases ritualizing moments of initiation and passage. In our culture, sport must be protected as a space in which such relationships between self and other can be embodied and explored—partly through healthy and inclusive rituals guided by the team's coach (who is, I would argue, always his or her team's true leader). Sport is—or ultimately should be—a safe space where we get to test out different versions of who we want to be. Coaches who choose to set as a professional goal their athletes' ability to intentionally transfer a sustainable team-oriented value regime to other areas of their lives often achieve a performance advantage, and invariably experience greater satisfaction in their lived experience, quite regardless of other outcomes.

Let's follow the *SMART* investment process to make this a reality in the athletic arena. In this chapter you will practice by...

S-M-A-R-T Model

Spotting	When you know your own strengths, you are a better observer of strengths in your student athletes and are more attentive to spotting what is good instead of trying to find fault.
Managing	Your strengths are a family of traits that can be combined, tapped and promoted for bringing out the best in you and your student-athletes.
Advocating	When you advocate with your own strengths in your work with student-athletes, you can effectively convey what you want and need.
Relating	Sports are relational activities, and knowing how your strengths match up with your student-athletes can enhance overall teamwork by connecting with and appealing to others.
Training	Once you understand and act on your own strengths, you can better help student-athletes spot, manage, advocate and relate strengths individually and on teams.

Spotting Strengths

Coaches and student-athletes learn a common strengths language in the athletic arena and clearly identify their respective strengths.

Good coaches can spot strengths in their individual players and collectively in a team. Some character strengths tend to be more associated with performance and others more connected to moral or relational character. However, these two areas are not mutually exclusive. Good coaches are able to play to their performance and relational strengths in ways to provide enjoyable and success-conducive environments with the athletes in their charge. Tom Lickona and Matt Davidson, leading character educators and authors of *Smart and Good Schools*, suggest that *performance* character focuses on the diligence, perseverance, and self-discipline necessary for a commitment to academic, athletic, and other areas of excellence. They claim that *moral or relational* character embodies the traits of "integrity, justice, caring, and respect—needed for successful interpersonal relationships and ethical behavior."

Character strengths such as hope, perseverance, creativity, and zest are but a few traits which, when habituated, provide sport participants the greatest opportunity to improve performance and enjoyment. Hope is about goal-setting and optimism, creativity is about finding alternative strategies to improve performance, and zest is about the enthusiasm that players and coaches bring to the field.

Mindful Moment: *Coaches Strengths*

What are my strengths? _____

_____

_____

How do these strengths help me as a coach? _____

_____

Are there shadow sides to some of my strengths? _____

_____

Spotting Player Strengths

A high school coach, who was very clear on how his performance and relational strengths helped him as a coach, once received a phone call from a former athlete ten years after that student's graduation. The former student-athlete invited the coach and his wife out to dinner to celebrate some milestone in his young career. During dinner, the former athlete explained the foundation of his success and thanked the coach for something he had said to him more than a decade earlier in the heat of athletic competition. The athlete assumed that the coach was as clear about remembering his words of wisdom as the athlete was. "Remember what you told me when I asked you about the right approach to an upcoming match?" And the coach smiled politely at him, realizing that he had no idea about what he had said or that something said in the heat of the moment could possibly have had so much influence on this young man.

"Remember, you said: 'This is not the time to try anything new. You are an accomplished athlete. Go with what got you there!'" His statement was about having the athlete play to his strengths. The young man went on to explain that this simple phrase had sustained him and motivated him to persevere in challenging times since. It had given him confidence to trust himself. As coaches, we have an authority that we are not always aware of or in charge of. Things that some coaches take for granted may have more impact on players than they could ever imagine.

Managing Strengths

In the athletic arena, managing strengths improves
coaches' and players' engagement and achievement.

Coaches create success-conducive environments when they help their athletes play to their own and their players' strengths sets. We interviewed one coach who had a player unknowingly and continually pressing the coach's strengths button of teamwork. The player was very independent and did not feel compelled to conform during practice drills and tactical situations. He did what he felt like doing in certain situations, which made the coach grind his teeth. The player was impulsive, but he was individually very competent in terms of scoring points. He was creative, passing and shooting the ball in ways that no other players had ever thought about. However, when the coach strongly pointed out the error in the player's ways when he didn't perform well, the player became highly anxious and performed poorly. Not until the coach realized that his player's top strength was creativity did he begin to find ways to help the player use his creativity in other ways that supported the team as well as this player's individual performance.

Managing *SMART Strengths* and Needs

Students often know a lot about their own strengths and needs. Listen as Caitlyn (whose name has been changed), a Culver Girls Academy junior, tells about her *Clifton StrengthsFinder* strengths through the *SMART* model. All students at Culver take the *Clifton StrengthsFinder* during their junior year. How do Caitlyn's strengths affect her athletic performance? As a coach, what is your reaction to her awareness of how her strengths impact her play and what challenges do they present for her in the hockey rink?

In Her Own Words: Caitlyn, age 17. Culver Girls Academy Junior

My *Clifton StrengthsFinder* strengths are *Competition, Achiever, Focus, Positivity*, and *Belief*. I can easily **spot** these strengths as they are evident in my everyday life. I am a huge competitor, and will push myself until I win. This ability to compete goes hand in hand with my second strength, achiever, as I will not stop until I have completed my goal. During hockey games, I use these strengths to make sure I stay focused, and I never let my mind stray away from what I want to get accomplished. While I am competing, I always maintain a positive attitude as I realize that when I stay positive, competing can be fun and also can be fulfilling. My final strength, belief, is important as it helps me trust in myself and believe that I can achieve my goals.

I definitely need to learn how to **manage** my strengths. Shadow sides are evident, especially competition. I am a huge competitor, and at times I will let my competitive nature take me too far. In hockey, my need to compete sometimes is for the worse as I lose my temper and act on impulse, which sometimes leads to checking someone illegally or taking a stupid penalty.

There are very few things that make me mad, but there is something about a person who does not seem to have a willingness to compete that pushes my strength buttons. In hockey, I always strive to be the best, and it makes me angry when those around me are slacking off, and not working as hard as me. I see this, and it can push me over the edge. I never have figured out why some people are content being average, and not using a competitive mindset, and not working hard in whatever they do. In a game last year during the hockey season, we were losing 3-1 and I felt that we still had a chance. I was diving for pucks, blocking shots, and back checking and fore-checking hard. It made me extremely angry when I realized that I was the only one that was still competing and giving it my all. When I get in situations like this, I simply need to **advocate** my needs and use my other strengths to get me out of my anger, as well as remember that we all have different strengths at work, even in a competition.

Competition gives me the drive and determination to succeed, but without an achiever mindset, finishing my goals would be much more difficult. Maintaining a high level of focus allows me to never take my mind off of my goal until it is achieved. One strength I have that is particularly good for hockey is positivity. Maintaining a positive mindset helps me to **relate** better with my teammates and shake off the apparent lack of effort of the others, and encourage rather than get angry.

A clear advantage of knowing her strengths is that Caitlyn knows not only why she is angry on the rink, but also how she can manage and control her anger. The coaches who work with her will benefit from knowing not just their own strengths but also their coaching traits and style.

Four Traits of Successful Coaches

Mark Boyea, a former athletic director at The Montclair Kimberley Academy in New Jersey, claims that for every 100 different coaches, there are 100 different styles. However, successful coaches seem to possess the following four traits: purpose, competence in teaching technical and strategic skills, the ability to relate positively to athletes, and a well-formed character. The figure below presents these concepts.

Four Core Traits of Successful Coaches

Purpose and Vision

- Goals, objectives, philosophy and underlying principles establish the guidelines of the program.

Skills and Competence

- Proficiency in terms of the knowledge regarding the sport
- Ability to teach necessary skills
- Effectiveness in communicating the priorities, goals, objectives, and culture of the program
- Organizational skills

Relationships

- Genuine caring about athletes
- Respecting players
- Concern for players
- Knowing and understanding players
- Ability to motivate

Character Habits

- Solid work ethic

In His Own Words: John Pirani, a special education teacher and coach at Winchester MA High School

I think as a younger coach, I was fixated on strategy more than anything else. I'm sure that was because I was insecure and felt the need to demonstrate my knowledge and ability. I really didn't see myself as a caregiver, leader, or role model until much later in my career. While there is no doubt that strategy is an important part of what we do, all the other stuff tends to be far more important in terms of being successful. For that matter, success is far broader than merely calculating wins and losses. Once I got that part straight in my head, winning and losing became easier. As a serious competitor, I don't mean to say that losing became easy, rather it is that I can be more comfortable with a loss if I know I have taken care of all the details that lead up to game day. While there have been days we have been beaten because I have been out-strategized, I don't believe that anyone outworks me or my staff when it comes to working with the whole student-athlete.

Mindful Moment: *Strengths Teams in Action*

How do my top strengths work in concert to help me fulfill the four core traits of being a successful coach?

Purpose and Vision _____

_____

_____

_____

Strength _____
An example of this strength in action. _____

_____

Skills and Competence _____

_____

_____

_____

Strength _____
An example of this strength in action. _____

_____

Relationships _____

_____

_____

_____

Strength _____
An example of this strength in action. _____

_____

Character Habits — *Other strengths that come alive in my coaching*

_____

_____

_____

_____

Advocating Strengths

After understanding how to identify and exercise strengths,
coaches and athletes can communicate in different
ways about their respective strengths.

Coaching Styles

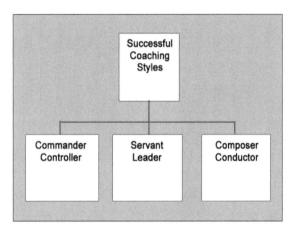

The coach plays an important role in orchestrating the completeness of the sport experience. We have found that there are three types of coaching styles that can make for productive and pleasurable experiences. This can also be said for parenting and teaching. No one style works best. Rather, there is a continuum and overlapping of the following three styles: *commander/controller, servant leader*, and *composer/conductor*. Much of this is based on the coaches' mindsets (more on this in Chapter Eight) and their ability to access the mindset of their respective athletes. Some experienced coaches assume that being a good coach is something they are—an internal quality that is evidenced when they easily, quickly, and perfectly perform their duties. Sometimes, this type of coach may have difficulty differentiating student-athlete's abilities and may tend to treat all players with the same expectations. Some coaches assume that coaching is something they do through the result of effort, prior knowledge, and strategy. (Refer to Chapter Eight for a more thorough review of mindsets). Some coaches operate in just the same way their past coaches modeled for them. In some cases, this is a productive state of affairs.

There has been more than one athletic director who had to let a coach go from a high school sports department because the coach wasn't able to adjust to what his student-athletes really needed. Coaches with growth mindsets can make the changes in themselves that can help their athletes adapt to a more effort-based way of thinking and acting.

In His Own Words: Alan McCoy, Athletic Director, Head Girl's Soccer Coach, Pingree School, Hamilton MA

As a younger coach I was fiery to a fault and put too much emphasis on winning as an outcome independent of any other factors. I think young coaches often feel the need to be successful in terms of wins before they will allow themselves to take a broader perspective on what they do. That was certainly the case for me. I remember working officials, pacing the sideline, using tactical fouls and sneaky plays. I also remember casting opponents as the enemy and thinking that portraying them as such was a good way to motivate the players in my charge. While my game intensity has lessened, my satisfaction with what I do has increased, and I have matured as a coach. I think mentoring by veteran coaches can have a profound impact on young adults coming into coaching and can help them gain a healthy perspective in a fashion other than trial and error, which is how many of us learned.

Commander/Controller. At one end of the continuum the coach may employ command/control. The coach sets the expectations, and the players fulfill the instructions. The main focus is on making sure every aspect of skill and team strategy is accounted for. This can be highly productive when the coach works with a new team with developing skills sets. It can be a disaster when the coach is overpowering with his or her expectations stated in a drill instructor manner.

Some coaches will spend more time in the command/control environment with a young team, where systems may not be in place at that time. Reinforcing fundamentals at all levels is essential, however, and many coaches spend a lot of time trying to convince their players of this necessity. Dee Stephan, former coach and athletic director at The Ethel Walker School and now head lacrosse coach at St. Joseph's College in Connecticut, sees about 75 percent of her coaching in the command/control arena. She feels women's lacrosse is a real strategy game and therefore she wants her players to really understand game tactics, especially the ball control side of the game.

Servant Leader. Robert Greenleaf, founder of the servant leadership movement says, "The servant-leader is servant first. It begins with the natural feeling that one wants to serve, to serve first. Then conscious choice brings one to aspire to lead. The difference manifests itself in the care taken by the servant to make sure that other people's highest priority needs are being served." There are great questions for coaches to ask themselves frequently: "Do those served grow as persons? Do they, while being served, become healthier, wiser, freer, more autonomous, more likely themselves to become servants? And, what is the effect on the least privileged in society? Will they benefit, or at least, not be further deprived?"

If the answers to those questions lead to the conclusion that our purpose is to serve (a conclusion that seems unavoidable), then we must be faithful to our service. We share the wonderful opportunity—and the privilege—of having a profound influence on others. Sam Osherson, a psychologist who specializes in mentor relationships, reminds us that by way of their experience, good coaches bring a shared wavelength to the conversation with the player. By serving the player at this level, they truly live in the skin of the young person.

The coach using a servant leader style understands that his or her responsibility is to ensure that the player's needs are addressed in order to derive characteristics of performance and mastery. He or she seeks first to serve players—to make sure the needs of players are taken care of so they can perform as well as possible.

Casey Jackson, whose coaching journey has taken her from New England to Colorado, believes that good youth coaches find ways to play weak and strong players who are on the same team.

In Her Own Words: Casey Jackson, Youth Coach

The number one question I receive from coaches is: "What do I do with my weak player? How do I hide her?" I tell them you have to get her out from being hidden, because she wants to hide, too." As a coach I have to help "Suzie Sizzlebritches" come to an understanding of her own gifts. On the flip side, you may have "Rhonda Rockstar," who wants to win a national title. You have to know how to tame and challenge her without letting her take the ball all the time. This is about teaching the stronger player to adjust to her other teammates. If they go coast-to-coast or ignore an open player and take a one-on-one, then they sit with me. Good coaches who are competent and passionate are better coaches when they are compassionate about the needs of their players. When this happens, distraction is minimized and trust increased.

Dee Stephan admits to being a servant leader 20 percent of the time. "I think I try to serve the players' needs. I constantly think about how they are feeling and whether or not they feel taken care of," she says. "I think with high school girls you can't help but use this style. They demand that they are taken care of. They speak their minds quite freely and if they are unhappy they just don't perform well. Success means to me that my players are having fun, learning and growing each game and supporting each other. I am proud that several players who have long since graduated still come home and check on Avon lacrosse to see the team play and reflect on their seasons."

Composer/Conductor. Some successful coaches are more hands-off with their teams. In this case, they act more as a consultant to the team. At this stage, the players all know their responsibilities on the field and carry them out with great success, akin to gears meshing together.

The composer/conductor acts as a consultant as the team takes care of business on the field. He or she is available to provide advice and counsel. Akin to an orchestra's brass, woodwinds, percussion and string sections, all players know their roles and responsibilities for their specific positions on the field, and their continuous interactions with the other positions. The coach waves his or her proverbial baton as the conductor, and welcomes discussion with players as a consultant.

John Wooden, a former high school teacher and coach who was eventually a Hall of Fame basketball coach at UCLA, is arguably one of the greatest college basketball coaches of all time. Wooden used his composer/conductor style to bring out the best in his players. Wooden once said that his coaching lessons came from his father, who preached a Seven-Point Creed including helping others and making friendships a fine art. He would be very calm during games, because the game was about the players and what they had learned in practice. "Let the players run with it."

Dee Stephan wishes she could be more than a five percent composer/conductor, but she realizes the reality is that lacrosse isn't the main sport for many of her players, and learning their roles and responsibilities on the field is an on-going process. Many times, the composer/conductor role only comes in when the team is ready to guide itself.

Balancing Coaching Styles

Kate Dresher claims there needs to be a nice balance of the three styles at the girls' youth level in Colorado. "If the drills and strategy are too complicated, you will lose them," she says. "Fourth and fifth graders need more creativity. They are such spatial beings. Of course it is important to challenge them with a little bit of competition, but it is equally, if not more, important for coaches to provide frequent positive reinforcement. They must allow for all players to be included in all aspects of the team. Playing capture the flag is a common occurrence in the youth program."

It is important to know that each of these coaching styles does not exclude the others. Also, they are not considered to be stages in a process. It is very possible and probable that many coaches will integrate all three of these styles at times. Some coaches spend the majority of time as commanders/controllers, while other split their time evenly among the three styles. It is important that each is delivered appropriately.

However, when a coach persists in one style when another might be more beneficial to the team, this typically contributes to miscommunication and ultimately a decrease in individual and team performance. Sometimes players may need more repetitive grounding in technique and strategy. This is not a time to let players be free-wheeling. Conversely, a team may be over-coached with drills and plays. Some players have difficulty sorting out the playbook in their heads and subsequently become so distracted that they may make errors in the game and fail. However, some coaches tend to be 100% command/control. When it is my way or the highway all the time, some players choose to take the path of least resistance, which leads to missed opportunity.

Mindful Moment: *Advocating Coaching Styles*

As a coach, what are examples of how you play to your players' strengths within different coaching styles? How would you estimate the percentage of time you use each style? If you are a parent, you can use this space to consider how one of your child's coaches leads. Here is a review of how each style functions:

Commander/Controller. *Work players who need more instruction.*

Servant Leader. *Find out about different abilities and motivations for each player. What strengths do they have? How do I play to their strengths? What are their other interests?*

Composer/Conductor. *Allow the players to lead themselves. Provide good counsel when needed.*

Review:

For each coaching style, list examples of how you or your child's coach has used this style. When you are finished listing examples, estimate the percentage of time you or your child's coach spends using each coaching style.

Commander/Controller. _____

_____

_____

_____

Percentage = _____

Servant/Leader. _____

_____

_____

_____

Percentage = _____

Composer/Conductor. _____

_____

_____

_____

Percentage = _____

Relating Strengths

Coaches and their players matter!
When you are more aware of each other's assets, you can better relate to them,
and in turn, use them to great benefit in the athletic arena.

For many years John Pirani has made sure there are good relationships between himself, his student-athletes, and their parents. His perspective on coach and parent responsibilities has never altered, including the 2000 and 2001 seasons when his teams won the Massachusetts Boys State Lacrosse Championships. His consistency of management has been crystal clear to his athletes and other stakeholders in the community (potentially overzealous parents) for years.

In His Own Words: John Pirani, Special Education Teacher and Lacrosse Coach, Winchester, MA High School

There are several adults who have the overall responsibility for many high school games—the coaches, the officials, and the attending administrator (not always attending, unfortunately). The adult stakeholders truly drive the bus regarding the flow and behavior of the game. Some will argue that the coach-official relationship is adversarial. And we know when this happens, more often than not, there are two competitions going on in the same game—one team versus the other team and both teams versus the officials. When this happens, it invites distraction from providing the best experience for all participants. Of course, some novice officials may inadvertently dictate the flow of the game, while some overzealous coaches may exhibit their lack of effort in preparing their team for the game, by scapegoating the officials. These scenarios are not either-or events. It is important to understand that the game is primarily for the players—an assumption that not all coaches and officials may totally buy into.

The game is made better when officials exhibit patience with players and coaches, especially with youth participants, while being instructive with youth and high school players. Good officials demonstrate a mastery of knowledge of the rules while embracing a healthy collaborative effort with coaches to ensure an appropriate experience for the players.

Parents aren't responsible for the contest. They are guests who have a wonderful opportunity to watch their children play. I speak to the parents collectively prior to each season and say, "I want you to be comfortable. I want your child to be comfortable. There shouldn't be a compelling reason to directly interact with your child during the game, so you don't need to stand on my sideline. Just watch the game and talk about it with your child over dinner." There is a compelling reason to empower parents to do what is right for their children.

Drew Hyland, a noted sports philosopher, once said that the goal of sport is to attempt to feel a sense of completeness as a result of the experience. When all sport stakeholders collaborate in the competitive environment and all the planets are aligned, we have the greatest opportunity to experience the pleasure, to be fully engaged in the process and find a sense of purpose and meaning in what we do.

Many coaches and athletes say that their former coaches have been models for their own coaching and playing styles. It was the relationships forged with those coaches that made all the difference to them. In the book, *Character and Coaching: Building Virtue in Athletic Programs*, John Yeager and his colleagues administered a brief questionnaire to a variety of coaches and athletes about their sport experiences. These coaches were asked to list and describe three strengths that they have derived from sport participation. It was found that coaches tend to describe teamwork, work ethic, and respect, whereas the high school athlete's survey viewed teamwork, fun, and perseverance as top strengths.

Also, the results of the questionnaire showed that the influential people in the coaches' lives were fathers, coaches, and peers. For the athletes, they were parents, pro athletes, and, importantly, coaches. Coaches were influential for the athletes because of being role models, being caring and concerned, and pushing a strong work ethic while building confidence in the athletes.

Mindful Moment: *Coaching Strengths and Models*

As an adult coach, what three strengths did you derive from your own participation in youth sports? _____

_____

Who were the most influential people in your sports life? _____

_____

_____

_____

How do you bring your strengths and role models to the field of play when you coach young people? _____

_____

_____

_____

Training Strengths — Building *SMART* Athletes

Strengths improve with deliberate practice on and off the athletic field.
Spot, manage, advocate and relate with your strengths individually
and in your relationships, and you will be able to use them
to develop these skills in your student-athletes.

Skill development in the athletic arena can be enhanced when coaches can get their players to understand how their strengths can help them improve performance and enjoy their participation in a sport. At Culver Academies, students take two strengths inventories and learn to integrate their results into their real lives. On the next page, read about how Aaron guides you through the *SMART* model. How do Aaron's strengths affect his athletic performance? As a coach, what is your reaction to his awareness of how his strengths impact his play?

In His Own Words: Aaron, age 17, Culver Academies

My *Clifton StrengthsFinder* strengths are *Strategic, Communication, Woo, Significance,* and *Context.* These strengths directly relate to me. I **spot** my strengths when I catch myself thinking of how to do things by either using my past experiences or the experiences of others. My biggest concern about my strengths is the over thinking and planning of certain things. The strategic strength of mine sometimes becomes too powerful and makes me over think even a simple task. However, I **manage** my strengths so they can complement each other nicely. I can notice when I am getting stuck in strategic thinking and easily think of a plan using the strategic part by using context of my past experiences to make the plan its very best.

This happens mainly on the athletic field. I **advocate** with my strengths and use communication and woo to make my plan known to everyone and to explain why I think it is the very best plan for this situation. I always can help to improve our game plan in all three of my sports. I understand situations well and can see the bigger picture than just the now. This context strength can have a down side, like when someone disregards the game plan and doesn't want to follow along when we have worked all week to perfect our plan of attack to give us the best chance to win. It really upsets me when someone does this. **Relating** is key, so I use my communication strength when this happens, and I try to talk to the player who is not following along and not executing the game plan that the team has decided to use. Now I am ready to **train** some of my other teammates to use their strengths more effectively and efficiently.

Young people can also learn through the coaches' sharing of his or her experiences as a coach or athlete themselves. John Buxton, the Head of Schools at the Culver Academies previously coached wrestling for thirty years at St. Paul's School in Concord, New Hampshire. His own experience and words of wisdom have been instructive and motivating for many of the athletes he has coached in his career.

In His Own Words: John Buxton, Head of Schools, Culver Academies

I had an unforgettable experience that occurred when I was in the eighth grade. I remember the details as if the match took place yesterday, and whenever I have been in a management workshop, a leadership or sports psychology class, or a serious conversation about sports or life with athletes or coaches, the specifics of the event rush back into my mind. I was thirteen, weighed ninety-nine pounds, and was wrestling for the varsity in the 110-pound weight class. Our team was competing in a significant pre-season tournament, against a number of larger schools with far more accomplished programs. It was the end of the day and I was the only wrestler from our school still competing. My opponent in the match for third place was a Mighty Mouse look alike, as big as a gorilla, with a five o'clock shadow. His muscles and his whiskers were enough to convince me that I didn't belong in this obvious mismatch.

I was somewhat skilled but seriously underpowered, so my strategy was to keep it close and not embarrass myself. Suddenly, it was the beginning of the third and final two-minute period, and I realized that I was only losing by two points, 5-3. I engaged myself in debate. Lose by two and it's a moral victory. Don't get pinned; too much pride for that. Don't risk putting yourself in danger just to be a hero. Keep it close and everybody wins. However, just when I had convinced myself that discretion would be the better part of valor, something also entered my mind. Escape, take him down, and win. What have I got to lose? If I don't try, I lose anyway.

The referee blew his whistle, and I exploded in a frenzy of activity. Everything I had, every ounce of resolve and effort was focused on the goal. But my attempts were thwarted. Try, fail. Try again, fail. Time was running out. Thirty-five seconds left in the match. I would not be denied. With five seconds remaining, the referee slapped the mat. I had pinned the gorilla. I had tamed the wild beast. I had overcome my own fear and had been rewarded for the effort. As the referee raised my hand to signify the victory, I fainted. I must have emptied the tank, pushed myself to the point of exhaustion.

When anyone asks me if I have ever had a moment in sports that influenced my character strengths or outlook on life, that match flows back to me immediately. It has taken on more importance for me than winning subsequent championships, playing three sports in college, or competing for national titles. Those two minutes taught me that I could influence the outcome of a contest or a situation. I would never be afraid to give my best effort, even if I was unsure of the outcome. I had a responsibility to myself, my team and to my opponent to give my best effort.

That match has influenced my attitude in my work, my approach to raising a family, and my philosophy as a long-time coach. The opportunity to recall and reflect upon that event and that decision-making process proved to be extremely significant for me. Since the event took place when I was thirteen years old, my focus, predictably was on the "I" aspect of the experience. A memorable moment later in my development would probably read quite differently. Nevertheless, the point is clear. We need to remember where we have been and understand where we are with our strengths, before we decide where we should go and how we can get there. My story has served me well throughout my life span. My experience happened to be positive and sustaining, but had it been negative, it would still benefit me to reflect upon it, understand it, and learn from it.

Mindful Moment: *Coaching SMART Review*

Spotting. *How do my top strengths come alive in my coaching?* _____

_____

_____

_____

Managing. *How do I use my strengths to manage the team and individual players? What strengths possibly go to the shadow side?* _____

_____

_____

_____

Advocating. *How do I best appeal to the strengths of my players and their parents?* _____

_____

_____

Relating. *What parent, player, or official behavior presses my strengths buttons? What other strengths of mine can I use to lessen the intensity of the button pushing?* _____

_____

_____

Training. *What can I do to help my assistant coaches, parents, and players to focus more on their strengths?* _____

_____

_____

In sports, as in academics and other areas, many coaches, teachers, parents, and student-athletes find as people more quickly adapt to achievements, expectations increase. There is always something more and something better. The development of sport-specific skill sets comes through trial and error until the skill becomes a habit and the athlete performs the movement with machine-like precision. We are all imperfect human beings, however, and not mechanistic automatons. We are social beings, we are thinkers, and we express emotions. As athletes and coaches chart their course towards reaching the goals that make athletic participation worthwhile, there is the need to balance machine-like behavior with human thoughts and emotions. Although there is great focus on performance, an emphasis on strengths of character may yield more enjoyment and satisfaction for coaches and young people in their quest towards overall well-being.

This chapter examined how coaches can understand and act on their own strengths to best provide student-athletes the greatest opportunity for improved performance and enjoyment. Chapter Five will focus on how adult mentors and young people can do strengths work to enhance their well-being. By managing stress, sleep habits, and learning to savor events, people can maintain and improve their overall well-being to deal with expectations and pressures.

Chapter Five

Strengths and Well-Being

The part can never be well unless the whole is well.
—Plato

James is constantly figuring out his next move as he navigates his life through high school and positions himself onto the fast track for college. He is in a pressure cooker to get top grades, perform well on the soccer field, keep a strong social profile, and maintain his participation in many other school activities. James' parents have hovered over him for the past six years to ensure that he follows all the steps to reach this goal. Although they won't admit it, his parents are worried that James won't be successful, and they truly believe that if he isn't successful, it means that they didn't do their job as parents. Since they can't bear the thought that they will be failing James somehow if they do not encourage him to seize every opportunity, they feel the need to push, push, push! James' teachers are pushing him, too. They each believe that their respective subjects are more important than other disciplines, and, subsequently, they want James' full attention. On the soccer field, much is expected of James, who is a four-year letter winner and senior co-captain. At the same time, James believes that to be happy, he must oblige his mentors. He, along with his parents and teachers, doesn't realize that they have lots in common with Alice in Wonderland, the heroine of Lewis Carroll's classic. They all are unwitting victims of the Red Queen Effect.

The Red Queen Effect

In Louis Carroll's *Alice Through the Looking Glass*, the Red Queen says to Alice, "It takes all the running you can do to keep in the same place. If you want to get somewhere else, you must run at least twice as fast as that!" James, his parents, his teachers, and his coaches have unknowingly adopted this as their mantra. "The Red

Queen Effect" is a term from biology that refers to predator and prey relationships in the animal kingdom. As the prey gets faster, the predator needs to find a way to get even faster, or it will starve to death. As the predator gets faster, the prey needs to find a strategy to avoid being eaten.

"The Red Queen Effect" is alive and well in many of our schools today. Young people now receive enormous quantities of information that they need to process. The perception of extreme competition to get into the right college is at an all time high. This bleeds over from the classroom to the athletic arena. John Corlett, from the University of Winnipeg, tells us that, "athletes are used to the Red Queen Effect. They train to become stronger, faster, and more skilled, knowing that other athletes are doing the same. Their coaches devise new strategies, knowing that other coaches will find ways to render them obsolete." On the surface, there is nothing inherently wrong with this. Some say that you just need to tough it out to keep up the pace for success. But at what cost?

Is More Better?

As James more quickly becomes accustomed to his achievements, his huge appetite for bigger and better things increases, as do his expectations. The joy (and relief) that James and his parents receive from his achievements in school as well as the numerous trophies from his youth soccer days to his high school championship team are short-lived, because the more James succeeds, the more is expected of him. While some people say that living in yesterday's glory may prevent them from looking towards the next challenge, the *Hedonic Treadmill* leads to youth and adults who need more and more to feel the same positive emotion. The *Hedonic Treadmill* is a term from psychology that explains how people adapt to positive and negative events and ultimately return to an earlier established level of well-being. Have we created a society of young people who are trying to do more things in their available time while expecting that performances can be endlessly improved?

Pursuing the Best

James is a maximizer, and he may pay a high price for this learned trait. A maximizer is characterized as someone who "will seek and accept only the best" claims Barry Schwartz, a Swarthmore College psychology professor and author of *The Paradox of Choice*. Schwartz says, "Why do a little less well objectively in order to subjectively feel better?" James is now looking for the perfect college. He has a long list that he has built up, but he's still not sure he has the best on the list yet. His parents have taken him to a wide range of schools throughout the country, but he's haunted by the idea that if he just looks harder, he'll find a college or university that is even better for him.

James tends to focus on the objective results of his actions, with little attention paid to anything else. For some maximizers, decreased levels of life satisfaction, pessimism, and lowered mood are common when life revolves around the perfectionist trait of pursuing the best. Even if an individual was to actually find the brass ring, there would still be disappointment and frustration.

Maximizing and Regret

The potential for regret for James and other maximizers may happen when they try to exhaust all the choices available. For instance, let's look at college choices for School A: The location is great. This school has a nice seasonal climate, blended with splendid views of the manicured campus. However, while the academic major the high school senior wants to pursue is offered at this college, it isn't regarded as a strong program. School B has a well-established and noted academic major that he or she is interested in. But the winters are harsh, and the school buildings seem a little bit worn. This is a good example of opportunity costs. If I choose School A, what will I be giving up in not choosing School B? When there are multiple possible combinations of variables that compare one school to another, a rising senior in high school may construct the imaginary perfect school that has the best of all the schools he or she is interested in. Unfortunately, there can be a sense of anticipated regret over his or her final choices, because the utopian school doesn't really exist.

In His Own Words: Barry Schwartz, Professor of Social Theory and Social Action — Swarthmore College, Author: *The Paradox of Choice*

As the experience of choice and control gets broader and deeper, expectations about choice and control may rise to match that experience. I have received countless correspondence from people and virtually no one says, "I am a maximizer and I am proud of it." Or "I choose to be a maximizer." The people who do write to me are all describing maximizing as if it is a disease that they can't control. They know it. It makes them miserable. It isn't mysterious. When juniors and seniors in high school are looking at competitive schools, chances are they have high achieving parents who keep on stressing how competitive the world is and how important it is to achieve and maintain. Even if parents don't mean to do this, they are behaving in that way themselves.

Spotting Strengths and Improving Well-Being

Young people, teachers, parents, and coaches learn a common strengths language they can use to enhance their overall well-being.

James' parents, teachers, and coaches can help him as he lives with some of his maximizing characteristics by encouraging him to play to his strengths. Adult mentors can help him spot and manage his own strengths to support his sleep, nutrition, exercise, and stress/mental health behavior. They also can help him see when he is going to the shadow side of some of his positive traits. Although flourishing in studies, outside activities, and good health may be a goal, in reality, living a balanced life and striving to excel may be a contradiction for many students. Faced with demanding academic standards, students like James are expected to make sound decisions. Some students are well-suited for this environment. They thrive on a busy schedule, while others may struggle with balancing day-to-day activities. For some, this is a healthy tension that helps to eventually promote self-discipline and organization.

On the other hand, many students end up "borrowing from Peter to pay Paul"— they have tipped the activity scales to one side and have difficulty righting themselves. They have either overscheduled themselves or are in a school, family, or community environment that promotes this. Focusing on strengths may be helpful in these situations so youth can fulfill their basic needs, which, in turn, may bring them happiness. If a student maximizer believes that "the best job is better than a good one" take heed, for the hedonic treadmill may sneak in and take the pleasure he or she derives from learning, training, and performing. Because there is always the potential for a disappointing performance, the maximizer is often more focused on preventing perceived outcome failure than enjoying the process, making it very difficult to savor later on. There is more on savoring later in this chapter.

Satisficing

With little food on the table when she comes home from school and no extra money to spend, Lali's focus on her studies at school is balanced with her need to work. She plans to get her Bs and will accept an occasional C so she is ready to go to the local community college when she graduates. It's not that she does not have goals, but that she is balancing her needs. As a satisficer, Lali may be moving "up" in the same general direction as a maximizer, but she is choosing "good enough" options over "the only acceptable" ones. While we may think that Lali is not challenging herself, or that she does not care, her hopes and behaviors are well-matched for her current resources.

Barry Schwartz suggests that an "alternative to maximizing is to be a satisficer." To satisfice is to settle for something that is good enough and not worry about the possibility, at least for now, that there might be something better. To satisfice, you will need to become aware of what Schwartz calls "the threshold of acceptability." Satisficers, he reminds us, may have very high standards. "It's just that they allow themselves to be satisfied once experiences meet those standards." They are happier, less depressed, and more optimistic than maximizers. While maximizers may stretch to develop creative problem solving or learn teamwork skills to make their work as perfect as possible—good for now and for the future—it comes at a steep price. Satisficers, on the other hand, may accept their current situation and work within constraints, resulting in more balance and well-being.

Managing Strengths for Overall Health

Managing strengths can help enhance overall well-being.

The World Health Organization (WHO) defines health as "a dynamic interaction and balance of the physical, emotional, mental, social and spiritual dimensions." The term wellness refers to the attainment of optimal health through the balance of these dimensions. This balance, by nature, falls within a spectrum or continuum, and a person's state of health or illness may be determined by the balance or imbalance of these factors.

Dimensions of Wellness — Six States of Health

At Culver, students learn to put their *SMART* strengths to use in a class specifically designed to expand the way they think about what it means to be healthy, beyond the physical. Here is a condensed version of what they study:

Physical	Good physical health is evident in people who are in a dynamic state of effective anatomical and physiological function including the circulatory, musculoskeletal, nervous, endocrine, and reproductive systems of the body.
Emotional	Emotionally healthy people recognize and express feelings appropriately and have the ability to control and balance these feelings with the other health dimensions.
Mental	Mentally healthy people have a sound intellect, the capacity to learn and to absorb as one appropriately perceives the environment. This may also be called intellectual or cognitive health.
Moral	Morally fit people have the capacity, regardless of the circumstances they might find themselves in, to consistently arrive at the best ethical decision possible.
Social	Socially healthy people relate well with others, including friends, family, and other groups. Being comfortable around others at various stages of the life span is a hallmark of good social health.
Spiritual	Spiritually healthy people are committed to a high level of faith or a belief system that provides a sense of meaning and purpose.

In Her Own Words: Donelle, age 18. Culver Girls Academy

People can change. Like trying to help a drug or alcohol abuser, sometimes it takes a loving family to support and change a person's food habits. My family used to eat pretty healthy but we have started eating more fast foods as we've all gotten older. My dad in particular increased his intake in fast food. He used to take a salad to work for lunch then he started going out for fast food. He became very overweight and I knew this wasn't healthy. I used my *Clifton StrengthsFinder relator* and *includer* strengths to tackle this. One day I said, "Dad, I want you to dance at my wedding." It was amazing how much of an impact this made on his food decisions. He now works out regularly and concentrates on eating healthy.

As a parent, teacher or coach, you employ different strengths to enhance your wellness dimensions. Optimal well-being includes each wellness dimension interrelating with each other. How do your strengths match up? When does the shadow side of a strength get in the way? For example, in figure on the next page, you will notice how a person's VIA strengths can influence the various wellness dimensions (+ for strength, - for shadow side of a strength).

WELLNESS DIMENSIONS (+ denotes strengths, - denotes shadow side)						
STRENGTHS	**Physical**	**Emotional**	**Mental**	**Moral**	**Social**	**Spiritual**
Zest		- Get too excited about big plays in the game				
Hope and Optimism						+ Strong sense of future-mindedness
Perseverance	+Disciplined to complete my work-outs			+Regardless of the situation, committed to what is right		
Social Intelligence					- Try to mind-read all the time	
Creativity			+Developing lesson plans			

Managing Stress

Although there is currently a great focus on performance in schools today, there is less emphasis on relationships and character formation. In the Josephson Center for Ethics 2008 study of over 29,000 youth, 64% claimed they had cheated on a test in the past year. In addition, approximately 10% of young people claimed anxiety issues and over 2.2 million youths experienced at least one major depressive episode within the past year. These issues are happening during formative growth periods and may be habituated into adulthood. Clearly something needs to be done not only to treat the results of life on the Hedonic Treadmill, but also to prevent depression, anxiety, and unhealthy behaviors.

From cradle to grave, there are countless demands or stressors that challenge the human system. Stress is a response to various stimuli that put demands on people. Hans Selye, an endocrinologist and a major pioneer in stress research, defined stress as a "non-specific response of the body to any demand upon it." He speaks of two types of stress: good stress or *eustress* and negative stress or *distress*. Both of these types of stress can cause similar physiological responses. Stress can also be a very good thing for people. It helps us respond to emergencies, keeps boredom away, and is a healthy response to good events.

However, if challenging and demanding experiences, whether real or imagined, are not resolved, then the integrity of the entire person, including the physical, emotional, mental, moral, social, and spiritual states, may be compromised. This may eventually lead to illness or disease. Much of the research and clinical work on the relationship between stress and disease has come from a bio-behavioral perspective, which has focused on trial and error behavior change. There are many stress management programs available, consisting of behavior modification skills, such as relaxation techniques, biofeedback, and cognitive restructuring (a strategy through which a person re-interprets thought processes).

Release Stress through Meditation

Michael Cohn, from the University of California, San Francisco, Barbara Fredrickson, University of North Carolina, and their colleagues found that loving kindness meditation can undo hedonic adaptation. They found that people who meditated during their seven-week study increased positive emotion and built personal resources including mindfulness, pathways thinking, savoring of the future, environmental mastery, and self-acceptance. Participants also increased their purpose in life, enhanced social support received, improved positive relationships with others, and decreased illness and depression symptoms.

In a follow-up study, Cohn and Fredrickson found that people from the study who had continued to meditate also continued to increase their positive emotions and personal resources. Interestingly though, regardless of whether participants continued to meditate (or what kind of meditation they practiced), all participants *maintained* gains in positive emotion found when they were interviewed at the end of the intervention, even when assessed more than a year later.

Cohn and Fredrickson suggest that because of the focus on mindful attention, the active, personalized, and adjustable elements, and the broad application of these skills and insights to many life domains, meditation practices have many benefits. Among these are:

- Increase in positive emotion and approach behavior
- More effective immune responses

- Increase in interpersonal emotions such as empathy and compassion

Benefits from meditation accumulate and persist. They can go on even through days without meditation practice. Children, adolescents and adults alike benefit from meditation.

In Her Own Words: Joan Young, former kindergarten teacher, now 4th grade teacher and educational coach/tutor.

I model being quiet and closing my eyes and taking some deep breaths when I get frustrated with my kindergarteners. I used to think I shouldn't let them see me get upset, even though I knew better. Sometimes when they are all sitting on the special rainbow carpet in front of me as I teach them a new concept or we read together, I get interrupted by some attention-seeking or impulsive behavior, which can be quite maddening, especially at the end of the day after several of these episodes.

One day I simply said to the students, "I am getting frustrated that we aren't showing respect to the person who is speaking." I am going to close my eyes and take a few deep breaths to calm down before I talk to you. The room fell silent as I did this. As I opened my eyes, the first time I did this, I noticed a couple of my kids in a meditation pose, eyes closed, hands with fingers together, chanting, "ummmm." It was quite precious. I realized that I had modeled a strategy of becoming quiet and calming down before acting. And it stopped me from saying something I might have otherwise said to the few students who seem to regularly seek attention in challenging ways!

Making Stress Work for You Stress — Hardiness

There is evidence that many people have acquired stress resilient behaviors. In the late 1970's, University of Chicago professor Suzanne Kobasa and Salvatore Maddi, Founder of the Hardiness Approach to Mastering Life, established a view toward life events which supports that stress is a normative part of life in a world that is constantly changing. Kobasa and Maddi claimed that individuals may have different responses to life stressors including people who thrive on stress. A person's level of stress and its connection to illness may be determined or dependent upon individual personality attributes that may have an impact on stress resistance. To support the claims that stress is not necessarily an uncontrollable reaction to a stimulus and that certain people have a greater level of stress resistance, they investigated the hardiness construct in three stages.

1. The **challenge** component of hardiness emphasizes that life is constantly changing and that hardy people are more capable of adapting to this change by healthfully responding to new situations.
2. **Commitment** is a term indicating a person's sense of purpose and meaning and dedication to a task or a person.
3. The relational definition of **control** emphasizes that the hardy person has a certain self-responsibility in acting or reacting to life events. This self-sufficient position stands in contrast to responding to stress as being helpless or victimized.

In others words, hardy people know how to welcome challenge, commit to goals that are related to a purpose, and look for what they can personally control.

Kobasa and Maddi also focused on the influence of stress resistance resources such as genetic predisposition and social support and their interaction with personality. They found that participants who had a genetic predisposition to certain illnesses and exposure to stressful life events experienced increased illness. However, those who were found to have a hardy personality showed fewer incidents of illness in spite of genetic predisposition and social support.

Take Sarah for example, a 7th grade special education teacher, who everyday wakes to the sun (even on an overcast morning) and is ready for whatever comes her way—an adolescent explosion in her classroom, a change in the day's schedule that she will have to adjust to, a surprise history quiz, a colleague with a family crisis. She confronts the school day with teflon resilience—no bad things will stick to her. Sarah is a "teacher." Whether she in the classroom, with her athletes at track practice, or at home with her two children, she is committed to her calling as an educator. "It is who I am and what I do," she shares. Sarah also knows what she can and can't control in her life. Her inspiration for this comes from the *Serenity Prayer*:

> *God grant me the serenity*
> *to accept the things I cannot change;*
> *courage to change the things I can;*
> *and wisdom to know the difference.*
>
> —Reinhold Niebuhr

When Sarah plays to her strengths of creativity, perseverance, love of learning, and kindness, she is better able to have a hardy existence.

Mindful Moment: *Hardiness*

As a parent, teacher or coach, how do your strengths support the three hardiness domains? Write down your strengths that influence each domain.

*These strengths help me adapt to challenges:*_____

_____

_____

_____

These strengths reinforce my commitment and dedication: _____

_____

_____

_____

These strengths help me understand what I can and can't control:

_____

_____

_____

_____

Beat Stress: Learn the Art of Savoring

Parents, teachers and coaches can help nudge young people in the direction toward overall well-being by providing them with strategies to learn the art of savoring. Savoring is the act of basking, luxuriating, marveling and being thankful. Although we live in an increasingly busy world, we can use our strengths to help us savor, while still keeping sight of achievement goals.

Four Ways to Savor
• **Basking:** receptive to praise and congratulations
• **Marveling:** losing self in the wonder of experience
• **Luxuriating:** engaging the senses fully
• **Thanksgiving:** experiencing and expressing gratitude
—Fred Bryant and Joseph Verhoff, 2007

Let's take a look back at James from earlier in this chapter, who is an unwittingly victim of "success depression," a concept coined by Steven Berglas, author of *The Success Syndrome: Hitting Bottom When You Reach The Top.* James achieves his desired goals, but he is generally incapable of taking pleasure in his achievements. No savoring for him. He has no clue to how to relish, delight in, and appreciate the good things in his life.

Fred Bryant, from Loyola University of Chicago, developed a model that focuses on a person's ability to savor:

- Avoiding: degree of personal control over bad things
- Coping: ability to cope with bad things
- Obtaining: degree of personal control over good things
- Savoring: ability to enjoy good things.

Based on Bryant's model, how can we help James help himself? James ought to look at ways to exert his own personal control over and his ability to enjoy good things. Learning how to bask, luxuriate, marvel, and be thankful at age 16 might be an onerous task for him. There are, however, a few cues that can help him access his "savoring from within."

Basking. James enjoys receiving praise and congratulations. However, he is on to the next thing within moments. Just providing an additional 5-10 minutes of basking may help to store some long-term memory and start the development of a mini-basking habit.

Marveling. If James can put his mind in slow motion for a moment, he may be able to cue into the wonder of different experiences, to see how cool what happened on the soccer field is, and to relive the "aha" moment in Physics class.

Luxuriating. By paying more attention to his senses and honing them, James may be able to access a state of savoring through sound, sight, feel, taste and smell that races his motor or soothes his soul.

Thanksgiving. James, like many other young people, tends to be self-absorbed. It is a natural part of the brain-development process of teens. We have found when children and adolescents frequently share gratitude with others, they are more engaged in school and relationships.

James deliberately practices to improve in the classroom and on the athletic field. By transforming his strengths to practice accessing his "savoring within" he may come to realize that the cost-benefit analysis of learning how to savor may get him what he wants more of in his life. James' parents and teachers could also learn a lesson or two!

Mindful Moment: 3XG Learn to Savor

Remember in Chapter Three that you learned how to shift your focus to good things that have happened in your life? Sometimes this is called a "gratitude journal," especially if you are collecting good things that happened and for which you are grateful. We call it 3XG: Three times good. You can use the same format for savoring.

1) Start by writing about what happened.

- *What happened? "Our family shared a wonderful hike in the White Mountains."*
- *What was good about it? "There had been a storm predicted earlier in the week but the weather was perfect."*
- *What do you want to remember about it? "The ascent was very challenging. There were times when I thought, gee, it is getting steep... maybe we should just stop where we were and turn back. My kids kept encouraging me, though, instead of the other way around. The view was spectacular and we all shared it."*

This person may want to savor by marveling at the view, perhaps by looking at photos of it taken on the hike. Another approach would be to give thanksgiving for having shared the view with the entire family. They might bask in the achievement of reaching the summit or luxuriate in the memory of the weather.

---

2) Then decide what type of savoring will tap into your strengths most. Record your "high point" memories in a way that will allow you to revisit them.

Basking _____

Marveling _____

Luxuriating _____

Thanksgiving _____

Anticipated, experienced and remembered savoring. People can amplify the intensity of positive events and positive emotion while in preparation for a future experience. They can feel the pleasure of experiencing the present while remembering the past. Try practicing all three until you find out what gives you most pleasure. Using imagination to anticipate what an upcoming event will feel like allows a person to possibly savor the moment while it is actually happening and have a greater memory of it afterwards. Learning breathing and imagery skills can help James and others with anticipated memory.

Inspiration savoring. Breathing is the rhythm of life. If one is not breathing, one is not alive. When the concept of breathing is reduced to a mere "involuntary physiological reaction," the significance of the breath's emotional, mental, social, and spiritual aspects is negated. The term inspiration, from a mechanical perspective, is the act of drawing in or inhaling breath. From a typical everyday use of the term, inspiration is also defined in Webster's Third International dictionary as "having an animating, enlivening, or exalting effect upon the working of some extraordinary power or influence." James' focus on his breath may help cue his imagery.

Imagery with the senses. Imagery can be the process of constructing mental pictures or images, either real or imagined, through the use of any sensory domain. Whether there is a resonating loud noise, a beautiful azure sky, or the soft sand of a beach that finds its way between the toes, an acrid smell, or a tasty doughnut, we constantly use imagery. The auditory (sound), visual (sight), kinesthetic (tactile), gustatory (taste), and olfactory (smell) dimensions of the human senses are cues that can assist James.

The use of imagery may be compared to a mental DVD library, a catalogued connection of thoughts which a young person has the power to create, recall, and consequently evoke a variety of physical and emotional responses. Even young people have amassed a great number of mental DVDs that they have stored in their long-term memory. Young people and adults have good movies, bad movies, and even horror movies of images that, real or imagined, have influenced their lives. When you use your strengths as part of the action in your savoring, you can create "strengths movies" to help reinforce how your assets can bring you what you want and need in your life. For example, here is an interesting visualization script written by a high school ice hockey player:

In His Own Words: High School Ice Hockey player

I put my hard sharp mouth guard in my mouth and click the snaps to my helmet. I walk to the door with an uncomfortable bouncing step. Then I step up onto the slippery shiny cold surface and push off. I glide and feel the cold air against my face and going through my jersey. The smell of my pads slips right up into my nose as I start to get warm and sweat. Then the bars in front of my face disappear and I notice the empty net at the other end of the ice. I look to my side and see the crowd with signs and hands next to their mouths through the glass. The yelling and cheering gets louder as more players enter the ice...

After a loud grunt of "Eagles," I make my way to the bench and sit shoulder to shoulder with my teammates. I can feel the pads against mine and hear the positive support coming from them. The slap of the puck and the click of sticks gets the game underway. I feel the little weight on the end of my stick as I skate down the ice. I'm not looking at the puck but looking around for other teammates to pass to. I can hear shouting "AC, AC...SHOOT!" I look and see the space the goalie is not covering. Without even knowing it, my body is telling me I need to get the shot off quickly if I am going to make it. As I look at the top right corner, I feel my stick come off the puck and my wrists curl to gain momentum. My pads slide against my body as I quickly follow through to slap the puck. I feel the stick flex in my wet palmed gloves. After the sound of the snap, the puck leaves my control and takes with it everything I taught it. It hits the back of the net and my arms become weightless.

Mindful Moments: Group Savoring for Class, Family, or Team		

As an adult mentor, choose a variety of events that your class, family, or team have experienced. What strengths do you and your group associate with the good moments? Do some strengths match up better with some savoring styles? You can use the following chart to help record the experience.

Savoring Domain	Event	Associated Strengths
Marveling	Observed students understanding material	Appreciation of beauty and excellence
Luxuriating		
Thanksgiving		
Basking		
Marveling		
Luxuriating		
Thanksgiving		
Basking		
Marveling		
Luxuriating		
Thanksgiving		
Basking		

Sleep and Well-Being

Sleep deprivation is rapidly becoming a major health issue for many adolescents as it can have a strong influence on academic achievement, mood regulation, and overall well-being. Young people are busier than ever before during their waking hours, participating in a plethora of activities while trying to balance their brain chemicals. Adolescent sleep research now finds that teens ought to be getting eight to nine hours of sleep a night, while we know that many have habituated themselves into four to six hour periods of shut-eye. There are a variety of factors responsible for this behavior. From a brain chemistry perspective, less sleep decreases brain serotonin levels, which can influence academic and athletic performance and overall subjective well-being. At the same time, young people are busier during the day than ever before, as dopamine courses through their system. Many teenagers are the epitome of maximizers. Between grades, getting into college, and the rising expectations of parents, they have to find ways to create more time. Have we developed a culture of adolescent maximizers who are doing more on less sleep with undesirable consequences?

Phase Delay

Mary Carskadon, a renowned sleep researcher, is alarmed by issues of sleep deprivation among our youth. She claims that teens typically experience "phase delay," where the release of melatonin (a hormone that supports sleep regulation) in their brains happens later on in the evening. This has been habituated over time. It is very different than being on the farm in the 1850s and going to bed earlier to get up earlier. With teens going to bed at midnight or 1 AM, they have adapted to a new circadian clock, which is much later than the average adult's clock. However, many will be up 6:30 AM and sort of ready to get the most out of an 18 hour or longer day. One of John's students was used to going to bed around 2 AM and then decided to cut it back to midnight, and laid awake for two hours. He had trained himself to go to bed at 2 AM.

Teenagers naturally need go to sleep later and wake up later. It is how the melatonin in their brains works. However, adults around the world have decided that it is better for teens to start school early in the morning, consistent with adult work schedules, when kids would normally still be asleep. Barbara Strauch, the author of *The Primal Teen*, discusses this problem: "That's left us with a disconnect between the amount of sleep teenagers need and the amount they're getting." This lack of sleep, which most teenagers believe will help them and alleviate stress, in fact only increases it. In a study of over 15,000 teenagers, James Gangwisch and his colleagues found that many adolescents who went to bed after midnight were more likely to become depressed than teens who went to bed before 10 PM. It is a false economy to trade sleep for accomplishment, especially when the stakes and drive to achieve are high.

Too Much Strength — Too Little Sleep

When we studied the relationship between character strengths, academic performance, and health behavior among high school freshmen and seniors, we found that having the VIA strength of "prudence" was significant for those student participants who sleep more than seven hours per evening during the typical school week. We have asked parents whether their children go to the shadow side (to an excess) with perseverance. Do they aspire to other performance-type strengths, doing so at the expense of sleep? Do strengths such as diligence impact self-regulation? There is a great self-regulation issue at hand that may not undo itself without behavioral change.

This is the case with Jenn, who was the epitome of a teenage maximizer. Between working to achieve good grades, planning ahead for getting into college, meeting the rising expectations of her parents and teachers, and working part-time, she tried to find ways to create more time. She ran the risk of bankrupting the currency of sleep as she diligently plotted her course to success. Below are some of Jenn's thoughts in one of her journals in a Health Issues class when she was a senior at Culver.

In Her Own Words: "Jenn" — High School Senior

A maximizer is a person who decides he/she has to do everything and anything. I am a maximizer, partly because I enjoy everything I do. I want to try new activities, and, quite frankly, it looks good on college applications. As Machiavellian as that sounds, countless high schoolers are doing more and more activities with hope that "padding" their resume will help them get into college. Other people are just natural maximizers. They feel that they have to do everything or be in charge of everything. This tendency to maximize generally leads to stress and the quality of happiness decreases. This is me.

As I have said "yes" to every leadership responsibility, I feel like I am being condemned for "choosing" to take on too much. At times I felt stuck between a rock and a hard place. Stress levels in people in these situations become higher as time progresses under these conditions. High stress levels eventually lead to people wanting to survive their day or week and in doing so, giving up components necessary to good health. But I do want it all.

An important question to ask is this: Will today's adolescent maximizers run the risk of bankrupting the currency of sleep and potentially decrease their subjective well-being as they journey to adulthood?

Nutrition and Physical Activity

Anytime I get the urge to exercise, I lie down and the feeling goes away.
—Oscar Wilde

Parents and teachers can appeal to young people's strengths to best shape nutrition habits. Accessing the strengths of persistence and self-regulation, for example, to support good nutrition habits, is important as there is a tendency for nutrition behavior to take a back seat in the accelerated pace of life in schools. In our research, we found that self-regulation was a strong predictor of optimal nutrition behavior and physical activity among adolescents.

Daily participation in exercise as well as participation in organized athletic programs at school and in the community helps shape well-being. Character strengths such as teamwork, self-regulation, hope, perseverance, creativity, and zest are but a few traits which, when habituated, provide sport participants the greatest opportunity to improve performance and enjoyment. This may explain the significance of citizenship (social responsibility, loyalty, teamwork) among athletes in our research.

Mindful Moment: Using *SMART Strengths* for Managing Well-Being

What strengths do you use to help self-regulate health behaviors?

*Sleep*_____

_____

Nutrition _____

_____

*Physical Activity/Managing Stress Where do you face challenges in these areas?*_____

_____

What would it be like if each of these areas of your life were in balance?

_____

_____

There are a variety of factors that influence the well-being of young people. Using strengths to promote good health can be a way to counteract some of the effects of stress and sleep deprivation, while stimulating savoring of life events, good nutrition, and physical activity. Self-regulation of health behaviors may be part of the recipe for building resilience in young people.

Relational and Training Strengths

Young people, teachers, parents, and coaches matter! When you are more aware of each other's assets, you can better relate to each other, and in turn, enhance each other's well-being.

In their book, *Promoting Well-Being*, Isaac and Ora Prilleltensky, from the University of Miami, make a strong case for the importance of positive relationships in achieving overall well-being. They claim that well-being is a positive state of affairs, brought about by the simultaneous satisfaction of personal, relational, and collective needs of individuals and communities. Support, affection bonding, and collaboration all contribute to this. When there is an integration of personal, relational and collective needs then people are "less likely to have heart attacks, more likely to resist the common cold virus, have less stress, are more resilient and have a more positive outlook on life." When we play to each other strengths, we directly help improve relationships.

This chapter examined how students, teachers, parents, and coaches can help young people and themselves use their strengths for improved well-being by managing stress, optimizing sleep habits and learning to savor.

What's Next?

Chapters One through Five focused on how strengths can be used to enhance the lives of students, teachers, parents, and coaches. In the second part of the book, *Building Resilience and Relationships*, we will show you how resilience is more than just the ability to bounce back from adversity; it is also the capacity to bounce forward in the presence of opportunity. We focus on developing clear-eyed, positive mindsets and springy resilience in parents, teachers, coaches, and young people. Also, we bridge the connection between strengths, resilience, and relationships. We provide tools that develop healthy relationships to mobilize and build high quality connections between educators, between students, between teachers and students, between parents and students, between teachers and parents, and between coaches and student-athletes.

PART TWO

Building Resilience and Relationships

Chapter Six

Positive Emotion: Becoming Better Mood Managers

*The emotions aren't always subject to reason, but
they are always immediately subject to action.*
—William James

Ella hates disappointing her parents and her fifth grade teacher. Although she knows they care for her, every time they roll their eyes she gets an uncomfortable feeling in the pit of her stomach. Fearful of making a mistake and being a disappointment to her teacher and parents, Ella connects school with anxiety. Her anxiety often distracts her from focusing on her work, thus increasing the likelihood of making mistakes. You don't have to be Ella to understand the importance of your emotional responses to events.

Fight, Flight, and Freeze with Emotions

Ella is a lot like her stone-age ancestor who, when confronted by a saber-toothed tiger, needed to make an immediate decision. Fight? Run? Play dead? Whatever decision is made, there is an immediate emergency response, an instinctual, protective mechanism in all humans, a type of survival instinct. As Ella's ancient ancestor decided on a response, his or her brain summoned certain chemicals to engage in a call to arms that prepared the body to fight, run away, or freeze. The brain stores this thought—whenever I see a threat, I need to run—along with the fear response. The connection between the eyes and the amygdala—the part of our brain that activates the physiological fight-or-fight reaction—is much quicker than the connection from the eyes via other brain centers to the pre-frontal cortex, the part of the brain that makes judgments. So people often have an initial arousal that occurs without any conscious thought. The quickness of that connection probably has a lot to do with why we are still around as a species, but it has its costs.

Unfortunately, Ella has habituated herself to go into the fight or flight response on a daily basis and for things that are not necessarily emergencies. Consistently responding to the saber-toothed tiger in the guise of a specific situation with a fellow student, parent, teacher, or coach is exhausting for her and can paralyze her ability to cope with stressors. Of course there are emergency situations when we must respond in that way, however, most day-to-day interactions are not of that magnitude. Unfortunately, many young people have habituated their negative emotional responses and call upon them in less stressful, non-threatening situations.

Jill Bolte Taylor, the neurologist who wrote *My Stroke of Insight*, makes the point that, even in situations that invoke a fight, flight, or freeze response, we are only in its sway for 90 seconds. After that, we are back in control. She says, "I define responsibility (response-ability) as the ability to choose how we respond to stimulation coming in through our sensory systems at any moment in time. Although there are certain limbic system (emotional) programs that can be triggered automatically, it takes less than ninety seconds for one of those programs to be triggered, surge through our body, and then be completely flushed out of our bloodstream. If, however, I remain angry after those ninety seconds have passed, then it is because I have *chosen* to let that circuit continue to run."

In the modern world, however, mortal threats (other than on the highways!) are now exceedingly rare compared to most of human history. We live in an opportunity-rich age where the rapid-response flight, fight, or freeze system can easily become counter-productive.

Negativity Bias

In addition to our hard-wired tendency to see threats that require us to fight, flee or freeze, we also have a tendency to pay too much attention to "bad stuff." Psychologists call this tendency a *negativity bias*. We are more likely to notice, remember, recall, and think about events that cause negative emotions than we are those that produce warm, positive feelings. As Florida State psychologist Roy Baumeister, says, "Bad is stronger than good." While negative emotions are important, they tend to result in a limited range of possible action. (More on this in Chapter Seven.)

So, if negative emotions narrow our thoughts down to flight, fight, or freeze, maybe positive emotions could help us and our children, students, or players be more productive. But is there any real evidence for the suggestion that positive emotions enable successful behavior? If so, how positive would we need to be?

The Role of Positive Emotions and the Fluffy Fallacy

Barbara Fredrickson, from the University of North Carolina, has studied positive emotions for many years. She has demonstrated in laboratory experiments that positive emotions broaden behavior responses, while negative emotion can narrow our responses.

Positive and Negative Emotion-Action Responses			
Positive Emotions Broaden		Negative Emotions Narrow	
Emotion	**Action**	**Emotion**	**Action**
Joy	Play	Anger	Attack
Interest	Explore/learn	Fear/anxiety	Escape
Contentment	Savor/integrate	Shame	Disappear
Pride	Dream big	Guilt	Make amends
Affection	Approach	Sadness	Withdraw
Relief	Relax	Disgust	Expel
Gratitude	Creative giving		
Elevation	Becoming better		
Love	All of the above		

"Do what feels good" is a phrase we often rapidly reject as short-sighted and irresponsible. However, we can be too quick to dismiss the importance of feeling good—the frequent experience of positive emotions. Such too-quick dismissal is what we call "the Fluffy Fallacy," the belief that paying attention to positive emotions is a trivial waste of time.

The Fluffy Fallacy rests on the assumption that concerns about whether young people and their adult mentors are happy, engaged, and enjoying themselves are somehow unserious or fluffy. Individuals operating under the Fluffy Fallacy act as if feeling good has no part in learning, achievement, and success. Stated this boldly, most of us start to question the Fluffy Fallacy, and well we should. As you have already seen in the chapters on strengths, individuals operating from their strengths experience more positive emotions and tend to produce more positive results. These two are related. The Fluffy Fallacy suggests that achievement and positive emotions are a zero-sum game where having more of one means having less of the other. It is a fallacy because, as it turns out, increasing our ratio of positive to negative emotions generally results in superior performance for individuals, pairs, and teams. Strong evidence points to upward spirals when positive emotions and meaningful achievements sustain one another for extended periods of high productivity and well-being. When it happens, we say, "I'm on a roll!"

Your Emotional ATM

Barbara Fredrickson's exciting and powerful body of work has helped us understand more about the role of positive emotions. She has established that positive emotions enable and prompt us to grow and connect. While experiencing positive emotions, we tend to think more broadly and display a greater range in our behaviors. Further, we tend to build and strengthen connections with others and our own internal resources, both physical and psychological. For example, in the presence of positive emotions, healing processes in our bodies increase and repair damage caused by our stress response to negative emotions. Positive emotions broaden what Fredrickson calls "our thought-action repertoire"—they build psychological, social, and physical resources for the future. Boosting the frequency of positive emotions is like boosting the frequency of deposits to your bank account—you've got something to draw on when you have to hit your emotional ATM for a resilience withdrawal.

How Positive Should We Be?

Most of us, when asked if we are a positive person, would respond with something like, "Yes, of course." We might think something like, "I am more positive than negative." Likewise, if we were asked if we are a positive influence on the relationships we have at home, school, or on a team of which we are a part, the answer would again likely be, "Yes." Again, this might well be based on a perception that we contribute more positive than negative interactions to the relationship. However, we now have empirical evidence about how positive we need to be, both personally and in relationships, including in school, at home and on the athletic field. It turns out to be significantly greater than simply being more positive than not.

Psychologist Marcial Losada spent many years in the business world studying the differences between productive and unproductive teams. He and his research team brought leadership teams from business units into their laboratory and observed them as they worked through actual business challenges for which the team was responsible. In other words, the performance of the teams was in no way artificial, although it was observed in a lab setting. Dr. Losada's team of researchers encoded their observations of the business teams along several dimensions to see how positively or negatively they interacted. As they analyzed the data, interesting relationships began to emerge.

Losada found that teams that were half positive and half negative, a 1:1 ratio of positive to negative, were locked in failure patterns that caused extremely poor productivity. Teams functioning at 2:1 positive to negative ratios were successful as long as they could follow a limited behavior pattern, but they had little flexibility and could not adapt to changing competitive environments. Obviously, their success was short-lived. However, as a team's positive to negative ratio reached 3:1, new patterns of behavior emerged that led to moderate levels of success. As teams reached and exceeded a 5:1 positivity ratio, they began to achieve top levels of performance.

When Losada collaborated with Barbara Fredrickson, whose research on positive emotions we discussed earlier, he strongly suspected the relationship between positive team interactions and team productivity would also describe the relationship of positivity to other forms of success, including personal happiness and relationship strengths. Regarding the daily emotional lives of individuals, they found that people who were flourishing came in at 3:1 or higher. Those who were below 3:1 but above 1:1 were languishing; they were experiencing some success in their lives, but not overall, and they were very subject to downward spirals when faced with adversity. Finally, at a 1:1 ratio of positive to negative emotions, the research subjects were unhappy and perceived themselves as unsuccessful in the most important areas of their lives.

We worked with a high school coach who was consistently at a 1:1 ratio. His players were not producing on the field, and several quit the team. After several years of good adult mentoring, he finally saw how a higher positive to negative ratio could work. He eventually worked his way to a 3:1 ratio. He enjoyed coaching more, and his players certainly were more satisfied with the experience. In fact, the overall team performance markedly increased.

Whether we're talking about an individual's interior life, the quality of a relationship, or the performance of a group, a 3:1 ratio of positive emotional experiences to negative ones should be the minimum goal, and 5:1 is optimal. That's 84% positive. The research also suggests that it is possible to be too positive when the ratio is around 12:1. Some people may take this as "if you can't say something nice, don't say anything at all"—a form of political correctness. It is important to understand that wanting high levels of positivity doesn't mean repressing all negativity.

Why Aren't Our Positivity Ratios Higher?

If, as the research seems to so clearly indicate, positivity ratios of 3:1, 4:1, 5:1 or even higher are necessary for optimal personal well-being, rewarding relationships, and productive organizational performance, why are so many of us operating at significantly lower levels personally, in our relationships, and in our schools? Higher levels of positive emotions cause our immune systems to function better. From an evolutionary perspective, doesn't it make sense that, over the course of thousands of generations, those individuals who, either because of genetic differences, or because of their experiences growing up in a tribe, operated at higher ratios of positivity would be more likely to survive and pass those traits on to the next generation, both genetically and culturally? Or, put another way, shouldn't we expect to find that human beings naturally tend to gravitate toward higher levels of positivity?

It may well be that a greater percentage of human beings today operate at a 3:1 positivity ratio than was the case thousands of generations ago. Robert Wright, in his book *Non-Zero*, suggests that cooperative, collaborative, positive-emotion-generating behavior has, in fact, been on the increase in human populations around the world for as far back as we are able to gather any evidence about the cultures and success of our ancestors. So, while we cannot go back and do detailed studies of the positivity ratios experienced by our distant ancestors in their daily lives, it is not unreasonable to assume that the gradual trend in human lives and societies is toward greater positivity ratios. As a result, the negativity bias doesn't serve us as well today as in the past. (In Chapter Seven you will learn skills to counter the negativity bias.)

Positive Emotions Improve Attention

Positive emotions help us to see the big picture and can increase the likelihood that we can perform under pressure. As we take in sensory information about the world around us, we can pay attention to either the particularities of that information or to the bigger picture—the overall pattern. In some situations it is important to be focused on details (local processing), and in others a more general perspective promotes success (global processing). Obviously, a student, parent, teacher, or coach who is able to flexibly shift back and forth between either more global or more local ways of processing is better able to adapt to the needs of any given situation and more likely to be successful.

Can Negative Emotions Increase Attention?

When Barbara Fredrickson primed research subjects in either a positive or negative direction with a video she had them watch, as predicted, those who were primed in a positive emotional direction generated significantly more entries for their list of things they wanted to do. So positive emotions broaden our attention and interest as we consider new things to do. But both negative and positive emotions are useful, as we have pointed out. Gary Strauss, from the University of Nevada, and Daniel Allen, from the University of Maryland School of Medicine, studied the influence of positive and negative emotions on attention. They found that negative emotions interfered with attention when there was high time pressure to complete a task. On the flip side, when there was less time pressure, positive emotions interfered with attention. You, or a student, may have experienced this attention dilemma when a deadline was about to be reached without the work having been completed. Becoming angry, guilty, or disgusted with the assignment (or the assigner) does not lead to more focus on the work!

Positive Emotions Help Us Connect

University of Michigan's Chris Peterson summarizes the findings in the Positive Psychology field to date by saying, "Other people matter." Playing to strengths and being aware of others' positive emotions can make a huge difference in how people connect in relationships.

At Texas A&M, Roger Goddard has studied how relationships in a school building strongly predict the amount of learning that students will achieve in a school year. In one study of hundreds of Indiana elementary schools, Goddard found that, after controlling for the effect of such things as race and socioeconomic background, it was the amount of trust teachers had in their students as learners that predicted the amount of learning those students would achieve in a school year. In other words, even in schools with similar characteristics as far as family income and other social elements, students learned more when their teachers felt a sense of trust. Although trust may not be considered an emotion, the presence of positive emotions can increase trust.

Balancing the Emotional Vocabulary

We have had numerous parents and teachers tell us that some fear, anger, shame, and guilt are productive at times—that these negative emotions are what motivate kids to work harder and get the job done. We agree that negative emotions are important, but they do not seem to help students perform under pressure. However, when young people tend to default to these emotions in a majority of situations, then we see the need for balancing the emotional vocabulary—to become more fluid in processing situations to elicit the most appropriate emotion. People need negative feedback to get better at what they do—but there is negative feedback and ineffective negative feedback, and negative feedback does not always require that the recipient experience negative emotions.

When a person feels fear, for example, the tendency is to want to escape. When people feel angry, they believe that their rights have been violated. They want to attack—either others (outwardly) or themselves (inwardly). Have you ever had a person tell you that they were disgusted with you? Disgust is one of the most powerful of the negative emotions. If you find a food disgusting, you want to spit it out. When someone feels disgust, he or she is motivated to expel a thing or a person. What goes through a young person's mind when teachers, parents, or coaches make known their disgust? Chances are the teachers and coaches are not totally disgusted, but the manner in which they share their frustration about a student's apparent laziness or a young athlete's error on the playing field can speak volumes to the child or adolescent.

Shame is an interesting emotion. When one feels shame, the tendency is to want to disappear. Shame is about feeling embarrassed or unworthy. Can shame help change a young person's behavior to be more positive? Maybe. But living in a shame-based environment, whether it be at home, school, or on the athletic field, doesn't bring out the best in a young person. If you remember from the Introduction, John's first grade teacher did a nice job of shaming him for wetting his pants in the classroom. When you are remorseful and responsible for making a mistake, there may be a sense that you violated the rights of someone else. If you wish to, but are unable to make amends, a cycle of expecting failure in pleasing another person may ensue. Some people claim that guilt is good for soul and can be helpful at times. However, living a lifetime of guilt may not bring the life satisfaction that someone really deserves.

There are certain situations when negative emotions are helpful or harmful for you and others. Fear may interfere with a student's ability to concentrate, while it may motivate another student who is procrastinating to complete an assignment. When we understand what situations trigger negative emotions, and when they are helpful and harmful, we can better regulate how we use negative emotions. Here is a chance for you to explore some of those times.

	It's helpful when...	It's harmful when...
Mindful Moment: *The Negative Emotions Litmus Test*		
Think of several situations when you tend to express the following negative emotions. When is it helpful for you and others? When is it harmful for you and others? (You do not have to fill in all the columns. Fortunately, there are not many positive uses of disgust.)		
Fear		
Anger		
Disgust		
Shame		
Guilt		
Sadness		

Todd Kashdan, a psychologist at George Mason University, and his colleagues studied previous research claims that people who are more skilled at differentiating emotions may be better able to self-regulate their emotions. They asked underage social drinkers to describe their emotions before and after drinking episodes. With the subjects using a hand-held electronic journal, Kashdan found that those young adults who could better distinguish and describe their emotions, were "less likely to drink excessively when in response to intense negative emotions."

The Positive Emotions

While negative emotions tend to more visceral in nature, positive emotions tend to be less prominent, and they can be fleeting. We can be awestruck one moment, interested by something else the next. We often experience brief moments of joy or contentment. A person can be angry for days, but positive emotions are more spread out over time and can recur more often.

When people are interested in something, their attention goes in that direction. When a good movie or book comes out, we see how the interest can become viral. When we are feeling content, we are feeling satisfied about something. Elevation is a positive emotion that is the result of being inspired by someone or something. It does just what it says—it elevates a person to another level.

For example, Frank's father expresses his thankfulness to teachers at Frank's school for their tireless efforts. In a case where a positive emotion can be expressed as harmful, Jodi, the ultimate *satisficer*, has always been content with getting C grades. However, she has become aware that her mediocre grade point average may not be sufficient to interest college admissions officers. When we understand what situations spark positive emotions, we can better control how we use positive emotions. In the *Mindful Moment* you have an opportunity to examine how and when you call upon your positive emotions.

Mindful Moment: *The Positive Emotions Litmus Test*

Think of several situations when you tend to express the following positive emotions. When is it helpful for you and others? When is it harmful for you and others? (You do not have to fill in all the columns. Fortunately, there are not many negative uses of joy and gratitude.)

	It's helpful when...	*It's harmful when...*
Joy		
Interest		
Contentment		
Gratitude		
Elevation		
Love		

Balancing Emotions when Making Decisions

Our emotions are major players in the important decisions we make. Becoming aware of the underlying values that drive student behavior and intuitive responses is an excellent first step toward improving the way they get along in the world. This is part of building character, understanding, and trust.

A fitting metaphor for the challenging realities of decision-making is University of Virginia professor Jon Haidt's "rider on the elephant." The rider (logical reasoning mind) can help steer the direction of the elephant (the emotional mind). The elephant, however, is very strong and, despite all the efforts of the rider, it may win out.

Jill Paolini

The rider can see farther into the distance, plan and sometimes anticipate things that the elephant will do and even explain what the elephant has done, but it is the elephant that is often in charge of our actions. This is something that we all need to be aware of about ourselves, since we all need to be able to work with our own elephant. Beyond that, sometimes someone else's elephant and rider will inevitably clash with ours.

Training the Rider

Training the rider to help regulate the elephant is very important. Fortunately, we have many strengths and strategies that make this possible. If you have ever trained a willful puppy, you may have needed a professional trainer to help you through rough patches. You, and the young people you serve, may benefit from having a trainer (friend, colleague, parent, teacher, or coach) because as any trainer will tell you, the animal learns what is taught. Beware the law of unintended consequences. You need to be skilled, confident, and consistent in your approach.

A trainer can help you learn to like and understand the elephant you've got without letting your rider overlook its bad behavior. Does your elephant tend toward impulsivity? Competition? Angry outbursts? Entitlement? Is it whiny? Does it overindulge? Look down on other elephants? Fail to accept its role in trouble and therefore its resolution? Your trainer can help you become more accurate about your contribution to difficult situations and help you figure out what you can change and what you cannot. It is also important to know that people can have gut reactions that lead them to moral behavior that their reasoning mind rejects. Here the elephant can be a friend. If someone is constantly aware of each decision they have to make during the day, it can be paralyzing. We need to make split second calls all the time.

Another trusted parent, teacher, coach, or student can be a trainer by helping a person develop self-regulation skills needed to "think before you do," perhaps by guiding you to make a list of tactics and identify strengths you will employ in the service of your goals. Ask your trainer to help you stay on track so that you can replicate tactics when faced with similar challenges. This develops self-efficacy, the belief about one's ability and capacity to accomplish a task or deal with an adversity, which is essential to the confidence and consistency you will need. The trainer may suggest that you find other elephants in your herd—your social connections—who support your growth so that you might collaborate with them. Even the best plans for self-improvement can be led astray by other wayward elephants.

Emotions Across Activities

Sports are a natural home for the expression of emotions, both for better and for worse. Although the magnitude of emotional responses may be greater on the athletic field, the same responses and consequences can be felt at home and in the classroom. Sport psychologists Jim Taylor and Mark Jones claim that the unpleasant emotions of frustration and anger may actually be helpful with athletic performance. Yet, at the highest levels of performance, athletes often report being in the zone, a state of flow where only the positive emotion of interest is evident, and only through the intensity of focused attention. If the athlete is continually frustrated or angry, however, then there tends to be a decrease in performance. For the most part fear, desperation, rage, panic, embarrassment, shame, and guilt decrease performance and can create a sense of learned helplessness, a feeling of despair. This can be seen at home and in the classroom, too. Pleasant emotions such as excitement, exhilaration, joy, and pride all tend to help a young person perform better.

Mindful Moment: *Positivity in School, at Home, and on the Athletic Field*

This 3-part activity is a way for you to evaluate positivity ratios, so you can see why some groups may flourish, and others flounder when it comes to relationships and performance.

Pre-Reflection

- *Think of a regular group activity that you participate in with young people as a parent, teacher or coach.*

- *Recalling your last group activity, think of the members of the group—be it spouse, sons and daughters at the dinner table; a department meeting at school, or a class; or a team at practice.*

- *In the time the group spent assembling, participating in the activity, and then departing, estimate the ratio of positive statements to negative statements during this group activity. Positive statements are those you would rate as likely to result in positive thoughts and emotions in those who heard the statement. Negative statements would be likely to lead to negative thoughts and emotions.*

Interaction Charting

- *Keep an interaction chart of all your activities for a week and evaluate for positivity and negativity. After each interaction during the week, put a plus or minus sign by the name of the person with whom you had the interaction. A plus indicates an interaction that you found energizing or otherwise positive. A negative indicates a de-energizing, negative interaction. At the end of the week, calculate the positivity ratio for your interactions with each individual.*

Post–Reflection

- *Are any of these relationships at or above the 3:1 positivity ratio? 5:1?*

- *Are there any relationships you would like to "Warm up?" Pay particular attention to relationships where a little warming might move the relationship to or above the 3:1 ratio. If so, try warming up that relationship for a few weeks, then reassess.*

- *Are there any changes you can make so you spend less time in low-positivity relationships and more time in high-positivity relationships?*

Flow

There are also situations where a person is so engaged in and enjoys the process of an endeavor that they are not even aware of their emotions. They are in a *flow state*. Mihaly Csikszentmihalyi, who has done extensive research on flow, claims that this state happens when a person's skill or talent for meeting a challenge is marginally equal to or above his or her current level of achievement (see figure below). If the young person's skill level is higher than the challenge, boredom sets in. In contrast, when the person's skill level is relatively lower than the challenge, anxiety enters the equation. Only when challenge meets skill can the individual be fully engaged in and enjoy the endeavor. When enjoyment is paired with enhanced performance, it is impossible for the relationship between challenge and skill to remain stagnant.

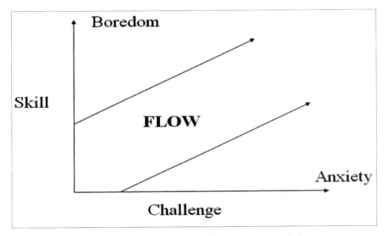

Reprinted with permission Mihaly Csikszentmihalyi,
Flow: The Psychology of Optimal Experience.
New York: HarperPerennial, 2008.

In Her Own Words: Cynthia Adams Harrison, Performance Consultant and former elite figure skater

I remember one night at the Broadmoor in Colorado Springs. There were two rinks and we would skate from 10 or 11 at night to 3 or 4 in the morning. Those were our training hours. I was in a big rink and decided to go to the little rink. Then there was the unbelievable moment. I remember going in and saying good night to others as they left. And I was alone. I had a mirror and my own little rink (the curling rink). I put on my music—not the regular dance music—and I was in front of the mirror, doing positions. I remember how much I loved being on the ice at that moment. I stopped for a moment and thought: "You know, if you just keep practicing, just keep moving, this will all pay off one day." I remember thinking that I want to be the last one on the ice, because I know that if I work really, really hard and I believe in this, and I am dedicated to what I am doing right now, good things will happen. I remember all of those thoughts as I just enjoyed the music, all by myself, as my partner had gone home, too. It was a total absence of anyone, and a total enjoyment of everything.

The IZOF

People get into the IZOF (Individual Zone of Functioning), by being a bit more relaxed, having a moderate level of arousal, or having a high level of physiological response. Yuri Hanin, a professor at the Research Institute for Olympic Sports in Jyvaskyla, Finland, has conducted extensive research in the area of performance arousal in sport. This has overlapping value to the classroom. The traditional understanding of performance and anxiety suggested the more emotionally aroused a person was, the better that he or she would perform. In sports, Hanin's work shows that sometimes coaches and athletes are *too* uptight, *too* psyched up for a contest, meaning that they are overly-aroused. When aroused, the physiological signs include increased heart rate, racing thoughts, profuse sweating, and tense muscles. However, when over-aroused, the signs may be related to relatively sub-par performance. There are other times when coaches and athletes are under-aroused— meaning they are in a lethargic, "I don't care," state of mind, and performance is again adversely affected.

The model in the figure below illustrates how people respond to arousal differently. For some people, it is best to approach competition when feeling calm and relaxed. For others, they need to be a little more excited. At the other end of the continuum, others do best when they are highly charged. This type of person benefits most from the energized pep talk by a parent, teacher, or coach. Hanin has shown that people can be in their own IZOF (Individual Zone of Functioning) at either the low, moderate, or highly-aroused level. A young person may be need to be at a higher arousal level to compete in a sports event, while needing to be very relaxed when taking a test in the classroom.

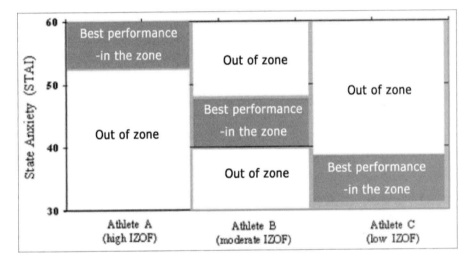

Reprinted with permission, Yuri Hanin, *Emotions in Sport.*
Champaign, Ill: Human Kinetics, 2000.

Performance goes up as arousal goes up—to a certain degree. As we increase arousal past this point, performance will tend to decrease, i.e., performance goes down as arousal continues to increase. In dealing with athletes, the advice is this: if you sense that your level of arousal is low, then you need to do something to get yourself up; and if you are too aroused, slow the system down. In the classroom or when doing homework, the same advice would apply. How do students keep themselves aroused at an appropriate level? For a student who wants to increase arousal, they might try stretching in their seat or socializing with another student when it is appropriate, focusing a short, even inhale/exhale of the breath (rather than long, deep breathing which is relaxing), or on forced yawning. This can happen at homework time, too. (Refer to the visualization information provided in Chapter Five).

Mindful Moment: *Knowing When You are In the Zone*

You at Your Best: What is your IZOF?

As a parent, teacher or coach, when have you found yourself in the IZOF? You'll know because your talents met your challenges, you emerged from the zone having lost track of time, and you would go back to that time if you could. _____

_____

_____

What was your optimal arousal level? Were you in the low, medium, or high range IZOF, and how could you tell? What factors contributed to getting you into that optimal state? _____

_____

_____

What were the factors that helped you stay in the IZOF? _____

_____

_____

_____

Would your IZOF level of arousal level work for you in another situation? Answer the questions for a different domain to discover the answer (e.g., the athletic field, an arts performance, or the classroom). _____

_____

_____

Honor and Emotions

The concept of honor is deeply ingrained in the study of evolutionary and cultural psychology. Human beings are genetically predisposed to human association. Our capacity to think into the future, anticipate and plan greatly exceeds anything demonstrated by any other species. We can reason about what needs to be done to anticipate and solve problems beyond the short term. Another piece necessary for survival is that human beings have a powerful ability to work in groups. We are genetically bound to this construct. Therefore loyalty to the group is a powerful driver. Competing motivations and a student's membership in a herd or a hive are dominant variables when weighing the pros and cons of doing the right thing. Even a brother and sister who incessantly tease each other circle the wagons to protect each other when threatened from an outside source like a parent or even a peer. At the beginning of each academic year, Culver Academies students are provided the opportunity to vote on maintaining the student-run honor code. Culver's mission to educate its students for leadership and responsible citizenship in society is rooted in the deep tradition of honor, and the learning laboratory at Culver exposes current students to real-time ethical challenges.

Culver provides students with skills of social perception, imagination, and reasoning as they navigate their journeys to adulthood. For any society to function there has to be a sense of honor so that people know that lying, cheating and stealing are wrong. This includes laws, customs, and rules aimed at having and maintaining order, and they are generally articulated in some sort of social contract among people. However, it is still challenging for students to tell on another student who has breached the honor code. Loyalty among the student community is very thick! The Rider and the Elephant are at play here. The reasoning mind of the student is saying: "He shouldn't have done that, and I know that I am supposed to turn him in. But the potential consequence of doing this among my peers is too great a risk." There may be fear and anxiety put forward by the elephant, or the student's response may not conjure up a lot of emotions—since he has established a "gut in the mind" response to the situation. The student might think, "I am going to keep my mouth shut. And that is that! End of story."

It is interesting to see how the students on Culver's Honor Council do business a bit differently. They have an incredible loyalty to the time-tested tradition of the Honor Code and take it extremely seriously. Therefore, their rider and the elephant experiences tend to come from making the right call on an honor case.

Social Norms and Emotions

Social norms are behavior patterns set by social groups. These behaviors often become what is normal for a given group, community, or society. A simple example in Western countries is shaking hands upon meeting someone. A more complex example is drinking alcohol. Among some groups, like high school students, a belief may develop that the social norm is partying with alcohol and getting drunk, when in fact the majority of students do not do that. What students believe about behavioral expectations of their peers is a potent driver of choices, especially when people are faced with a moral decision that may influence his or her relationship with others.

Tim was a high school junior in a parochial school when he faced such a moral dilemma. He arrived at a school-sponsored event after drinking with his friends, who also attended the same event. They entered at different times and, at first, only Tim was questioned by the school administration. However, the principal knew to ask if Tim had any friends attending the event and he answered, "Yes." Suddenly Tim knew that he would have to make a choice: whether to rat on his friends and risk their friendship by telling the truth or lie in hopes of saving them but not himself.

Students generally operate on a paradigm where loyalty takes precedence over honor. This has a lot to do with the development of an adolescent's brain. Although they are compelled by raw, brute emotion to be loyal, they need some sense of honor to maintain order and to grow in and as a community. At stake in a situation like this was much more than friendship. For Tim, his friends were an important group to protect, and with them he had many positive memories that had created a deep well of positive emotions. The principal was clever to ask the "friends" question, and ultimately Tim chose truth over loyalty, and of this he was *proud*. Of course this was the right thing to do in the principal's mind, and Tim was rewarded by not having charges filed with the police department and not having the incident reported on his college recommendations, for which he felt both relief and gratitude.

Although part of Tim's motivation was to protect himself, he did lose those friends (all of whom lied to the principal when questioned individually) and they were suspended. If you recall the *Positive and Negative Emotion-Action Responses* table from earlier in the chapter, you'll see that the action for *pride* is to dream big, for *relief* is to relax, and for *gratitude* is to give back. Tim graduated #6 in his high school class, is now a very successful student at a highly selective college, and has many new friends. His parents and his school could not be happier to see the way he has changed for good.

Psychological research consistently shows people overestimate their own goodness compared to that of others. In any situation of conflict or social comparison, our self-perception is distorted because we look at ourselves in a rose-colored mirror. Many times a day, as we observe or interact with others, our rider keeps the elephant on course by reminding it to (or not to) act. But sometimes, like Tim, the rider must clean up after his elephant.

In this chapter we showed you how parents, teachers, and coaches can use a more positive emotional vocabulary at home, at school, and in sports to build resilience in young people. We discussed the benefits that positive emotions have on strengthening learning and improving sports performances, as well as building overall optimism at home and at school. We hope you understand how parents, teachers, and coaches can enable positive emotions by helping young people shift focus to be more creative, tolerant, generous, imaginative and productive.

In Chapter Seven, you will extend your understanding of emotions and their effect on planning and choice. You'll learn and practice skills for becoming more optimistic and resilient that will work for you and for the youth you mentor.

Chapter Seven

Building Resilience with Flexible and Accurate Thinking

I am an optimist. It does not seem too much use being anything else.
—Winston Churchill

On a beautiful spring afternoon, a softball and baseball team played home games. In the baseball game, the batter hit a grounder to Darren, the shortstop, who failed to catch it, as it took a bad hop before it reached his glove. In the heat of the moment, he said to himself, "The ball took a bad bounce." Darren continued to feel confident in his abilities and to enjoy the game. His teammates and coach yelled out: "Shake it off." They noticed Darren's erect posture and energetic movements and were confident that he would continue to play to his expected level of performance for the rest of the game. The coach remembered that Darren was scheduled to bat in the next inning and thought, "Good. He is one of our better hitters."

On the adjacent softball field, shortstop Samantha bobbled a ground ball that hit a little rock as she was trying to make the play. As she watched the ball roll into left field, she thought, "I just don't have what it takes to play this game." She began to lose confidence in her abilities and started wishing she was doing something else. Just like at the boys' game, her teammates and coach told her, "Shake it off!" They noticed Samantha's slumped posture and slowed movement and began to wonder whether she would recover from the error. The coach remembered that Samantha was scheduled to bat in the next inning and thought, "She's normally one of our better hitters, but maybe I should let someone else bat in that slot. She's not likely to get a hit after making that error."

© Ashleigh Brilliant   www.ashleighbrilliant.com

Optimistic and Pessimistic Explanatory Styles

Nothing differed in these two stories up until the point where each player thought about their error. However, from that point forward, not only did Darren and Samantha begin to feel and behave differently, but other players and the coach, too, began to think, feel and act differently. Samantha and Darren were expressing different *explanatory styles*. We each have an explanatory style. Martin Seligman and colleagues explain that we begin to develop this way of explaining the causes of negative events in our lives during childhood.

Briefly, explanatory style is based on three two-dimensional attributes of a person's evaluation of why a negative event occurred:

- *Duration.* Do we believe the bad event will last forever or temporarily?
- *Scope.* Do we believe that the bad event affects everything in our lives or just a small part or it?
- *Control.* Do we blame ourselves or others for the event?

For instance, an event can be a consequence of stable, long-in-duration causes versus unstable, short-term causes. Darren's explanation of why he did not catch the ball was temporary (the ball does not always take a bad bounce). The causes can be broad in scope, affecting many areas of performance versus specific causes.

The cause was specific (took a bad hop). And the cause can be more or less controllable by the individual. In this case, the ball was outside his control (nothing to feel bad about). This sort of explanation frees him up to try again and expect a different and better outcome next time. It was not his fault, it will not happen every time, and he is not globally incompetent. Robert Brooks, a Boston area psychologist and co-author of *Raising Resilient Children* and *The Power of Resilience*, has a lot of experience working with young people and explanatory styles. He claims that one of the key points about explanatory style is how honest we are with ourselves. Blaming the ball on a bad hop can serve to work against realistic accomplishment. Sometimes, youth will blame factors outside their control that were in fact in their control. Thus, if Darren made an error and it was not a bad hop, a more adaptive pattern of thinking would be, "I made an error, that can happen. I'm going to put in more time practicing my fielding."

Samantha, on the other hand, explained her event very differently. She is responsible, it's always going to be this way, and she will always struggle with everything about softball.

Thoughts and emotions are intertwined to the point where we rarely stop and separate them. But, as researchers have teased apart the strands of thought and emotion, clarity has emerged: thinking affects feeling. Our emotions are shaped by our beliefs about our experiences, thus, if we are thinking less flexibly and accurately about a situation because of our thoughts, we can become stuck in one set of feelings. Most importantly, as a result, we are likely able to act in only limited ways. The great news is that we all have the ability to think about our thoughts and to reshape our thought patterns to become more flexible, accurate, and productive. This chapter will help you learn to do this and to teach you skills that your children, students, and athletes can use to shape their thinking for building optimism and resilience.

The Case for Optimism

A key component of resilience is optimism, especially the kind of realistic optimism promoted by flexible and accurate thinking. There are hundreds of well-designed research studies that have evaluated the effects of optimistic thinking. Researchers agree that those who typically think about themselves, the events in their lives, and their goals in positive, optimistic ways also are more likely to have good health, good relationships, and to successfully pursue their goals.

One important study helps make the case for working to develop a more flexible and accurate thinking style. A national study begun in 1979 looked at data about more than 10,000 young people, aged 14-22 when the study began. Tim Judge and Charlice Hurst, researchers from the University of Florida, compared the income of participants as they aged, based on their high school grades. They discovered that those who had 4.0 high school grade point averages (straight As) and who also had some of the qualities of positive, optimistic thinking described above, were on average making twice as much money as they approached age 50 as their more negative, pessimistic thinking peers who also made straight As.

In fact, the pessimistic straight-A students were making less than not only the optimistic C or D students, they were making less than even the pessimistic D students. The difference was even more pronounced for the 1200 SAT scorers. The more positive students who scored 1200 were making over *three times* as much on average ($134,000 compared to $42,000) as their pessimistic classmates who scored 1200. The more pessimistic students with a 1200 SAT ended up making *less* than students with a 600, whether optimistic or pessimistic.

A large body of research also exists on the effect of helping students or adults with pessimistic thinking styles learn to counter that tendency and think more flexibly and more accurately. The data shows that both youth and adults can change their patterns. When they do, they begin to experience the stronger relationships, better health, and greater success that come with realistic optimism. In the stories that began this chapter, Darren thought optimistically about missing the ground ball, whereas Samantha thought pessimistically.

Common Links Between Thoughts and Emotions

It will help you learn to more easily identify what thoughts might be driving a particular emotion and action if you know that research has identified common links between certain types of thoughts and corresponding emotions, and that those thought/emotion pairs often lead to particular types of actions. This is particularly true of the emotions most of us do not want to experience: the negative emotions. For example, if we think that someone or something we value is gone from our lives, we will likely feel sadness and want to withdraw. But if we think someone has violated our rights, anger and a tendency to want to attack are more likely feelings. Here are the common connections between types of thoughts and emotions and actions:

Negative Emotional Links		
When I Think...	**I Feel...**	**I Do...** (tendency)
My rights have been violated.	Anger	Attack
I am threatened and have no coping plan.	Fear/ anxiety	Escape
I have failed to meet standards.	Shame	Disappear
I have violated someone's rights.	Guilt	Make amends
I have lost something valuable.	Sadness	Withdraw
My morals or sense of right and wrong have been violated.	Disgust	Expel

Why Just Negative Emotions?

You may have wondered why the chart above only lists negative emotions. Research has shown us that most individuals make the greatest gains in resilience by learning to recognize and challenge the thoughts they have when faced with adversity. Further, when you're able to successfully challenge the negative thoughts or beliefs that lead to negative emotions by finding more flexible and more accurate thoughts, the result will be either neutral or positive emotions, thus improving your positivity ratio. (More on this is in Chapter Six.)

The rest of this chapter will give you some deeper understanding of challenges you might run into, tactics for overcoming those challenges, and some suggestions about two specific challenges with youth where these skills open new pathways to success. However, it is important to remember that flexible and accurate thinking is not easy, or we would all be doing it already.

Challenges to Flexible and Accurate Thinking

We do not approach each event in our lives with a completely open mind. Rather, we are inclined by both personal habits of thinking and patterns that seem to be deeply wired in all human beings. In other words, we are more likely to think some thoughts than others. The personal habits of thinking affect the types of explanations we generate when we encounter adversities. The deeply-wired patterns include an extra-sharp sense of negatives and a tendency to focus exclusively on evidence that supports our beliefs. Each is a challenge to flexible and accurate thinking. Let's look at each of these challenges and some ways you can overcome them.

Challenge #1: Habits of Thinking

As we pursue our goals in life, we run into obstacles, adversities, and challenges. As a first step toward moving forward, we often look for an explanation. We want to know why. Unfortunately, for some of us, our habits of thinking cause our efforts to work against us. Some of us tend to explain things by pointing to causes that are broad in scope, long in duration, and leave us little control. This leads to hopelessness and keeps us from moving forward. To understand this better, let's return to the stories of the two ballplayers that began this chapter.

Remember that both Darren and Samantha failed to field a ball hit to them. Nothing differed in these two stories up until the point where each player thought about their error. Darren thought, "The ball took a bad bounce." Samantha thought, "I just don't have what it takes to play this game." From that point forward, not only did Darren and Samantha begin to feel and behave differently, other players and their coaches began to think, feel, and act differently. Samantha and Darren were expressing different habits for explaining events.

Darren and Samantha demonstrate key differences in habits of explanation. Individuals can tend toward explaining events by suggesting causes that are:

Optimistic because:	Pessimistic because:
Temporary: "bad hop"	**Permanent:** "don't have what it takes"
Specific: bad hop applies to one play	**Broad:** lack of ability affects all parts of the game
Boost Control: bad hops happen to all, but most games are determined by skill. Darren is in control.	**Diminish Control:** not having "what it takes" means Samantha has no control over her performance.

An optimist is more resilient because he or she sees that causes of bad events are short-term and specific, and that leaves the optimist in more control. A pessimist, on the other hand, loses energy and motivation when faced with adversity because he or she tends to see causes that are permanent (will keep creating problems in the future) and broad (will affect many activities or areas of life). This point of view tends to diminish the pessimist's control. These tendencies are simply habits, and over time we can train ourselves to have new, more productive explanatory habits.

What about Good Events?

When things go well, optimists and pessimists reverse their explanations. Optimists see long-lasting, broad causes that are within their control. Pessimists see good events as having fleeting causes that are specific and outside their control. If Darren, the optimist, makes a great play, he will likely think, "All my hard work in practice is paying off!" Notice that he can keep working hard, that hard work can improve other areas of his play, and even other areas of his life, and that how hard he works is within his control. On the other hand, Samantha, the pessimist, might think after making a good play, "Got lucky on that one!" Darren's beliefs will boost his energy, focus, and commitment when things go right and keep them from dropping when adversity strikes. His thoughts will help create winning streaks and upward spirals of performance. Samantha's thoughts will bring her down when adversity strikes and do little to boost her up when she succeeds.

It is easy to see why hundreds of research studies have shown that those with a positive explanatory style—optimists—are more likely to succeed in many areas of life, such as sports, business, and relationships, including marriage. The good news is that our explanatory style is within our control. We can learn to challenge pessimistic thoughts and replace them with more flexible, accurate thinking. In so doing, we are both *more* in touch with reality than when we are unduly pessimistic, *and* we are more likely to achieve our goals.

The Power of More Flexible, Accurate Thinking

Whether a person is a realistic optimist or an Eeyore, the gloomy character in the Winnie-the-Pooh stories, explanatory style can be a powerful motivator of behavior. Pessimists too often see roadblocks and impossibilities instead of just hard work and a little challenge—the kinds of things that make us feel good about our accomplishments later. Optimists may occasionally work harder at a goal that they ultimately abandon than pessimists would have (though research indicates this is rare), but they also gain skills and experience that help them with the next goal. Optimists may also give other individuals a little more of the benefit of the doubt than pessimists, but again this simply opens up the possibility of better and more satisfying relationships. Knowing that you can use your thoughts to recreate the reality within which you live can have powerful—and good—consequences.

Challenge #2: Two Thinking Biases

What if you are now convinced that you might be more successful and happier if you developed a more flexible and accurate (optimistic) explanatory style? Or, perhaps you would like to help your children, students, or athletes learn to think in more optimistic ways. How hard will it be? For a time, it will be tough. Then it will become easier. And the reason for both is the same: Humans have some deeply-wired biases that make it difficult to challenge our thoughts, *especially* our pessimistic thoughts.

Negativity bias is the tendency we have to notice, remember, recall, and give weight to bad things more than we do good things. Negativity bias, which we also mentioned in the last chapter, is the first of our deeply-wired tendencies that tends to keep pessimists stuck with rigid, often inaccurate thinking. We see, remember, recall, and give weight to bad things—negative occurrences—more than to the good. For a pessimist confronted with an adversity or obstacle, the negativity bias makes it easy for him or her to remember and give importance to other bad things that have happened in the past, and times he or she failed to overcome the challenge. The pessimist finds that it is easy to remember lots of bad things from the past, so why not look for causes that are permanent and broad in scope? Why not decide you have little control over events? Thus, the negativity bias supports pessimistic explanations for adversity, explanations that rob us of motivation and cloud the ability to see and move forward on pathways to success.

Negativity bias, however, is not the only deeply-wired tendency you will have to counter to successfully move from a habit of pessimistic explanations to a more optimistic style. There is a second such deeply-wired tendency, but, unlike the negativity bias, this tendency can be turned to the cause of optimism.

The confirmation bias causes us to notice, remember, recall, and give weight to observations and thoughts that confirm what we already believe. Once our explanatory style causes us to jump to an initial explanation about why something happened, that explanation can become our belief, and the confirmation bias kicks in to make sure we notice, remember, recall, and give weight to only those pieces of evidence that support our version of things. You may have tried to talk someone else out of an overly negative way of seeing something only to have them stubbornly (at least that is your belief!) focus on just the aspects of the situation that supported their pessimistic, depressing, helplessness-inducing view of events. That was the confirmation bias, and it is *much* easier to see in others than in ourselves.

As you begin developing a more productive explanatory style by becoming more flexible and accurate in your thinking, you are going to need to be especially careful not to let the negativity bias and your confirmation bias pull you off track. The best way to do this is to slow down and think carefully.

Resilience is comprised of skills that can be learned. An important place to begin is *thinking it through*. You can use the *Negative Emotions Links* chart on page 189 to help you work through your feelings and behaviors. In the activity on the next page, you can practice sorting out the *facts* of an event from your thoughts about it and determine the emotions that were reinforced by those thoughts.

Mindful Moment — *Think It Through*

Think of a recent time when things did not go your way. It may have been at work, at home, or with friends. Were you . . .

- *Sad*
- *Embarrassed*
- *Angry or frustrated*
- *Guilty or ashamed*
- *Afraid or anxious*
- *Disgusted*

What happened? *List just the facts, and try not to analyze.*

Who? _____

_____

_____

What? _____

_____

_____

When? _____

_____

_____

Where? _____

_____

_____

Think (List your thoughts or beliefs as the event happened.)_____

_____

_____

_____

Feel (What emotions went with those thoughts or beliefs?) _____

_____

_____

_____

Do (What did you do?)_____

_____

_____

In the *Think It Through* activity above, you used the first resilience skill to identify the basic "I think, I feel, I do…" pattern for an event where things did not go your way. The second skill, which we call *RAMP Up* will teach you how to change your thoughts and notice that by changing your thoughts you could also change your emotions and perhaps find different pathways to move forward.

As you do, you may need to *RAMP Up* your challenges to your thoughts. When you *RAMP Up*, you reject and rethink evidence, generate alternatives, minimize the initial evidence and plan a route ahead.

For the following activity return to your *Think It Through* example.

Mindful Moment: *RAMP Up*

Reject and Rethink:
Look for evidence that would cause you to reject and rethink your first thought. **What have you missed?**

Alternatives:
Generate other ways of explaining the event. **Can you think of causes with shorter duration, narrower scope, and that leave you more in control?**

Minimize:
Create some wiggle room. If you cannot reject or develop an alternative, **can you at least narrow the duration and scope of the cause in your first thought?**

Plan:
Sometimes our thoughts are more about "what next" than "why." When challenging "what next" thoughts, a plan to achieve better outcomes can help. **What steps can prevent the worst and make the best more likely?**

At first, this will seem like a lot of work. However, by thinking through your reaction to events carefully and thoroughly, you will find the best ways to challenge your own thoughts. After some deliberate practice you will find yourself challenging broad, permanent causes of adversities that diminish your control even as they pop into your mind. Further, you will more easily and quickly see the evidence that points to more optimistic explanations featuring specific, short-term causes that leave you in control. Keep using *Think It Through* and *RAMP Up* until it becomes automatic. If you get stuck, ask a friend to *Think It Through* with you.

The Benefits of Emotional Vocabulary

As you pay attention to how you react to events—what you think, feel, and do—you will begin to develop more awareness of your emotions. The same will happen for your children, students, and athletes as they learn these skills. You will be developing the ability to more carefully and accurately identify emotions in yourself and in others. This skill alone has benefits. Since the publication of *Emotional Intelligence* by Daniel Goleman, much has been written and said about the importance of emotional intelligence. But for many, emotional intelligence remains mysterious and thought of as something you either have or do not have. In truth, EI is a set of skills and capabilities that, to a large extent, can be learned, and the foundation for these skills is the ability to accurately recognize and name emotions.

John Gottman, a researcher at the University of Washington, notes in *Raising an Emotionally Intelligent Child* that helping a child accurately name their emotions is an important first step in achieving emotional control. Frequently, just identifying and acknowledging a child's emotion will allow them to achieve better control over their behavior in the moment. Further, this effect does not diminish as children become teenagers. There is something about thinking, "Hmmm… I am experiencing anger because I thought…" that turns anger from something that controls us to something we can think about and control. This can be a very powerful benefit.

Remember: Learning to Think Flexibly and Accurately Will Take Work!

When you are dealing with your own adversities and problems, remember, your thoughts will, at first, *seem* right to you. You will be convinced that you are seeing the situation correctly and that your thoughts accurately reflect the truth of the matter. This is the confirmation bias we have already discussed. Your emotions in particular will back into your thinking to convince you that you are correct. For example, if an event occurs and you think that a violation of your rights was involved, that thought will lead to feelings of anger and the sense of anger will make it difficult for you to entertain the possibility that the situation did not involve a violation of rights. By practicing noticing your thoughts, you have already begun to give yourself a chance to challenge them. With practice, the skill of thinking flexibly and accurately becomes easier, to the point where it even happens in real time. At that point, you will be functioning like an optimist.

Mindful Moment: *Combining Thinking It Through and RAMP Up*

We have learned that resilience takes practice and that using these tools as a team will pay dividends. Now it's your turn to put these tools together.

Think It Through

First, think of a recent time when things did not go your way. It may have been at work, at home, or with friends. Were you . . .

- *Sad*
- *Embarrassed*
- *Angry or frustrated*
- *Guilty or ashamed*
- *Afraid or anxious*
- *Disgusted*

What happened? *List just the facts, and try not to analyze.*

Who? _____

What? _____

When? _____

Where? _____

Think *(List your thoughts or beliefs as the event happened.)* _____

_____

_____

Feel *(What emotions went with those thoughts or beliefs?)* _____

_____

_____

Do *(What did you do?)* _____

_____

_____

RAMP Up

Reject and Rethink:

Look for evidence that would cause you to reject and rethink your first thought. **What have you missed?** _____

_____

_____

Alternatives:

Generate other ways of explaining the event. **Can you think of causes with shorter duration, narrower scope, and that leave you more in control?** _____

_____

_____

Minimize:

Create some wiggle room. If you cannot reject or develop an alternative, **can you at least narrow the duration and scope of the cause in your first thought?**_____

_____

_____

Plan:

Sometimes our thoughts are more about "what next" than "why." When challenging "what next" thoughts, a plan to achieve better outcomes can help. **What steps can prevent the worst and make the best more likely?**

_____

_____

_____

_____

Flexible and Accurate Thinking in Practice

Let's look a little more closely at how more flexible and accurate thinking can lead to more optimistic outcomes. Imagine that Brandon, an 8th grader, walks into the cafeteria and sees his friend Jose across the room talking to two of their classmates. Jose looks up, sees Brandon, raises his hand, looks back to the two boys with him, says something, and the boys laugh. You may be wondering what Jose said, but Brandon does not wonder—he knows. Or at least he thinks he does. The simple explanation of the pattern here is:

Think It Through

Event (Just the facts: Who? What? When? Where?)

    Who: Jose
    What: Said something to two of our friends and they laughed
    When: Today
    Where: In the cafeteria

Think (List your thoughts or beliefs while the event was happening.)

On no! Jose told them about the dumb thing I did. I asked him not to say anything about that! ...

Feel (What emotions went with those thoughts or beliefs?)

Embarrassment ...

Do (What did you do?)

Went to another table, sat with kids I did not know and did not talk to them...

RAMP Up	RAMP Up	RAMP Up
It's also true that...	Now I will feel...	Now I will be able to...
Rethink: *Jose usually keeps secrets. No reason to think he didn't this time.* **Alternative:** *Jose is a funny guy. He makes me laugh all of the time. I bet he just told one of his crazy jokes.* **Minimize:** *Anyway, even if he did tell, everybody does dumb things sometimes.* **Plan:** *I'm just going to go over and act normal. If anyone says anything, I'll laugh it off and figure out what to do later.*	*Relieved; a little anxious, but not nearly as much, and maybe a little bit happier—he is a funny guy and a good friend. I might be a little anxious, but I can deal with it. I'm proud that I'm not falling to pieces; I can handle this!*	*Sit with my friends. That's what I'm going to do tomorrow.*

Reality: Sometimes You May Need to Go Deeper

Like every other human being, you and the students you mentor are complex. Sometimes, the thoughts you have in the heat of the moment will not account for your emotions; you will find your emotions confusing. Being confused by your emotions is not the same as being confused by the situation. Being confused by the situation is, "I don't know why he is doing that." Being confused by your emotions is, "I don't know why I am feeling like this." Confusion about your emotions can take several forms.

- First, your emotions may seem way out of proportion to your thoughts. You think, "That wasn't very considerate," and you are wildly angry. Or you think, "He went WAY over the line there," and you feel nothing.
- Second, your emotions might not match your thoughts. Refer back to the *Negative Emotional Links* Chart on page 189. You might have a thought that would be in the family of "violation of rights," but instead of feeling angry, you feel sad. That would be confusing.
- Third, you could have emotions that flip back and forth making it hard for

you to make a seemingly simple decision.

- Fourth, and finally, you could find yourself unable to carry through on firm commitments to make changes in your behavior that, on the surface, you truly desire.

We all carry deep beliefs—strongly held thoughts about the way the world is or should be—that usually work for us. But, sometimes they can be triggered without us realizing it. In many of these situations, the real thought or belief (often a firmly held belief) is below the surface of the thought that crossed your mind at the moment. When that happens, we get confusion, either in our emotions or in being unable to make desired behavior changes. The good news is that we can still *Think It Through*. However, when we realize that something is not connecting between what we think, feel, and do, it is time to dig deeper.

The trick to digging deeper is to ask yourself what is really going on with you until you get to an answer that explains your emotions or behavior. Do not ask yourself why you feel the way you do. That just kicks your confirmation bias into gear and you will generate all sorts of reasons to justify your emotion. The point is, as the event happened, your thoughts and emotions did not make sense. They confused you. Sit down with and complete a *Think It Through* exercise for the event. Then choose the thought that seems most tied to your emotions and, assuming that thought to be true, ask yourself what would be so bad about that. Then make your answer to that question the subject of another "what" question. For example, "What about that really bothers me?" or "What would be the worst part of that?" Keep going until you reach an answer that makes sense out of your emotions. You will likely feel the rightness of that answer. In other words, you would be able to say, "Well, no wonder! If I believed that, it makes total sense that I felt _____."

Interpersonal Resilience

Imagine how these thoughts and feelings can interact when people do. This is a good reason for families, faculties, and teams to train resilience skills together. In June of 2006, John, Sherri, and Dave were scheduled to hold the first strengths seminar for Culver faculty. Nancy, a leadership instructor, was one of the first faculty members to register for the class. A day before the event, Nancy asked John if she could miss part of the first session. Could she leave "ten to three" to bring her children to get their pre-summer camp physicals? John immediately responded no, that Nancy could not miss that amount of time on the first day of the seminar. He thought, "Five hours is a big chunk of time, and Nancy will miss the important early information. I have put a lot of energy into getting the ball rolling with the seminar. *How dare she* make a commitment and then ask me this? No way!" Nancy ended up making other arrangements for her children and was in attendance for the entire first day. John had not given the request another thought.

On day two of the seminar, Sherri was introducing the connection of thoughts to feelings and actions and asked if anyone had an "adversity" he or she would like to share so that it could be modeled for the class. Nancy immediately raised her hand and said, "I do. And my adversity is John Yeager!" John was aghast at her statement. "Who, me?" he thought. Nancy proceeded to tell the group about her conversation with John the day before, and about how angry she was that he didn't understand her situation and would not let her leave at "ten to three." It became clear she meant leaving at 10 minutes before 3 o'clock, which was when the seminar ended that first day. What John had thought, and reacted to, was that she wanted to leave from 10 o'clock until 3 o'clock. There was a rush of laughter throughout the classroom as Nancy continued to share her top-of-mind thoughts during the event.

Nancy's thoughts were:

I thought John was a reasonable person, that we were friends. What's ten minutes to him? Who does he think he is? Now I'll have to find someone else to take my kids to their doctor's appointments. I really should be going with them. I'm not a very good mother sometimes. I should have planned better. The pace of work here can make family time so challenging. John was being unreasonable. I was so furious with him. Instead of trying to get John to see things my way, though, I took action by having someone else take my children to their appointments; however, I remained unhappy about the way I had been treated.

Meanwhile, John was thinking:

I have worked so hard to put this together. Why is she doing this to me? I need to put my foot down and say, "No way." Who does she think she is, asking to miss one-third of the class? I can't believe she bothered to sign up. We're all busy here—she needs to plan better. Besides that, I am not feeling well. I've got to hold myself together. Leaving for that length of time (which he believed to be five hours) is unacceptable. I made it plain to her.

Because both John and Nancy gave each other an immediate emotional response, neither of them was left with any choices. Nancy understood that the reason she was reacting so strongly, instead of asking for clarification, was that John's "no" answer reinforced her belief that she was being a bad mother by needing to be somewhere else when her kids needed to get their camp physicals. (If she had not been aware of this strongly-held belief, she would have needed to dig deeper, but in this case it was at the surface of her mind.) John, on the other hand, was consumed with a combination of negative emotions: anxiety about not feeling physically well that day, coupled with anger that a participant in the program we had all worked so hard to create was going to miss so much time. His positivity ratio was down, so he did not think as broadly as he might have and did not connect with Nancy in ways that would have let her provide more information that might have clarified the miscommunication.

Giving John and Nancy a Re-do

Imagine what might have happened if *either* John or Nancy had stopped to *Think It Through*. John, in just writing "10 to 3" might have begun to wonder about that—five hours for camp physicals? Using the *RAMP Up* model to challenge that thought, he might not have been able to reject it outright, but he could have considered the possibility of an alternative. In this case, just considering that Nancy might have meant something different than the meaning he had jumped to would have been enough. One clarifying question to Nancy would have resolved the whole matter.

Nancy, on the other hand, might have challenged her thought that John was just being unreasonable. Applying *RAMP Up*, she could have looked for reasons to rethink her thought, and this would have reinforced what she was already thinking, that John was normally a very reasonable person. Again, just considering this possibility might have led to the one additional question that would have cleared the whole matter up. But, for both John and Nancy, the flow of negative emotions from their original thoughts washed away the opportunity to broaden and build and led to actions that could have created long-term bad feelings between them. This example makes clear the benefits that can occur when a family, faculty, or team learn these skills together. With group proficiency, negative cascades can be stopped when even one person decides to *Think It Through*.

Resilience Skills Benefit Social Networks

Sixteen-year-old Martina, who is supposed to be studying for a physics test, is instead texting the girl she thought was her best friend. Full of anger and fueled by indignant thoughts like, "You don't even deserve to know me," Martina has sent things she may later regret, and this has consumed the energy and focus she needs to do her school work.

At the other end of the house, Martina's mother, Jan, has just gotten home from work and is making dinner. As she chops up vegetables for stir-fry she thinks, "I can't believe I am wasting my time doing this and getting no help from anyone. Everyone else would rather have pizza delivered every night. They won't even appreciate this healthy food."

At his house, the physics teacher, Mr. Kronstadt, is busy writing the test Martina will take tomorrow. He's remembering the day he taught about Newton's Laws of Motion. The First Law says that any change of direction or increase in acceleration requires a force to be applied. That's why, he thinks, only some students will pass this test, since the rest of them will be glued to a TV, cell phone, or computer screen instead of studying. Since Newton's Third Law says that for every action there is an equal and opposite reaction, Mr. Kronstadt cleverly thinks those students will be getting a reaction they deserve when they don't pass this test.

All three of these people have something in common: They are unaware that their thoughts are actually getting them *more of what they don't want*. Martina doesn't want to lose her best friend or fail her physics test, Jan doesn't want to feed her family unhealthy food or work in the kitchen alone, and Mr. Kronstadt doesn't want his students to fail to learn. But because they are each unaware of the impact a change in thoughts could have on their feelings and actions, there is little chance that things will improve.

Mindful Moment: Resilience in a Network

We have learned that resilience takes practice and that using these tools will pay dividends for individuals and pairs of people. Each one of the characters in the resilience network above could use the two resilience skills that you have learned. How would you use these tools with this group?

Think It Through

Negative Emotions List:

- *Sad*
- *Embarrassed*
- *Angry or frustrated*
- *Guilty or ashamed*
- *Afraid or anxious*
- *Disgusted*

What happened?
List just the facts, and try not to analyze.

*Who?*_____

_____

*What?*_____

_____

*When?*_____

_____

*Where?*_____

_____

Think *(List person's thoughts or beliefs as the event happened.)*_____

_____

Feel *(What emotions went with those thoughts or beliefs?)* _____

_____

Do *(What did person do?)* _____

_____

RAMP Up It's also true that...	*RAMP Up* Now person can feel...	*RAMP Up* Now person will be able to...
Reject and Rethink: _____ _____	_____ _____ _____	_____ _____ _____
Alternatives: _____ _____	_____ _____ _____	_____ _____ _____
Minimize: _____ _____	_____ _____	_____ _____
Plan: _____ _____	_____ _____	_____ _____

Self-Forgiveness

These skills can also help students learn how to forgive themselves, especially when forgiveness is modeled by important adults. How a parent, teacher or coach responds to, and forgives, a child or adolescent can have lasting consequences. A constructive style of responding can foster self-forgiveness and learning in a young person, while a reactive style can foster guilt, shame, and avoidance. When a young person has violated the rights of an adult, there is interesting phenomena that happens. The fear, shame, and guilt associated with a young person who asks a significant adult for forgiveness sometimes provides the motivation to prevent a similar transgression from happening again. However, even a heartfelt apology to the parent, teacher, or coach, followed by adult forgiveness, can result in a lingering case of a lack of self-forgiveness in the child.

Research distinguishes self-forgiveness and interpersonal forgiveness, especially in relationship to empathy. Julie Hall of the University of Rochester Medical Center and Florida State University's Frank Fincham have shown that empathy facilitates interpersonal forgiveness, but inhibits self-forgiveness, "as empathic transgressors may be so concerned about those they have hurt that they find it difficult to forgive themselves."

Kevin Danti, a 9th grade humanities teacher at the Culver Academies, provides a cogent example of the role that adults can play in fostering self-forgiveness in youth. Kevin builds close relationships with his students during the year. One morning, seven students showed up for class who were not prepared to make their scheduled PowerPoint presentations, even though Kevin had reminded the students about the assignment several times during the week.

In His Own Words: Kevin Danti — High School Humanities Teacher, Culver Academies

Upon seeing that half my class was unprepared, I felt they had betrayed me. My first reaction was disappointment, with an undertone of anger. The mood of the class went from upbeat to down instantly. I knew those students were empathizing with me. They were feeling my disappointment and emotion because I could see it in their faces, and they were punishing themselves instantaneously as they just sat in silence and hung their heads. They didn't make eye contact with me. They were not blaming anybody but themselves, because they felt my disappointment. They were not making excuses and were not trying to rationalize anything. They wanted to empathize with me because I had already created an atmosphere of close relationship with them—one that I value and they value. I caught myself and said to them, "I understand that there were different factors that contributed to the lack of preparedness. I really appreciate the honesty when I asked if you were prepared, but will still hold you accountable to the process." The whole mood immediately changed in the class. Everything turned upbeat.

Thinking, Empathy, and Forgiveness

As adult mentors we can help young people by being mindful of the nexus where our disappointment can promote self-forgiveness or self-loathing in youth. Fortunately, we can help them be more internally directed in those moments. When Kevin caught himself reacting to his students, he acknowledged his disappointment and then provided a pathway to self-forgiveness. He was able to help the students re-frame their thinking to, "You know what, I messed up. I understand why I messed up, and I am going to try and not do that again. But I am okay with it. I am going to make amends."

Through awareness about their style of response to a young person's transgression, adults can provide a better climate for self-forgiveness that isn't confounded by fear, guilt, and shame. The magnitude, frequency, and intensity of the adult response should be measured so that the young person's empathy for the offended adult doesn't rise to the level that they are flooded with negative emotions. When this destructive flooding happens consistently, young people tend to project blame and start using excuses to avoid accountability and honesty. Without self-forgiveness, they may assign responsibility elsewhere because they want to avoid the bad feelings. This can result in creating unfounded realities about the teacher or the assignment. This removes the student from culpability, which creates the short-term gain of relief, but it prevents learning and reconciliation. Fear, shame, and guilt can sometimes help young people understand the nature of their transgressions. However, the empathy a child feels for an angry or disappointed adult should not override the need to self-forgive.

Emerging Maturity

Along with learning to self-forgive, maturity can offer a greater pathway to success. Obviously, every young person faces developing maturity. Often, immaturity is characterized by a failure to think things through. The ability to have a second thought, and one very different from the first thought, is a hallmark of maturity. Teenagers face special challenges here as modern brain research has shown that, as a general rule, they are less able than older individuals to both feel strong emotions and think rationally at the same time.

The *Think It Through* and *RAMP Up* exercises (pages 194-196, 198-199) can help. Repeated practice at analyzing exactly what happened and what they thought, felt, and did can help sensitize young persons to the need for flexible and accurate thinking. By analyzing how they respond to adversities, obstacles, and challenges, they can develop a better sense for the need to *Think It Through*. Occasionally, that heightened sense of the need to think will cause a young person who has learned these skills to stop and wait for emotions to pass and think more deeply before acting. Even one such occasion can save untold heartache. As the occasions begin to become more common, the perception of others is that the young person is more mature.

This chapter revealed how parents, teachers, coaches, and students can shift how they respond to various fears and negative self-talk by being more flexible and more accurate in their thinking to drive their emotions to healthy actions. We addressed the differences in optimistic and pessimistic thinking. In the next chapter, we will uncover how people who have different mindsets—fixed and growth—deal with challenges and adversities.

Chapter Eight

"Smart" is Something I Do:
Student Mindsets That Work

Is success about learning—or proving you are smart?
—Carol Dweck

Simon, a fourth grader who had just taken the Massachusetts high stakes test called MCAS, came to see Sherri at the end of his long day. He was very teary and said, "I am the stupidest kid in my class!" Sherri calmly responded, "Tell me what happened." Simon explained, "I was the second to the last person done in my class. Everybody else but one kid finished before me." Sherri then asked, "What did you think about that?" The boy replied, "I was thinking I was stupid because it took me so long to finish." Sherri wrote down an alternative thought for him: *I worked harder than every other person in my class.* Sherri then asked him, "Do you think that is true?"

The boy said, "I know I worked harder than everybody else because I was there second to the last." Sherri inquired, "How did it make you feel to think about that? Read it back to me." Simon replied, "Well, I am a very hard worker and that is one of the best things about me." Sherri continued, "At another time when you have to take a test like this, are you going to think, 'I am stupid because it takes me so long to finish' or will you think, 'I am a very hard worker. I am the hardest working student in my class. I am going to use all the time they give me and make sure I get all the way to the end.'" Simon said, "I will know I am a hard worker, and I have done my very best job." Sherri asked, "Will this let you feel better than if you think that you are stupid, because it took you longer than everybody else?" Simon smiled and chimed, "Well, of course!"

Sherri helped Simon to begin to make a shift from operating in a fixed mindset toward having a growth mindset. Those with fixed mindsets assume that smart is something they are—an internal attribute or quality that the student cannot

211

see or know, but that is evidenced when the student easily, quickly, and perfectly performs work, especially tasks that other students do not perform as well.

Two Types of Mindsets

Carol Dweck, Stanford University professor and author of the book *Mindset*, was inspired in her work by Martin Seligman's research about explanatory styles (introduced in Chapter Seven). While teaching at Columbia University, Dweck noticed that her students shared one common experience but had two different reactions to it. The common experience was that school was hard, and the students were all behind in their work. Sometimes they weren't interested in the work, and they felt dejected about this. She noticed two different things. Some of her students she talked with said, "This is hard, a lot of work and I don't know if I can do this." They got up in the morning, went to class and did work, got food, got exercise and got sleep and then did it all over again.

At points over the semester and as exams approached, these students didn't feel good about how things were going. They were not happy, but they were still func-tioning. If Dweck sent them to the counseling center, they would be told that they were not depressed because they were still working. They felt miserable at the moment, even though they were still performing. However, for other students in that same class, the pressure was ebbing and flowing. They didn't feel

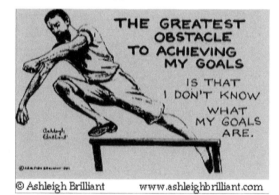

THE GREATEST OBSTACLE TO ACHIEVING MY GOALS IS THAT I DON'T KNOW WHAT MY GOALS ARE.

© Ashleigh Brilliant   www.ashleighbrilliant.com

good. They stopped going to class. They stopped doing their work. They didn't get enough sleep and didn't eat right. Basically, they went into a complete tailspin.

By the time anybody found out and tried to help the students, it was too late to salvage their work for the semester. So Dweck asked the important question: "What is the difference between the students?" When she asked them how they felt, she said the responses were the same, "I feel stressed and worried that I can't do the work." But some students were functioning and some weren't, so she began to investigate. What she found that differentiated the two groups of students was the fact that they were working using either a growth or a fixed mindset.

In a fixed mindset:

Failure means I'm not smart, or I'm a loser: a global, over-generalizing tendency.

In a growth mindset:

- Failure means I didn't work efficiently enough or my strategy wasn't effective.
- Failure means I need to engage more and seek new strategies: a local, specific tendency.

You may see connections between mindsets and explanatory style, discussed in Chapter Seven. The growth mindset tends to be more flexible in thinking about events than the fixed mindset.

The Growth Mindset

The growth mindset can be learned. Robin's five years of training with the oboe, for example, has been both a challenging and rewarding venture. When she hits off-notes, she quickly recovers as she realizes that her effort and deliberate practice will eventually yield positive results. If Robin thinks, "That was an off note," it will open up the possibilities of improved playing compared to "I stink at the oboe." (Remember the power of *Think It Through* and *RAMP Up* from Chapter Seven?) Those with *growth mindsets* believe that "smart" is something a person does—the result of accumulated effort, prior knowledge, and strategy. Upon encountering a challenge, the student with a growth mindset will dig in, work harder, seek help, try to find new approaches, and eventually master the material.

The growth mindset is about effort and the motivation to persevere, which can come from inspired belief and a sense of purpose. Parents, teachers and coaches have an important role to play. When failure happens, it hurts, but students with a growth mindset learn something from their errors, and more importantly, they learn to focus on what went well and use that knowledge to succeed next time. They develop what we call an appreciative eye.

The Fixed Mindset

On the other hand, the fixed mindset can cause trouble for students who have always found school easy and achievement a given. For example, Joseph couldn't understand what was happening at school. He was a straight-A student up through fifth grade. Joseph's parents and teachers had even told him he was gifted, and he identified strongly with this intellectually capable view of himself. Into the second term in middle school, however, he was struggling to earn Bs. Had he lost it? Was he not "A-student" smart anymore? Was he a smart kid imposter? Here is what Joseph might have said to himself: "I am in 8th grade at the middle school. No more easy stuff. I got a C. What am I going to do? I am going to be very reasonable about this. I don't want you to know how stupid I am. Smart isn't about work, it is about what you've already got. You can't really make up for a lack of intelligence with hard work. What strategies do I have? Hard work isn't going to make me any smarter. This is me. This is who I am. I have got to hide this. I have got to quit working. Now, at least I can say that I didn't try. And if I can drop this course, let's drop it. Is there a lower math course?"

Mindset in a Standards-Based School Culture

Having a growth mindset can be tough in a high stakes standards-based environment. The standards are often being set by people two generations away from the current students, who have not taught in a classroom for years, and who set goals and standards for teachers who are then expected to use strengths they may not even have to deliver in the classroom. Teachers become stuck in the standards box and may feel a growth mindset is beyond them, too. Students who appear to meet the standards quickly become "smart kids" and those who don't, aren't. There is no doubt that without literacy skills in both language arts and mathematics that students are at an incredible disadvantage in life. A potential problem with the focus on standards, though, is that skills acquisition becomes the goal, not the means, of preparing students for their future. Students need to believe that school is not just about performing tasks and being done with your education. It's about learning to learn and knowing that you can get smarter when you do.

When what is valued is tightly focused on being mathematically, logically, or linguistically smart (or only smart in a limited number of other ways), kids (and teachers) learn to perform and get it over with. A student may say, "I got a high fail on my Algebra test on parabolas. But it doesn't matter because there is another test next week on stuff I get, and the teacher said we won't be doing any more parabolas this year." But it does matter, because the student has missed the opportunity to learn that he can learn! He is disengaged from the process and is instead relieved by the teacher's promise that the misery is over. He has learned to accept a fixed mindset.

The Power of Mindsets

Getting young people to develop an appreciative eye, one that looks for possibilities, can be a challenging task and can be influenced by the mindset of the adult mentor. When working with teachers and coaches, Dave provides an example of the power of fixed and growth mindsets on young people and how a mentor can influence them.

Turning Mindsets — The E-Lab and I-Gym

Dave says to the coaches and teachers, "Let's imagine that we want to teach our students how to turn—we want a world of turners, and this class is untrained. We are going to send the students to one of our two fine turning schools. One half of you will be going to the E-lab Turning School, and the other half attends the I-Gym Turning School. Let's go to our respective schools.

I am going to start with the E-Lab school. 'Good morning students! Glad to have you at E-Lab. We have produced many outstanding turners, and I am confident that many of you will live up to that standard. I want to get you on your way. If you would all stand up and turn for me. Thank you very much.' Each of the participants turns in a complete circle. Dave looks at them and, pointing to each one in turn, says: "You are now an 'L.' and to others, "You're an 'L' and to the rest of them, 'You're an 'NYL.'"

Next, Dave asks the I-Gym turners to stand up and he says, "Please turn for me as I come by. Good effort with your balance. Your expression shows your passion for turning. Yes, very controlled. You've got some spin to it. Turn balance good. Some speed. All of you have some very good turns. What we are going to do in the next few weeks is further develop those qualities for you. Please sit down."

Dave then asks the class what was different in how he dealt with each group. Most say something like, "You were more supportive of the I-Gym group. Eventually, someone asks about the "L" and the "NYL" he assigned the E-Lab group. 'L' stands for loser, and the 'NYL' means you're not yet a loser but come back tomorrow, and we'll see if we can find the point where you become a loser!"

In E-Lab you are labeled by your current performance. This is the fixed mindset. In the other, you will be more willing to work hard at becoming the best turner you can be. This is the growth mindset.

The fixed mindset leads to haves and have-nots—the smart and the not-smart. Students in the E-Lab think that being able to turn or not is who they are—a characteristic. This is the **Entity** approach to looking at intelligence. Here is how a person with this mindset may think: "I have a certain amount of intelligence and all that the school is going to do for me is take me to where that level is. I am sent signals every day about how much intelligence I have and if I didn't reach my intelligence limit today, it could be tomorrow. Whenever it happens, that's the signal. Since there is nothing I can do to get smarter, I might as well stop where I am. If I've got enough smarts to do algebra, then I'll do algebra. If I have enough to analyze a poem, I'll do that. Every morning I get up wondering if I find out today that I'll get the signal that I have reached my limit of smart."

Other students go every morning to an I-Gym—an **Incremental** gymnasium— a place they are going because smart for them isn't fixed, and it isn't a characteristic of who they are. Smart is a result of the knowledge they have gained, the efforts they are making and the strategies that they are using. They always learn something new, always find or develop a new strategy or get assistance to develop a strategy in the belief that they can always work hard and they can continue to improve over time. They think, "So, if today I got a message that I did not understand the algebra, what does that mean? It means I need to learn some new things, develop some new strategies, work harder, and then I can do better at this. I have the intelligence I need to improve my performance." The growth mindset is predicated on incremental steps that a student pursues.

Some schools can develop a culture that sends a message like an E-lab: Some of you are perfect; some of you haven't failed yet, but you likely will; and some of you are just losers. Schools where students compete to prove how smart they are can leave students worrying that if they aren't among the smartest, then they're not smart at all. Sadly, some students come to believe that a need to work hard for success is a sign of failure—a belief that "you must never let them see you sweat." A more productive message is promoted by the I-gym: We are about work, about effort, and about strategies for gaining knowledge and achieving at our personal highest and improving levels.

Appreciative Intelligence

Don't worry if your job is small and your rewards are few.
Just remember that the mighty oak was once a nut like you.
—Bullwinkle Moose

Tojo Thatchenkery and Carol Metzker, authors of *Appreciative Intelligence*, have studied how people think about being smart. Working from the premise that being smart results in being more successful, they interviewed a number of people who had been very successful—such as lawyers, artists, and educational leaders. They identified factors that related to the thinking behind success and realized through their data that these successful people can see the "acorn and the mighty oak"—they see the potential of an idea, and they sense the possibilities, but more importantly, they can imagine the possible outcomes. "It's an acorn—not going to grow into a mango, but an oak is a distinct possibility!" This appreciative intelligence is about being in touch with the possibilities that have a pathway to the future. This is a skill that students and their adult mentors can cultivate.

A great example of the appreciative eye is seen in the amazing story of Ernest Shackleton's expedition to Antarctica during the First World War. The ship, aptly named *Endurance*, became trapped in floe ice, and the crew was forced to abandon ship. For over a year, Shackleton and his crew lived on the floe in which the *Endurance* was trapped, surviving the fierce Antarctic conditions as well as the sinking of the ship. Eventually, the crew arrived at Elephant Island, near the southern tip of South America. In a lifeboat, using dead reckoning navigation skills, Shackleton and five members of the crew eventually made it to the inhabited island of South Georgia. Shackleton quickly organized a rescue of the 22 men who had been left on Elephant Island.

One of the stranded men had his birthday while awaiting rescue and wrote that it was one of the happiest days of his life. Everything went wrong with the intended expedition. However, due to perseverance and optimistic behavior, everyone survived. When he returned to England, Shackleton visited the school where he had finished 8th grade. The headmaster of the school said he was sorry that he didn't remember who Shackleton was. Shackleton replied, "I didn't know who I was then, either!" The appreciative eye looks for that which is positive—and possible—seeing how the future can unfold from the present. How do we get young people to develop an appreciative eye?

Teachers, Coaches, and Mindsets

We are attentive to the fact that there are many experienced teachers and coaches who have employed methods of good instruction over the years and may be resistant to making philosophical and strategic shifts in the daily business of their classroom. Experienced teachers with fixed mindsets may assume that "being a good teacher" is something they are—an attribute or quality evidenced by the ease with which the teacher performs in the classroom. The fixed mindset teacher may tend to treat students with the same expectations and may even believe that students have fixed minds, leading to trouble differentiating students' abilities and intelligences. Teachers and coaches with growth mindsets know that being a good teacher is something a person does—the result of focusing on continual improvement. Upon encountering a challenge, the teacher with a growth mindset will dig in, work harder, seek help, and try to find new approaches to reach students. In addition, teachers with a growth mindset will teach students to do the same.

Deliberate Practice

Of course there are differences in capacities among individuals, but fortunately the brain rewires itself according to what we learn, and because of neuroplasticity, it can be altered through adulthood. We now know through neuroscience that the brain is continually changing. Since neurons that fire together wire together and neurons that no longer fire together are pruned (shed to adapt to better brain functioning). Given different experiences, a person can achieve competence even in a field for which they may have little natural talent. In the same way, a talent may be lost or squandered because it is never used or never developed through dedication and practice.

Even people with natural talent have to work long hours over many years and develop it to achieve elite levels. Florida State's K. Anders Ericsson, an expert in the study of deliberate practice, reminds us that while people can become proficient at everyday tasks with relatively simple repetition, and that even specialized skills specific to one's profession can be learned within weeks and months, very high levels of achievement appear to require many years or even decades of experience to yield exceptional levels of performance. Research has found that in numerous and diverse areas such as professional endeavors (e.g. medicine), software design, professional writing, decision-making, teamwork, the visual and performing arts, sport and motor skills, education, and games (such as chess), there are people who have not stopped increasing their exceptional skill. For them, expertise is not about reaching an endpoint but about continually improving.

When teachers and coaches are more attuned to what separates successful performers from others in the classroom, athletic field, and stage, they find it is not the raw ability of a student, but the ability of the student to make the most of their inherent ability by focusing on their aspirations to yield optimal performance. Deliberate practice requires concentration, mindful repetition, and practice. This doesn't mean everyone can be an elite athlete or an accomplished artist. But it does mean that young people can strive to perform their best at their ability levels—both as individuals and as part of a team.

The Physical Genius

Malcolm Gladwell, the author of *Blink* and *Outliers*, wrote an instructive piece in *The New Yorker*, entitled "The Physical Genius." He claimed "What sets physical geniuses apart from other people, then, is not merely being able to do something but knowing what to do—their capacity to pick up on subtle patterns that others generally miss. This is what we mean when we say that great athletes have a feel for the game or that they 'see' the court, the field, or the ice in a special way." Gladwell asserts that the physical genius *works* for top performance rather than wishes for it. This provides the athlete with the knowledge of what to do at the right moment on the playing field. He goes on to say, "If you think of physical genius as a pyramid with, at the bottom, the raw components of coordination and, above that, the practice that perfects those particular movements, then this faculty of imagination is the top layer. This is what separates physical geniuses from those who are merely very good."

Praise and Frames of Mind

Teachers can alter student mindsets through stories, direct instruction about mindsets, and certain types of praise that promote or detract from student learning. Carol Dweck suggests we can give praise to the process or give praise to a person. *Process praise* is more about the specific effort and strategy the youth puts forth: "You kept scanning the field for an opportunity to set up the goal." Dweck claims that praise for effort can increase a person's enjoyment, persistence and performance after a challenge. *Person praise* is based on assessing a behavior or performance: "You are really smart! You are our team's top scorer!" Process praise is about effort and can promote more of a growth mindset, while person praise can promote more of a fixed mindset.

We know a variety of athletes who have gone off to college with significant scholarship packages. One student-athlete we'll call Alex found himself under a great deal of pressure by well-meaning parents and the boy's head coach. They said things to him like, "You are the best! When you are out on the field, you are always our leading scorer! That's why 'X' university wants you." Was Alex talented? Sure thing. However, during his senior high school year, Alex wasn't living up to the expectations that the coach and the parent had set earlier on. In fact, following a poor performance in one game, Alex feigned a small injury that took him out of the contest.

The head coach spoke with Alex about getting back on the field for the next game. He mentioned different ways that Alex could improve on the field—trying something different and seeing how that would work. Alex went out in the next game and played well, scoring three goals. The coach helped Alex take the pressure off himself and focus on a growth mindset, at least for that game.

Deliberate practice with growth mindsets needs to be reinforced by coaches to help athletes continue to play with effort and imagination. This translates seamlessly to the classroom: Jane's teacher says to her, "I have been noticing that you have been taking notes in class and how it has been paying off." Jane thinks, "I have been doing better. Note-taking is hard for me but I will try it again."

Carol Dweck's research has also shown that teachers of students in the younger grades tend to frame their praise in different ways for boys than for girls. When the boys didn't do well, they were told, "You need to pay better attention. You need to work a little harder." When girls failed, teachers tended to say, "That's okay, I know you tried. No need to pay attention to this score, all you have to do is to work a little bit harder and pay attention to do that." When teachers and coaches praise, they should watch how young people are approaching their studies and activities, because when they do succeed it is possible to focus specifically on what is working and if they have failed, to help them look for a new strategy: "I noticed that you tend to highlight material in the book. How about taking notes also?"

Mindful Moment: *Your Mindset — Fixed or Growth?*

1. Make a list of your top five high moments of the last month. For each, tell why the event happened. For instance, if you write, "Our team won the championship," you might add, "We have an outstanding coach," or "The other team was no match for our power," or "This team was meant to win."

_____

_____

_____

_____

2. Evaluate what you have written by thinking about each event this way: Have you explained the "why" of the event in a fixed or a growth mindset way? Is your "why" thought permanent and broad in scope? What would make it possible for your event to be repeated?

_____

_____

_____

_____

The Double Whammy of Incompetence

"I thought I did so well this time." Sarah looked at her test which was marked D+ on the last page at the bottom right-hand corner. She had spent hours studying the material on the exam, and yet her performance was very poor. Students like Sarah are often described as "not knowing what they don't know." Well-meaning teachers often think the student is merely missing critical information, perhaps because they need to study harder. Meanwhile the incompetent student often continues to perform at the bottom of the class, even after attending extra help sessions, and the teacher is surprised at the ongoing poor performance. It just makes no sense.

Statistics professors will remind you, tongue-in-cheek, that in the fictitious town of Lake Woebegone, all the women are strong, all the men are good-looking, and all the children are above average. In 2010 there were 1.65 million new college graduates in the US alone, according to the Christian Science Monitor. Nearly every one of them who prepared a resume and a cover letter in search of work will fall victim to the *Lake Woebegone Effect*, whereby they will believe that armed with a college degree, lots of knowledge, and maybe even some time spent in an internship, they should be swamped with job offers.

Statistically, of course, it is just not possible for everyone to be above average. As psychologists Justin Kruger and David Dunning found in studying incompetence, the people most lacking in the knowledge and skills for doing well are most often unaware of this fact. By believing that they are not just smart but smarter than their peers, the students were unable to benefit from accurate social comparison and recognize the difference between competent behaviors and incompetence. Thus they failed to gain insight into how they might change for the better.

Miscalibrating Your Competence

Competence or the lack of it may be the result of many things, including good versus poor preparation and efficient versus inefficient neurodevelopment. What highly competent and less competent students share is this: both miscalibrate the perception of their own and of others' performance. The difference is that competent students believe their peers have done only slightly better than they have, and so they work to apply success strategies that they believe will make a difference in their performance. Incompetent students, on the other hand, believe they have performed significantly better than their peers and therefore do not take advantage of strategies to achieve greater success. How's that for a counter-intuitive finding?

In a series of four experiments first published in 1999, Kruger and Dunning found that students performing in the bottom quartile tended to be unable to recognize that their performance was poor compared to that of their peers. Students whose actual performance was at the 12th percentile, for example, overestimated their expected scores by 50 points! They were four times more likely to miscalibrate than their competent peers. They overestimated both their actual scores and their ranks compared to peers. As a consequence, it is very difficult for such students to make the necessary changes to deliver a better outcome alone, since they believe that they are doing both personally well and better than their peers. In contrast, top students underestimate their performance compared to peers, thinking their peers have done better than they actually have, though not by nearly as much as the poor performers think they have out-scored their peers.

All of us have to work at accurately calibrating our metacognitive or "thinking about thinking" skills. When a person is incompetent because of lack of knowledge, skills, or experience, metacognition is difficult. Things that get in the way include several that we have discussed at length in this book:

- **Negative Explanatory Style:** personal, permanent, and pervasive explanations about why things go poorly, such as blaming the teacher, coach, or a parent without seeing personal contribution
- **Fixed Mindset:** the belief that intellectual or other ability is a fixed trait to be accepted as is
- **Inaccurate self-awareness:** moving on confidently instead of accurately comparing oneself to an objective measure or competent peers
- **Misapplication of strengths:** for example, being unrealistically optimistic or failing to be honest about the need to self-regulate

You Can Recalibrate Your Thinking

The good news is that people can significantly recalibrate how they think about how they think and thus learn to develop a growth mindset. When these metacognitive (how we know about knowing) strategies are used in specific problem-solving settings, students increase the accuracy of their self-appraisals. In fact, once bottom-quartile study participants gained the metacognitive skills and self-awareness to note their thinking errors, they applied strategies and performed as well as previously more competent students.

Mindful Moment: *Adjust Your Effort*

A sign in Sherri's office reads, "It's not how hard you work; it's how you work hard." When you connect the dots between your efforts and your achievement, it is more obvious what works.

What do you do to be competent and to replicate your good work?

_____

_____

_____

How would you help a peer, colleague, or student replicate their good work?_____

_____

_____

_____

Below are some ways to get started. Joseph T. Hallinan, author of Why We Make Mistakes: How We Look Without Seeing, Forget Things in Seconds, and Are All Pretty Sure We Are Way Above Average, *reminds us that we must regularly re-calibrate our metacognitive skills even if we are sure that we are already competent.*

Here are three important ways he suggests that we can adjust our metacognitive skill and self-appraisal:

- *Keep a written record of hits, misses, and never-attempted items to prevent us from an after-the-fact view through rose-colored lenses.*
- *Value being happy, because happier people make quicker decisions both more accurately and with less back-and-forth.*
- *Know how strengths may cloud your vision, making you think you are more virtuous, and thus higher achieving, than you really are.*

Strengths and Mindsets

Erik Erikson, the noted social psychologist, viewed the social life span as a series of eight progressive and sequential stages. Successful transition from stage-to-stage, or the inability to resolve crisis within each stage, determined a person's psychosocial health. He called this process the "epigenetic principle" and claimed that the acquisition of good character habits developed from a favorable transition throughout each of the stages. Erikson's stage theory is common reading in most psychology texts. However, it is essential to analyze the relationship that healthy psychosocial transitions may have on a person's development of the application of their character strengths throughout the lifespan. Remember that we said earlier in this chapter that people exhibit a growth mindset when they believe "smart" is a result of the knowledge they have gained, the efforts they are making, and the strategies that they are using. As you can see in the figure below, Erikson points out the two dimensions—transition or crisis—at each developmental level. He associated these attributes with certain virtues, which can be translated into strengths language.

Erickson's Model of Psychosocial Development		
Age	**Transitions/Crises**	**Virtues**
Infancy	Trust vs. Mistrust	Hope
Toddler	Autonomy vs. Shame	Will
Early Childhood	Initiative vs. Guilt	Purpose
Childhood	Industry vs. Inferiority	Competence
Adolescence	Identity vs. ID Confusion	Fidelity
Young Adulthood	Intimacy vs. Isolation	Love
Middle Adulthood	Generativity vs. Stagnation	Care
Older Adulthood	Integrity vs. Despair	Wisdom

Adapted from Erikson, E.H. *Identity: Youth and Crisis.* New York: W.W. Norton, 1994

For example, a newborn is exposed to the opportunity of trusting (or not) the primary caregiver, who is/are typically the parent/s. Trust establishes hope and allows the young person to take risks based on that level of trust in the progressing stages. In the transition to the autonomy vs. shame stage, the toddler "puts his will against the will of others—even that of his protectors." There are respective character strengths that relate to successful psychosocial transitions that follow hope and will. Care and wisdom, for example, may be more fully acquired during middle and later life; however, the early exposure and experience is essential to healthy development. Unfortunately, there are young people who have cultivated fixed mindsets about the world they live in by way of the consistent mistrust, shame, guilt and inferiority they have experienced. This has also prevented them from forming positive character traits.

Strengths, Mindsets and High Risk Youth

We have spent a good amount of time helping build strengths among well-adjusted adolescents—young people who are at a plus level in their lives. Then John had the opportunity to work with high risk youth, ages 12-20, who are members of a residential treatment center. Most of these young men grew up in a life of abuse and eventually became violent abusers themselves. Many of them have developed a fixed mindset toward their limitations for success in the world. Each youth has already been involved with the Department of Corrections. As part of their program, they are strictly supervised by counselors. They must remain in the sight of a counselor at all times due to impulse control issues. Trust issues are a huge concern and the program provides them with pathways to better cope and function with moment-to-moment living.

All of the young men with whom John and others worked for three days at Culver grew up in environments that didn't foster trust and they defaulted to the crisis side of Erikson's stages of psycho-social development. This included a shame-based climate that has led to immense degrees of guilt and inferiority. These young people come from deficit family models and after being cast away at very young ages, they were eventually adjudicated and sent to residential treatment, their last stop before jail. As part of the three-day program, the boys faced a variety of group and individual challenges. These activities were designed to magnify trust, autonomy, initiative, and industry. When the boys started working on the challenge course (collaborative games and eventually the low and high ropes courses), John observed some of the crisis pieces coming out in some of their behaviors, but also witnessed bits of trust, initiative, and industry.

After exposure to the ropes challenges, John met with the boys to chat about their signature strengths (each of the boys had previously completed the VIA-Youth). It was very interesting to review the individual and collective results of their signature strengths. The majority of the boys had *spirituality* as one of their top strengths. Prior to the ropes activities, the boys toured the campus, and John noticed several boys who were visibly moved by the architecture of the inside of Culver's chapel. The house of worship was a safe haven for many of them. That evening, they discussed how *spirituality* was a leading strength for the majority of the boys. They remarked how this characteristic comes alive daily for each of them. Later, one young man said that his belief in God is similar to the "belayer on the ropes course"—always protecting him from falling and other dangers. The strengths the youths least endorsed were *caution, prudence, humility,* and *modesty.* This correlates strongly in that these characteristics are just being developed through the modeling, dialogue, and consequences process while they are in this program.

The intention of the strengths discussion was to help the boys know their strengths and see ways that they could express and use the strengths they wanted to develop. A program like this creates a fertile environment to help people to become more aware of some strengths that may cloud their vision and other strengths that they are not using enough. Remember from Part One of this book that having knowledge of what strengths look like in action can be a valuable instrument in the tool box of life skills. Individuals then can have the cues to pull out the strength when they want or need to. The more that the strength is habituated, the greater the odds are that it will be realized as an outcome in healthy growth-oriented behaviors. While this is asking a lot of a young person who has been exposed to neglect and abuse, Nansook Park and Chris Peterson find that "being able to put a name to what one does well is intriguing and even empowering."

The boys were divided into several groups and were instructed to complete strength trees (graphic representations of their strengths). They were provided with a large piece of newsprint-butcher block paper and a variety of markers. The most challenging aspect of the activity was having them try to link their strengths to others in their respective groups. They are at a point in their lives where it is still difficult to see the relationship between the influence of their actions/behaviors on others, and the ability to trust others to be part of their lives. One boy's *appreciation of beauty and excellence* came out in a wonderful graphic representation with his group. He was extremely proud of his drawing, and John helped him see how he could use this strength even more in moment-to-moment living.

John and the facilitators noticed how the shadow or excess side of the boys' top strengths could create problems in the groups. One boy, who had *leadership* as his top strength, was having difficulty motivating his small group to get rolling on their strengths representation. He was getting very frustrated, and one could see the shadow side of his leadership defaulting to biting sarcasm with other group members. With some timely prompting by the residential staff, he gradually got the rest of his group on board and their final product was quite good. In fact, they were the only group to draw strong connections between each others' strengths in the development of a team.

The three day experience may have slightly nudged these young men to play to their strengths, to begin to look at life through a growth mindset, and hopefully set reasonable goals for their future. (More on goal-setting is in Chapter Nine.) Psychologist Robert Brooks says, "The more that children are engaged in activities in which they use their strengths, the less time they have available for self-defeating or counterproductive behaviors, and the less interest they have in getting involved in such behaviors." And with positive feedback, encouragement and reinforcement by adult mentors, in this case the residential staff, the young people can use their strengths or "islands of competence" to navigate the world they live in.

In Chapter Eight, we introduced you to two different views of intelligence that influence young people—fixed and growth mindsets. Teachers can help alter student mindsets through stories, direct instruction about mindsets, and certain types of praise to promote or detract from student learning. In the next chapter, we will provide tools and techniques for parents, teachers, coaches, and students to set and achieve realistic goals that are engaging and meaningful.

Chapter Nine

Wishing and Willing:
Goal Setting, Engagement, and Meaning

If you don't know where you are going, any road will take you there.
—Lewis Carroll

Will, an eleven-year-old little league baseball player, was not known for being a good hitter. In fact, he often didn't swing the bat at all, and he was called out on strikes nearly every time he came to home plate. It was agonizing for his mother and father to listen to other angry parents saying awful things about their wonderful son all because he couldn't—or at least didn't—hit the ball. At the end of the season, Will came to the plate in a critical situation. True to form, the bat didn't leave his shoulder for three pitches. After the game the dejected son said to his proud and caring father, "Dad, I really wish I could hit." His father was elated and said, "Yes. I will find you the best help available. We will make you a hitter." Will's reply was, "But, Dad, I don't want to work at it. I just want to hit." Will had not yet learned the difference between wishing and willing.

Wishing, Willing, and Hope

Wishing is the first step in setting goals. We start by wanting things to be at least a little bit different than they are and may dream about what it would be like if a miracle happened to make the wish come true. Before a wish can become a dream-come-true, some other things need to happen. First of all, a person needs to have at least some hope that the wish could come true. Hope building allows people to explore this possibility. Sean Doyle, a North Carolina attorney and father, who holds a Master of Applied Positive Psychology degree from the University of Pennsylvania maintains, "Wishes tell us something about what it means to be human. They frame for us our vision of what is important."

In His Own Words: Sean Doyle, Poet, Lawyer, and Consulting Psychologist

While they are not the same thing as hope, our wishes have a hand in the motivation, passion, and clear goals that make our hopes possible. When times are hard, sometimes wishes offer the comfort we need.

Of course, we are not always good at guessing what we want, or what will make us happy. As a result, sometimes we wish for the "wrong" things. But this, too, says something about who we are, and what it means to be human as we go about stammering and stumbling through life. Ultimately our wishes connect us to one another. No matter where we are from or where we are going, when we hear the wishes of others, we realize that we are not alone in our dreams.

Sean's child attends TY Joyner Elementary school, and was pictured on a poster developed by documentary artist Liisa Ogburn. Sean says, "Lisa asked 63 first graders this question: 'What do you wish for?' and they told her that they wanted people to be brave all the time. They also wished people were nice and always shared. The first graders did not want people to lie or use bad words, and they wished people would love one another. They wanted everyone to have a home and to be healthy."

These are wonderful wishes, and as the children grow older, it will be important that their adult mentors—teachers, parents, and coaches, help them make the shift from wishing to willing. Unfortunately, wishing has become magical thinking for the many people who have high expectations, but haven't developed a strong will to develop a vision and a plan, and subsequently, they are not able to enjoy the rewards of their aspirations. As you recall from Chapter Seven, one of the goals of building resilience is developing a certain tolerance to ambiguity and to potential failure in the process of attempting challenges. Developing the will (remember the "Six Ways to Eat a Potato Chip" in Chapter One) that leads to good character in the form of habits and improved skills (as opposed to merely wishing them to happen) is central to the foundations that help people awaken their dreams to make them a reality.

Goal setting is essential to individual and collective success for all people, at all levels of development. Luck happens, but goals do not achieve themselves! Therefore we define a goal as an ambition, target, or aspiration that will require awareness, planning, and action to attain. It is important to distinguish between *subjective* and *objective* goals, in that goal setting is most effective when adult mentors help youth establish clear and consistent aims. Subjective goals are based on individual judgment or discretion, thereby making them difficult to measure. Often subjective goals are represented by such hoped for outcomes as working harder, having fun, or doing one's best.

Wishing, Willing, and Hope

give to the poor people

Guns were not inveted.

AllPeople haveo home.

to travle across the world.

"Wishes tell us something about what it means to be human. They frame for us our vision of what is important."
Sean Doyle

Although these outcomes are desirable, it is nearly always more effective to establish *specific* and *measurable* goals, such as attaining a specific standard of proficiency on a task in a specified time period. Examples of objective goals for an athlete might include increasing the number of throws and catches over a certain period of time or proper execution during drills or shuttles based on a percentage of successful catches. Also, it is more effective to set personal and team performance goals rather than outcome goals based on comparisons with other athletes. "As well as…" or "better than…" goals may exist in the feelings that we have about what we would like to attain, but they are not effectively specific. In a classroom, students often set goals of doing better on the next test, improving a grade, or turning in more homework, which may be worthy ambitions, but for many they are too general and thus may be difficult to attain. With such competing and confusing ideas, it is good to know that there are research-based goal setting strategies.

Goal Setting

We were very fortunate to attend University of Pennsylvania's MAPP program with classmate Caroline Adams Miller, an expert in goal setting and lead author of the wonderful book *Creating Your Best Life: The Ultimate Life List Guide.* In it Miller, a goals coach with an international reputation, identifies approaches to goal setting that are research supported and which lead to improved well-being. She suggests that goal setting is a bit more complex than most people think. You may have seen the acronym SMART applied to goals, where "r" stands for realistic. Miller says, "Having a 'realistic' goal may not stretch your imagination and abilities as far as possible, while a goal that is very audacious might be appropriate for your particular emotional make-up and situation, but not someone else's." Based on her extensive research into effective goal-setting and performance, she believes there are ten aspects to effective goal setting.

According to Miller, goals ought to be:
- Specific and challenging
- Measurable and have the opportunity to produce feedback
- Approach (exciting and magnetic) and not avoidance
- Value driven
- Able to create feelings of independence, connectedness, and competence
- Based on pre-commitment and accountability
- Intrinsic (not extrinsic)

- Non-conflicting and leveraged
- Written
- Capable of stimulating the "flow state"

To help you understand how to set and achieve goals—and this works not just for your students and children but for you, too—we will look at some common goals in the world of families, teachers, and coaches, and show you a model for achieving goals that takes advantage of both the "means" (paths taken and skills needed on the way to a goal) and "nutrients" (elements such as well-being or positive emotion that support the means) of goals. Later in the chapter you will have an opportunity to use our approach, so you might want to be thinking as you read along about a goal to use in this activity.

Below Sherri shows a structured way to think about the research-based elements of goal setting that she has used successfully with her coaching clients, both adults and students. The table presents the relationship among the means and nutrients so you know *what* to do as well as *why*, and at the bottom of the chart you connect your goals to the *SMART Strengths* model you practiced in Part One of this book:

Means and Nutrients for Goal Setting and Attainment	
Means	**Stimulate Growth Through These Nutrients**
Specific and Written: The goal needs to identify exactly what will be accomplished and may need to be broken down into very tiny, sequential steps on the way to something big.	**Challenging:** Easy goals don't feel worth it, and sometimes a person needs something "big" to capture their imagination and focus. You may need to work backwards from the "big picture" to the incremental steps needed.
Measurable: If it cannot be measured, there's no way of knowing if a goal has been accomplished.	**Provide Feedback:** Regular and incremental review feedback ideally comes from an objective source, e.g. a stopwatch, measuring tape, video, or rubric.

233

Approach versus avoidance: Goals are something to accomplish rather than avoid, e.g.: take steps to get a good grade rather than avoid a bad one; win a game rather than avoid losing one.	**Intrinsically valuable**: The person doing the work wants to achieve the goal—not just doing it for someone else, like a parent, teacher, or coach, or to avoid making that person angry, sad, etc.
Leveraged: Take advantage of and contribute to other goals.	**Nonconflicting**: Won't harm accomplishment of other goals or be in opposition to your values.
Use your Strengths: S-M-A-R-T	**Engaging**: Using strengths in the service of attaining goals puts you into flow state where you build well-being resources.

Making Goals Specific

Before we delve into specific goals, we'd like to point out that subjective goals can be helpful for those just beginning the study of a discipline. Edwin Locke and Gary Latham, noted researchers in goal setting, state: "When people lack the requisite knowledge to master a task, because they are in the early stage of learning, urging them to do their best results in higher performance than setting a specific difficult goal." Shane Lopez and his colleagues at the University of Kansas-Lawrence, based on the pioneering work of C.S. Snyder, have shown that there are three important aspects of goal setting: 1) goals thinking; 2) goals pathways, or strategies; and 3) goals agency, or ways to sustain motivation towards reaching a goal. In the chart above, goals thinking and pathways fit into column one, while goals agency fits into column two. Both are important.

Teachers, coaches, and parents can help young people set and achieve realistic yet challenging goals. Establishing goals through deliberate practice can lead to positive well-being, to more engagement and interest, and can both enhance life satisfaction and help prevent the negative emotions associated with failing to reach a goal.

The Procrastination Paradox

Marissa was languishing in her Pre-calculus class. After the first quarter grades went home, she was embarrassed to have earned a C-, and when her parents asked what happened, Marissa said that she was sure she could do better. She made a goal to try harder so that her disappointing grade would improve. By the end of the next term, things had not improved and the teacher noted in Marissa's report card that she had failed to turn in some assignments and had not attended study sessions. These two things alone, he assured her parents in a phone call, would make a huge difference not only in Marissa's grade, but more importantly, in how much she learned. The first semester grade was disappointing. Marissa thought that she had been trying harder—she cared so much about doing well. However, she had no clear plan. Her confidence eroded, she slipped into procrastination patterns that found her leaving homework incomplete or undone on her desk at home and waiting till the last minute to study. The results, of course, were disastrous.

One thing that Marissa needed was a personal *site team*. When we work with adults in a school to teach them the *SMART Strengths* approach, this is what we call the group of people in a school who support one another. As they set out to attain goals both individually and together, people need *meaningful feedback*. It will be essential to have others—a combination of peers and leadership—who expect and deserve accountability. Marissa will need to choose these people carefully. A friend who lets her feel sorry for herself or who ruminates with her is not a good candidate for her site team, nor is someone who is always seeking to perfect her efforts without appreciating what is already there, moving her toward her goal. (More about the appreciative approach is in Chapter Ten.)

Marissa will want her *challenging* goals to be stated—actually written down and shown to someone she is accountable to—in an approach format: "I want to increase my quiz and test performance to 85% or better" rather than "I do not want any test grades lower than a C." She will also need to become much more aware of the things that conspire to let her procrastinate and build benchmarks that will show her she is making progress toward the bigger goal of "85% or better." For Marissa, benchmarks may sound like this: "I will complete all homework to the best of my ability. If I have trouble I will do the following in order, until I understand: 1) Call Nina for help. 2) Go to the teacher's website. 3) Go to Math Lab. 4) Raise my hand in class to get clarification. 5) Attend Extra Help."

When she is successful along the way, Marissa will be able to show incremental growth. Her site team and teacher will be able to provide *objective feedback* that she can connect to her benchmarks. Since Marissa plans to attend college, attaining this goal is both *nonconflicting* and *leveraged*: it will contribute to that bigger goal. She does not just want to attend college to please her parents and the other adults in her life, so the goal is also *intrinsically valuable*. She can intentionally use her *SMART Strengths* in the service of the goal, which is more likely to put her into the *flow state*.

As mentioned in Chapter Six, students can best achieve goals through engagement and interest by accessing their individual zone of functioning in their quest to reach the flow state. There are five indicators that a person is in the Flow State:

- Concentration
- Action and Awareness Merge
- Self-consciousness disappears
- Sense of time becomes distorted, and
- The experience becomes its own reward.

Mastery Goals versus Performance Goals

Mastery goals are ones focused on helping a student see how well they are progressing when compared to their own previous achievement through learning, understanding, and individual progress and knowledge. *Performance goals* focus on the importance of avoiding mistakes, outperforming other students, and meeting extrinsic objectives such as high grades, standards, and awards.

A focus on mastery goals tends to build intrinsic motivation and creativity, along with positive feelings about learning, and it develops more perseverance (think grit), self-advocacy and curiosity, as well as higher academic engagement. A classroom with a mastery focus is also more student-centered and individualized, and its students attribute success to effort rather than just ability.

Most schools, interestingly, are structured around performance goals. As mentioned in Chapter Eight, Carol Dweck's work has found that everyone tends to have one of two basic mindsets: the fixed (performance) mindset, where you believe that your talents and abilities are either something you have or don't have, or the growth (mastery) mindset, which is characterized by knowing that abilities can develop over time with effort and practice. Many teachers and school districts say they value the very things that a mastery focus develops, yet schools are also performance oriented, with data-driven goals for higher math and reading scores, graduation rates, and college acceptances.

Calibrating Progress Toward Goals

Research in the classroom has shown that students with performance-approach goals—those in which a student sets goals to outperform others—tend to score high on exams. Those students who have performance-avoidance goals—trying to avoid performing poorly among their peers—tend to score lower than students who aspire to approach goals. Of course, competence or the lack of it may be the result of many things. What highly competent and incompetent students share is this: both miscalibrate the perception of their own and of others' performance. The difference is that competent students believe their peers have done only slightly better than they have, and so they work to apply success strategies—the growth mindset. Less competent students, on the other hand, often believe they have performed significantly better than their peers and therefore do not take advantage of strategies to achieve even greater success. Marissa, in the example above, will need to be careful to use her own progress and not that of her peers to judge her performance.

Encouraging Love of Learning in Students

It should not come as a surprise that classrooms with a performance goal focus have students who are more competitive with peers and less personally interested in learning, since the adults in such environments use extrinsic motivators such as grades, and they generally reward conventional responses. The current push to reward teachers for student performance uses the same approach. If creativity can encourage curiosity, and curiosity along with other VIA strengths like love of learning and perseverance help to predict GPA, it would make sense to nurture more divergent creative thinking.

We would argue that the best teachers are able to think like their students, anticipating bumps along the learning road that may either cause a breakdown or instead catapult students to new heights of learning. Remember that effective goals are *value driven*. Revisit your strengths and you will find that these relate to your own core values—what matters most to you. Don't forget your strengths buttons, either. These connect with your ability to "will" goals alive!

Mindful Moment: *Writing a Goal Plan*	
Means...	***Stimulate Growth Through These Nutrients***
Specific and Written: The goal needs to identify exactly what will be accomplished and may need to be broken down into very tiny, sequential steps on the way to something big.	**Challenging:** Easy goals don't feel worth it, and sometimes a person needs something big to capture their imagination and focus. You may need to work backwards from the big picture to the incremental steps needed.
What is a goal you want to accomplish?	*Why is this goal challenging for you?*
Measurable: If it cannot be measured, there's no way of knowing if a goal has been accomplished.	**Provide Meaningful Feedback:** Regular and incremental review feedback ideally comes from both an objective source, e.g. a stopwatch, measuring tape, video, or rubric, as well as your personal site team of one or more people to whom you are accountable.
How will you know that this goal has been achieved?	*How will you receive meaningful feedback, both objectively and from your personal "site team"?*
Approach versus avoidance: Goals are something to accomplish rather than avoid, e.g.: take steps to get a good grade rather than avoid a bad one; win a game rather than avoid losing one.	**Intrinsically valuable:** The person doing the work wants to achieve the goal—not just doing it for someone else, like a parent, teacher, or coach, or to avoid making that person angry, sad, etc.

Is your goal stated in a way that shows it is something you are attracted to and which will involve you?	*Who are you doing this for? Is your goal something that will make you feel more . . . Skilled? Independent? Connected? Happy?*
Leveraged: Take advantage of and contribute to other goals.	**Nonconflicting**: Won't harm accomplishment of other goals or be in opposition to your values.
What are other goals you have that are related to this one? How will achieving this goal specifically contribute to other goals?	*Cross-check (and maybe check with your personal site team) to be sure your goals are a good fit for each other and your values. Are they? How do you know?*
Use your Strengths: S-M-A-R-T	**Engaging**: Using strengths in the service of attaining goals puts you into flow state where you build well-being resources.
*List up to five of the strengths you feel most aligned with how you will use them in the service of attaining your goals. **Think: Spotting, Managing, Advocating, Relating and Training your strengths.***	*Anticipate your success! What will it be like when you achieve your goal? Write your imagined future:*

Trust and the Realization of Goals

Integrity is like homogenization is to milk—a single consistency throughout.
—Edwin J. Delattre, *Teaching Integrity: The Boundaries of Moral Education*

One way to increase student attention to their strengths in the classroom is to establish an authentic, trusting environment, where students trust their teachers and vice versa. Integrity is important in teachers and students alike. Good teachers, for example, are "promise keepers." When teachers are clear and consistent with their expectations in the classroom and for work at home, young people tend to respond more positively, because they trust the process. Trust creates less distraction and doubt in young people, and inevitably more attention, so that there isn't any hesitation about what the teacher or another student says.

Ken Bain, a professor at Montclair State University, has lessons for teachers at all levels of school, from kindergarten through college. He suggests that teachers ask themselves the following question: "What do I promise to provide to my students?" Whether it is a lesson plan or course outline, Bain believes that a *promising syllabus* is one that the best teachers adopt because it engenders trust, rejects power as the sole domain of the teacher, and sets authentic course goals. The three parts of the promising syllabus are:

The Promising Syllabus

1. Laying out the promises and opportunities that the course offers—the kinds of questions it will help students explore and answer and the types of skills they will develop as a result
2. Explaining what the students will be doing to realize the promises, giving them a sense of ownership for their own learning but also a sense of engagement with the teacher
3. Summarizing how the teacher and students will understand learning and evaluate it, building in some flexibility for adjustments

Adapted from Bain, K. *What the Best College Teachers Do.* Cambridge: MA: Harvard

Here is an excerpt from a Promising Syllabus for "Health Issues," a class at the Culver Academies.

The Promise: Health Issues 12ᵗʰ grade

- I will do my very best to provide you with a variety of learning activities to help you acquire a deep understanding of personal, community, national, and world health issues to support this process.
- I expect you to engage in student-centered discussions, group work, report writing, and survey/investigations.
- We will have an emphasis on critical thinking and moral interpretation of health information and health behavior.
- I will provide you with different ways of addressing health issues to gain a high level of understanding of the biochemical, sociological, and psychological concepts we will explore with relation to the need for happiness, the pursuit of happiness, the roots of addiction, basic desires of human nature and the seeking of personal and social fulfillment.
- It is important for all of us to be here, be on time, and to do our part in cultivating a learning environment that is respectful and comfortable.
- Your written assignments may be emailed or handed in on the due date.
- I promise to have your papers and journals graded within 48 hours after they are submitted.

Some teachers balk at a *promising syllabus*, because it takes away their wiggle room—their ability to make changes and potentially break their promises to their students. The plan or outline ought to instead be a binding document of trust. The development of trust in young people is the first stage of social development, and trusting the teacher and course expectations is a first step to success in the classroom.

Mindful Moment: The Promise

Write a Promising Syllabus:

1. What will you promise your students? "I promise to..."

_____

_____

2. What activities will the students participate in to help fulfill the promise? (reading, presenting, group work, research, etc.)

_____

_____

3. How will your strengths appeal to students' strengths to make the promise a reality?

_____

_____

4. What will the students have learned by the end of the term, semester, or year?

_____

_____

What makes the promising syllabus different from standard behavioral goals and objectives is that it tells students what the teacher will do to help students realize the outcomes for the lesson or class. The invitation and promise is an important part of school engagement that involves the relationships students have with their teachers and other students. When students have a clear sense of purpose in classroom activities, they become *partners in the process,* rather than subjects under the teacher's command. John Murray, the CEO of Advance Path Academies, asserts that as teachers we many times need to "capture the heart before engaging the mind"—especially with young people who are struggling in school. And it is only through healthy relationships that creativity, passion, and empowerment can be conveyed.

The Practice Plan

The practice plan in the athletic arena is similar to the *promising syllabus.* When coaches share the objectives of the practice with their players in a short briefing at the beginning of practice, it provides the players with an understanding of the structure of the time. Good coaches are able to make course corrections mid-practice and can bring the team together for that. And at the end of the practice, a debrief is in order: "So what did we just accomplish today? How does this set us up for tomorrow's practice or for the next game?"

The importance of proper goal-setting in sports cannot be overemphasized. If the goal is about developing skills, the fundamentals of the game revolve around the development of second-nature habits through on-going repetition. Improving skills, techniques, and tactics through the means of a structured goal setting system can enable the realities of improvement to be more satisfying and beneficial to the player and coach. We studied stakeholders in the game of lacrosse and ninety-nine percent of the participants who were surveyed agreed or strongly agreed that it is important for teams or programs and coaches to clearly outline goals and objectives that establish appropriate guidelines for both players and adult mentors.

One Goal

Having a clear purpose is essential and should be understood and declared by all stakeholders. Although this ought to happen at every level of sports, John was moved by a keynote talk by Dom Starsia, the University of Virginia men's lacrosse coach, at a convention a while ago. John has known Dom since they first played together on a club lacrosse team back in the 1970s. He is arguably one of the best coaches in Division I, and he conveyed, through his talk and a pre-season letter he sent to his 2003 team, what really matters most to attain success in the Virginia program. Dom talked about having "one goal" in mind for the whole team, since many games are, in fact, decided by one goal.

In His Own Words: Dom Starsia, University of Virginia men's lacrosse coach.

I have often said that the difference in play between two teams in a one-goal game is so disproportionate to how the two teams feel about themselves upon the game's conclusion. What is the difference in play between the two teams? Sixty minutes, or more, of lacrosse, all those groundballs, those individual battles, deflecting a pass, making a save, etc., and one final shot determines the outcome.

The top programs attain (and maintain) their status because they believe in the philosophy of their program—style of play, standard of behavior on and off the field, respect for each other, practice environment, etc. In turn, a player on one of these top teams is already one of the very best college players in the country. So how does someone at this level improve, how does a program at this level improve itself, how do you improve your chances of having the winning result in one of these close games?

WORK HARDER! Sure—but there are a limited number of hours in the day and everyone works hard.

WORK BETTER! Definitely—always modifying the lifts, adjusting practice, trying to improve the individual workouts, thinking of creative ways to improve our business. We spend most of our time with this one.

What I am certain of is that as you move toward the top, greater effort is required for any improved results. This is not meant to discourage—the rewards at the top are also much more meaningful.

Habit: Competence through Deliberate Practice

The lessons are straightforward: There is no path to excellence at anything except the deliberate, purposeful formation of daily habits that make the specific form of excellence possible. There are no shortcuts, and mere talent is not enough.

—Edwin J. Delattre

More often than not the initial process of improvement, guided by practice, requires that young people be willing to make choices that are different from what they feel like doing in the moment. A student who has developed a strong character can call on a foundation of well-formed habits in aspiring to realize their goals.

Young people can continually stretch their abilities through deliberate practice—focused and effortful rehearsal. Deliberate practice, of course, requires a good degree of patience and perseverance.

Young people who are committed to improving their performance in the classroom or on the field quickly learn that one of the most significant sources of both difficulty and joy comes from the ability to rise to challenging goals—they don't back down from momentary lapses in motivation. The ability to stretch beyond one's perceived ability or desire and to continue is contingent on asking, "What is the right action—what needs to be done at this time to reach my goals right now?" This allows the student who has difficulties in math to continue working with his teacher. This allows the high school track athlete to push a little harder on the last lap of the mile. And with this effort also comes the joy, satisfaction, and meaning of the process. Amy Baltzell, a sport psychologist at Boston University, states: "When the body and mind adapt to higher demands, the adaptation leads, inevitably, to a heightened sense of engagement and enjoyment, a 'dog-with-a-bone' type of satisfaction."

Great Expectations?

Neena is hoping to be back in college soon after a rather disastrous semester has left her "withdrawn/failing." She has never been a stellar student, not even in elementary school. A review of report cards finds a pattern of "talking in class, socializing instead of working," "inconsistent work production," "could be a good student," and "needs to apply more effort."

In art classes she consistently earned As, and she loved being part of the theater productions at school, but as she says, "I don't want to be a starving artist, so I am going to get a degree in business." Ask Neena how she feels about reapplying for next semester and she says, "This time will be different. I just wasn't ready before. I'm just going to do my work this time. That will change everything." Maybe, but not likely.

What Neena doesn't know is that her years of self-defeating behaviors—procrastination, disorganization, inconsistency, and excuses—are symptoms of more than just needing to work harder. Neena needs to work smarter, too. As "grit" researcher Angela Duckworth reminds us, "Self-discipline is the ability to marshal willpower to accomplish goals and uphold standards that one personally regards as desirable. That is, self-discipline isn't the capacity to do what other people order you to do." To establish a level of competence, Neena and other goal setters ought to engage in deliberate practice as seen through three different lenses we first introduced in Chapter 3:

Self-regulation: Practice requires goal-setting and perseverance. Edwin Locke and Gary Latham claim that one factor explaining why people may not reach their goals is that they underestimate how hard it will be to do the work necessary to achieve them. But beyond improving the ability to anticipate how difficult a goal may be, people need to manage the resources of self-regulation. Students like Neena may need incremental practice to build this set of skills.

Self-efficacy: Remember that this develops as the student works through both independent and directed trial and error, and the pathways and actions that have led to success are recorded so that they can be replicated. Albert Bandura of Stanford University says, "A resilient sense of efficacy requires experience in overcoming obstacles through perseverant effort." Students who struggle can learn where they have the ability to do their own work through mentor-designed mastery experiences as they gain realistic confidence in applying their SMART Strengths. Practicing until the point of success reinforces how you will need to be able to replicate—or even improve—a performance.

Self-determination: Determine what is valuable to you. Yes, there are necessary extrinsic motivators along the way, as any coach or parent or teacher will tell you. But when you choose a habit of mindful, intrinsic practice—bolstered by approach goals—your success is for "you", not just what someone else wants to see from you.

Remember that goals you establish for yourself, appreciate, and value are more likely to result in success. When you are enthusiastic about a goal it is more aligned with what you want to do, as opposed to what others expect from you. When you connect the dots between your efforts and your achievement, it is more obvious what works. What do you do to be competent and to replicate your good work? It is worth recording this so that you can get more of what you want. You might try Sherri's version of Martin Seligman's Three Blessings Exercise: Three Times Good or 3XG. (This exercise is also presented in Chapter Three as a *Mindful Moment*.)

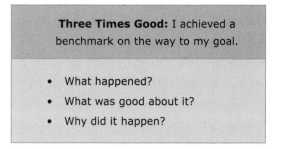

Three Times Good: I achieved a benchmark on the way to my goal.

- What happened?
- What was good about it?
- Why did it happen?

Sometimes adults fail to see what makes a goal feel *leveraged* for a student. One of the reasons that many young people retire from youth competitive sports by the age of 14 is because their goals are not in sync with their parents' and their coaches' dreams. Caroline Miller says, "Goals must not only be harmonious with our desires and dreams, they must also be leveraged. What this means is that the accomplishment of one goal will be enhanced by the accomplishment of another." For example, a student's goal to do well in high school in order to be more attractive to a college is doubly rewarding. That's something that parents can get behind, too.

In Her Own Words: Eleanor Chin, Principal: Clarity Partners Coaching

For several summers, our daughter went to a camp where one of the activity choices was archery and she chose it every year. Each year she came back with trophies that we acknowledged, but in retrospect, did not give much weight to, among the requisite awards for participation in activities.

After three awards like this, she came home with a new one, a golden arrow. When we asked her to explain, she said that the counselors made up a new award for her, so that someone else could win the award she usually got. Still, this didn't register to us as anything to take serious note of. Duh! Then one day, as Emma and I were driving, we passed an indoor archery range near our house—one that none of us had noticed before—and Emma pointed it out, somewhat excitedly.

I finally woke up and asked if she'd be interested in taking lessons. She answered with an enthusiastic "yes." She began taking those lessons at age 12. By 13 she wanted to do local tournaments and by 15 she had won her first silver medal at a national tournament. Although she had her struggles with it, she continued shooting and continued to love archery.

She ended up being recruited for the Columbia University Division One Women's team and continued shooting until she graduated college. To this day at 23, she still loves it. Although she's taken a break from it, she's currently looking for a range to shoot at in NYC where she lives. She maintains many friendships from all over the world from her archery days.

Imagery and Goal Setting

When we focus and practice positive imagery (Refer to Chapter Five), our imagined thoughts have a greater opportunity to become reality. The more conscious we are at using our senses for good, the more adept we become at creating positive future scripts that link the mind to the body. Laura King, a University of Missouri researcher, has investigated not only the benefits of writing about challenging past experiences, but also imagining the future and writing about it. Her work with college students showed that those who wrote about their "best possible future self" showed decreases in illness and more overall optimism. Although King claims that the emotional effects of writing may influence physical effects, they may also impact the mental, moral, social, and spiritual dimensions of well-being.

Goal Setting Portfolios

With the emergence of the digital age, electronic scrapbooks are finding a place in our schools. The portfolio is a tool that allows adolescents to capture and reflect on their goals, aspirations, and accomplishments throughout their school career. Pictures and stories of elations and even frustrations form a medium for students to demonstrate and express what matters most to them as they track their academic, leadership, athletic, and wellness development. This allows students to 1) foster self-awareness and reflection; 2) gain a greater awareness of goals achieved and goals for the future; and 3) more meaningfully and purposefully connect the dots of their school experience through tracking their life satisfaction. At Culver Academies, seniors construct individual digital portfolios of their high school experience.

This process gives students permission to explore and examine their remembered pleasures in their journey. We provide seniors with their Culver Admissions Essay that was completed with their application as eighth graders. Without fail, the seniors are astounded at what they wrote and how they have grown over the past four years. This chronological reflection of where they have come from, what their Culver experience has been like, and their aspirations for college becomes a wonderful medium for identifying strengths and the constellation of emotions experienced during their secondary school career.

The portfolio invites students to access their *anticipated memory*. By placing representative documents in the portfolio (i.e. written journals, audio and/or video-tape) students may be more readily able to access a proper goal-setting mindset. By attending to their *anticipated memory*, students catalog thoughts for the future that help to frame and realize their hopes and dreams.

Piloting Your Dreams

A student from Culver's class of 2006 aspired to become a U.S. Navy fighter pilot. He placed a vivid video of a jet pilot taking off from an aircraft carrier into his portfolio. He said that watching the video reinforced his goal to attend the United States Naval Academy, a step along the way to becoming a Navy pilot. He was very specific with his goals as a Navy Midshipman. They were exciting and magnetic, derived from his strong value system. His goals were written in his high school portfolio, as he made a pre-commitment to follow these aspirations. His goals have stimulated frequent experiences of flow. For his final semester at the Naval Academy, this young man was named Brigade Commander, the highest position within the Brigade of Midshipmen.

During the primary and secondary school years, students participate in many events and experiences that help them to establish their autobiographical map. Stories, pictures, and animations of their "best selves," collected over this time, have the potential to assist young people in developing more meaningful lives. As students attend to their own stories, they look for cues that uncover their beliefs and sense of purpose. By doing so, they are more able to identify with their own joys, elations, frustrations, and troubles. The portfolio presents stories of tough calls, illusions, allusions, and residues that form the fodder for the development of healthy life goals. The portfolio becomes a vehicle in which the student can paint a multi-faceted picture of aspiring to become a "whole person." It allows them to bask and marvel in who they are, what they have done and what they hope to become.

Poverty and Goal Setting: Building A Future Story

Over 50% of Triton School Corporation students live in families whose incomes place them at the poverty line or below. Elementary school principal, Jeremy Riffle, and his teachers have focused on strategies to "help erase some of the back story" to bring out the best in students who have grown up in generational poverty in this rural community in North Central Indiana. Many of his teachers have attended seminars with Ruby Payne, the author of *A Framework for Understanding Poverty*. Payne, an expert in understanding the mindsets of poverty, middle class, and wealth in the United States, claims that there are four reasons one leaves poverty:

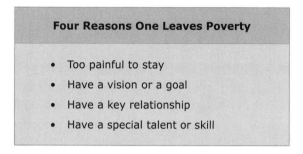

The second point, that the student has a vision or a goal, is something the adults at this school have built into the curriculum. Jeremy and his teachers have focused on what Payne calls the child's development of a future story. Payne maintains that a lot of students don't have a future story because they live in the moment from day to day. The future story simply says, for example, that if a child likes Peyton Manning, the iconic quarterback for the Indianapolis Colts, a number 18 jersey or a book about Manning might be a perfect gift. Very few young people will approach Manning's position on the spotlight of the football gridiron, but maybe they can relate to some of the challenges that he went through and be motivated by his deliberate practice to succeed.

Unfortunately, some impoverished children are worried at the moment about what they are going to eat and what clothes are they going to wear. People of poverty tend to look at the here and now because they are simply trying to survive. Providing them with a future story allows them to look beyond 24 hours to a future, and whether it means coming to school tomorrow, graduating high school, going to post-high school education, or beginning a career, it's about finding something students really enjoy and giving them motivation. Christine Cook, the Instructional Coach/Data Assessment Coordinator at Triton Elementary School believes that it is important to present possibilities for the future that most students of poverty aren't building within their families.

The realization of goals is not always an easy task. It takes a good amount of "willingness" to take the chance to set important goals. Louis Pasteur once said, "Chance favors the prepared mind." Start creating those chances with your students and with yourself! This can lead to a healthy appreciation of living and learning with each other to make better families, schools and teams.

In Chapter Nine, we discussed how teachers, coaches, and parents can help young people set and achieve realistic yet challenging goals. Establishing goals through deliberate practice can lead to positive well-being, to more engagement and interest, and can enhance life satisfaction and help prevent the negative emotions associated with failing to reach a goal. In the final chapter we will examine how building high quality connections through respectful engagement, task enabling, and trust can create and maintain flourishing relationships in schools.

Chapter Ten

High-Quality Connections and Appreciative Questions

In a high-quality connection, people feel more engaged,
more open, more competent. They feel more alive!

—Jane Dutton, *Energizing your Workplace*

Every first Friday of the month during the school year, Jeremy Riffle, who you have met earlier, hosts either *Muffins for Moms* or *Donuts for Dads* at Triton Elementary School. Parents are invited to have breakfast with their children at school. Once the children go to their classrooms, Jeremy engages parents in a discussion of hot topics at school, such as Internet safety and standardized tests. He also describes learning activities that mothers and fathers can do with their children outside of school. Parents find these occasions interesting and non-threatening. They break bread communally. In the process, they learn more about the school and the education of their children. These occasions increase the number of high-quality connections between parents and school staff.

Building High-Quality Connections

Jane Dutton, an organizational psychologist at the University of Michigan, coined the term "high-quality connections" for interactions that are "marked by mutual positive regard, trust, and active engagement on both sides." Any point of contact between people can potentially be a high-quality connection, even something as fleeting as an encounter in a grocery-store line.

According to research by Dutton and others, high-quality connections have numerous benefits for individuals, contributing to greater well-being, reduced stress, increased engagement, and increased ability to learn. They also have benefits for communities and organizations, contributing to enhanced cooperation, increased organizational loyalty, transmission of purpose, open dialogue, and adaptability.

Schools are complex environments. They include many kinds of relationships among people with different values, purposes, and ways of making meaning. One way that schools can contribute to the larger community is by encouraging high-quality connections between students and students, teachers and teachers, teachers and students, parents and students, teachers and parents, coaches and parents, and coaches and student-athletes. Those high-quality connections can have an energizing effect on life at school, and they can have a strong positive impact on the surrounding community.

Dutton organizes her book about establishing high-quality connections around strategies that increase the following qualities that are just as important in schools as they are in workplaces:

- Respectful engagement
- Effective task enabling
- Trust

Jeremy Riffle uses the three strategies with parents in his school community, encouraging them to have high-quality connections with their own children, other children, other parents, and teachers.

In His Own Words: Jeremy Riffle, Principal, Triton Elementary School, Bourbon, IN

Muffins for Moms and *Donuts for Dads* is for parents to put aside their busy schedule once a month to take the time to have breakfast with their children. This time serves 3 purposes. First, it facilitates the connection of parents with their students away from a television. Second, the parents are able to build relationships within the community and to discuss ideas of how they can continue to be the best parents they can possibly be. Third, it allows me to inform parents on the happenings of Triton Elementary and allows them to get open and candid answers from me about why we do what we do.

We have averaged approximately 40 fathers and 60 mothers with each group meeting alternate months. This has been well received and has allowed Triton Elementary to continue to build its reputation in the community as we strive to be a lighthouse for our students. My constant reminder to parents that I have an open door policy and the fact that my assistants share that view helps us to continue to build trust. This cures a lot of ills when times and circumstances get tough because they know that we have cared long before there was an issue that we have to resolve.

Respectful engagement, task enabling and trust are essential components for school flourishing. In the next several pages, we will break down each of these skills to help you better understand their importance.

Skill 1: Respectful Engagement

Respectful engagement involves paying attention, showing consideration for others, and treating them with high positive regard. Dutton describes respectful engagement as

- Conveying presence, for example, not allowing oneself to be distracted by television or other technology
- Communicating affirmation
- Effective listening
- Supportive communication

Parents, teachers, and coaches who engage respectfully are good listeners. They pay attention to what children say and do, and then express genuine interest. They look for value in other people. Respectful engagement makes other people feel that they have been taken seriously and are genuinely wanted and needed. Respectful engagement can help students perceive things about themselves that otherwise might be hidden from them. Mason McIntyre, the Athletic Director at the Triton School Corporation, has found students who engage with each other respectfully can see strengths in each other. He can then use the language of strengths to make their observations clear.

In His Own Words: Mason McIntyre, Athletic Director, Triton School Corporation

There was a junior, Kylee, who was in my Triton Leadership group last year. Students were nominated by teachers and coaches to be part of this program. I thought she could be a leader, and she has now really blossomed into a good leader. But it took some nudging from the other members of the group.

At a meeting, another girl in the group said to her, "You know, Kylee, if you stepped up and told the other girls what you were concerned about, they would listen to you." Kylee didn't really see that at the time. She was kind of laid back about the whole thing. She felt she was only a leader because somebody had told her she was a leader, and it wasn't something that she really wanted to do.

Kylee and I have talked about leadership since then, and she realized that one of her top VIA strengths was *leadership*, while *developer* and *includer* were two of her top *Clifton StrengthsFinder* assets. She also had *positivity* which I think at that time meant to her that everything had to be "peachy." However, since then she has really stepped up to the plate and has been more positive with her peers by helping them and including them in all the things she is doing.

Skill 2: Task Enabling

According to Dutton, "Task enabling comprises the various strategies that people use to facilitate the successful performance of others." Teaching is one form of task enabling that obviously belongs in schools. Other important forms include:

- Designing tasks to make them more natural for others to perform, for example breaking them into chunks that seem doable
- Advocating for people, for example providing them visibility and speaking out for their interests

- Nurturing, for example making tasks fit the developmental needs of the individual

When parents, teachers, and coaches perform task enabling effectively, they help young people see greater value in themselves and feel a greater ability to master challenges. This is about really investing in young people, helping them to "fish for themselves," as stated in the old proverb. Often it means helping them learn to work interdependently with each other. Dutton says "task enabling through teaching happens whenever one person offers information, guidance, or a morsel of advice that enables others to conduct their work easily."

Nancy McKinnis had an interesting task enabling experience as a leadership educator at Culver. When members of the student-run *Leadership Committee for Africa* at Culver Girls Academy realized the magnitude of the HIV/AIDS issue in Africa, they said they wanted to help. However, they felt that it was a daunting task. With a pandemic across the continent, they wondered how a small group of high school girls from North Central Indiana could make a difference at all.

Nancy connected them with Christel House South Africa (CHSA) and helped them organize a trip to Cape Town and Johannesburg during spring break. CHSA is one of five schools worldwide that share the stated mission, "To help children break the cycle of poverty and become self-sufficient, contributing members of their society." The Culver girls taught leadership skills and other activities to students at Christel House. The experience included visits to historic sites, meeting individuals who served disadvantaged children, and learning about South African history and culture. One of students recognized that she was doing task enabling for Christel House students by helping them identify and use their strengths.

In Her Own Words: Phoebe Hall, Culver Girls Academy student

On the second day, we began our work at Christel House Academy, South Africa, which is by far the experience I treasure most. Our workshops focused on their high school students, specifically those that had been identified as leaders within their new prefect system, which is modeled in many ways after Culver Girls Academy.

I had the opportunity to plan and execute one of the three workshops. The goal of my workshop was to identify personal leadership strengths and discuss ways to own and use these strengths in daily life. I decided to use storytelling as a way to talk about how we use our strengths in our moments of success.

Because there was a lot of emphasis on discussion in the workshop, I had the opportunity to learn a lot about the lives that the children at Christel House live. I met peers that spoke as many as 4 or 5 languages and balanced school pressures with fears about basic needs that I take for granted.

The biggest success in the week of workshops was seeing the quietest members of the groups learn to own their strengths and make them part of their identities. During each session, we did a "360" in which members of the group assessed each other's strengths and wrote them down. It was amazing to see members of the group unanimously decide, and reassure quieter or more reserved classmates that they were kind, courageous, and intelligent.

As Phoebe demonstrates, students can be task enablers for each other. For example, older students can serve as mentors and supporters for younger students. Students at the same level can learn task enabling skills in the process of working on team assignments or tutoring others. When it is explained to students this way, they see that it is not a one-way street. Both the one helped and the one doing the helping learn something from the experience.

In the *Fluency Partners* program at Triton Elementary School, sixth graders use their strengths to help the second graders in the building continue to build their reading skills. During the last half hour of every day, the chosen sixth grade students get the second grade students and work with them on teacher-given reading practice. The sixth graders went through a three session training to learn research-based practices so that they could make gains with the second graders who needed extra practice.

The sixth graders have used their strengths to mentor, teach, and build relationships with the younger children. The sixth graders have taken ownership and responsibility to live out their strengths and to give back to their school community by giving up their own study time to share their talents and abilities with the younger students in their building.

Skill 3: Building Trust

> *You must trust and believe in people or life becomes impossible.*
> —Anton Chekhov

One way to encourage high-quality connections at school is to establish a safe and authentic environment that leads to mutual trust between students and adults. When parents, teachers, and coaches are clear and consistent with their expectations, young people tend to respond positively because they trust the process. Trust reduces distraction and uncertainty. Jane Dutton says, "Acting with trust means acting toward others in a way that conveys belief in their integrity (consistency between thought and behavior), dependability (honesty and reliability), and benevolence (desire and willingness to care)." Building on these ideas, Aneil and Karen Mishra constructed the ROCC model for characterizing qualities that lead to trust:

R stands for reliability, delivering on commitments, acting so that people believe that you will do what you say you will do.

O stands for openness, transparency, and willingness to share information that other people need to know.

C stands for competence, that is, what you produce is high quality and usable.

C also stands for compassion, that is, when others are open with you, they know you will respond with empathy and consideration.

This model can be useful as a diagnostic tool when you want to evaluate whether you are acting in a way that supports trust.

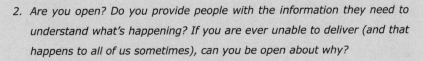

Mindful Moment: *The ROCC of Trust*

Think about the following questions in terms of your relationships at school with teachers, students, parents, or coaches.

1. *Are you reliable? Can people depend on you to deliver on your promises? What could you do to increase your reliability?* _____
_____
_____
_____

2. *Are you open? Do you provide people with the information they need to understand what's happening? If you are ever unable to deliver (and that happens to all of us sometimes), can you be open about why? What could you do to increase your openness?* _____
_____
_____
_____

3. *Are you competent? Can other people depend on what you produce? What could you do to increase your competence?* _____
_____
_____
_____

4. *Are you compassionate? Do people feel you will treat them with consideration and respect if they are open with you? What could you do to increase your demonstration of compassion for others?*
_____
_____
_____

Trust is the bedrock of supportive relationships. Adults with behaviors that engender trust are role models for students, helping them see how to behave towards each other. This can be said of the *promising syllabus*, mentioned in Chapter Nine.

Using the language of strengths can be a powerful way to help students build trusting relationships since it leads to greater competence, willingness to be open, and compassion for people with different strengths.

Using Strengths to Build Trust

At Triton Elementary School, 5th and 6th grade students and teachers are aware of their strengths and are able to use them to enable trust within student groups whether they are working on research projects, small group activities or differentiated assigned tasks based on what the students do well. The second wave of strengths-based leadership allows students to learn more about the strengths of others, including their teachers, so that they may gain trust by understanding how and why people do what they do.

Ruby Payne, the author of *A Framework for Understanding Poverty*, says that no learning takes place without a significant relationship being built first. It is our goal as educators to get to know our students' strengths which will allow us to put students in situations where they will succeed—experience being reliable and competent—and understand how to finish. So many times we ask our students to lead yet very rarely do we give them the opportunity to lead in practical ways. We continue to strive to not only model but also give our students the opportunity to find themselves in situations where their strengths can come to light.

Student-Student Trust: Effective Group Projects

Students engage in many group projects in the course of their education. One way to make these group experiences more effective is to help students learn the skills of team formation that lead to trust, such as exploring the strengths that each member brings to the table, making promises to each other about what each will contribute, and understanding the importance of keeping those promises.

Teachers who are particularly adept at using group projects make sure that many different kinds of strengths are required to achieve group goals. Thus, the most effective team assignments cannot be accomplished with just verbal and analytical strengths. These projects require other kinds of understanding and other ways of contributing, so that all students learn that they need the contributions of every student on the team in order to meet the goal.

According to Carol Rolheiser and Stephen Anderson at the University of Toronto, teachers who use cooperative projects need to address the following hurdles, "(1) recognizing when cooperative group activities could be used to effectively enhance student learning, (2) shifting from the rote use of procedures (e.g., assigning roles to small group members) to the application of principles that can be enacted in multiple ways (e.g., positive interdependence to ensure cooperation); (3) structuring small group activities to make collaboration essential to the learning process and to include individual as well as group accountability; (4) incorporating both academic and social goals and skill development; (5) finding effective ways to monitor small group activity across the class; and (6) anticipating and preparing students for the complexity of small-group learning tasks." In all of these steps, a primary goal is helping students learn how to trust others and how to be trustworthy.

High-Quality Connections in Action

There are many behaviors that parents, teachers, and coaches can use to encourage high-quality connections within the school community. We will share three behaviors that are both relatively easy to learn and profound in their potential impacts.

- The power of naming
- Green light responding
- Using appreciative questions.

The Power of Naming

The late song master Jim Croce portrayed an instinctive understanding of high-quality connections in many of his ballads, including the song, *I've Got a Name*. Greeting a student by name can have a profound impact. There is something special, almost magical, about the experience of greeting by name that can bring pleasure, engagement, and meaning to both the greeter and recipient.

As a substitute teacher in a Boston area high school in the late 1990's, Mark Harris worked hard to learn the names of his students.

In His Own Words: Mark Harris

To remember faces it is not enough to associate them to names; faces can blend in the mind, and mistakes can be made. With the face one has to recognize the body, the voice, the posture, the habits, the responses. A person is a system of being in the world, and a name is the tag we attach to that total system. It encompasses quite a lot, not just a face.

When I think of 'Mickey Phelan' or 'Claire Darcy,' I associate a hundred things with each of them; remembering a constellation of details about a student, paradoxically, is much easier and makes remembering the name and fact a piece of cake. The students whose names I have a hard time summoning up are the ones I don't know much about. The elements of names, the 'Mikes' and the 'Caitlins' and the 'Murphies' and the 'Mitchells,' are not unique, but they stand for and indicate persons who are unique and uniquely valuable.

A positive salutation can enhance pleasure and meaning and often brings a smile to one's face. The process of greeting or tendering a "hello" or "good bye" by saying someone's name, paired with a handshake or pat on the shoulder, can elicit a slight visceral response in both participants. Of course, one must know which of the senses are most comfortable to elicit in others. We are attentive to the various cultural nuances of gestures, eye contact, and touching, and hope that people find their way to greet others in a comfortable and engaging manner.

Human beings have different motives, desires, and appetites. Most people, however, yearn to be listened to, taken seriously, and feel wanted by others. Naming people out loud is a form of respectful engagement. It is an authentic interchange that says: "You matter." We value close relationships, and we want them "just because," not because of what they can do for us. Relationships are important in and of themselves, not just because they lead to other outcomes. Still, the power of naming can bring out the best in self and the best in others in the domains of family, school, and sports.

Green Light Responding

Kind words can be short and easy to speak, but their echoes are truly endless.
—Mother Teresa

One of the best ways to make positive experiences salient and memorable is to relive them out loud with a trusted other. Shelly Gable at the University of California at Santa Barbara calls this *capitalizing* on the experience. Her research shows that taking time to talk about good experiences substantially increases their impacts on individuals. There needs to be at least one listener. One way that listeners can help people benefit from their accomplishments is to respond enthusiastically and to ask questions that help them relive good experiences out loud.

Let's take the story of Emily Wright, a tenth grade science teacher. She excitedly entered the teacher's room abuzz with the "Aha" moment she just observed in several of her students, "The lights just went on—they finally understood it!" Without hesitation from the back of the room, nestled behind yesterday's crossword puzzle, came a growl, "Don't get too excited. It took them all semester to finally . . ." Before the school's resident keeper of the nightmare could finish his reply, Mr. Burton's oratorical voice took over, "Well done, Ms. Wright! You have persevered! Tell me how you helped them get to this understanding."

Mr. Burton saved the day by using Green Light Responding, a term we use for what Shelly Gable calls *Active Constructive Responding* (ACR), the process of responding with appreciation and asking questions that make a person relive the experiences out loud. Sharing a personal positive event provides an opportunity to build social resources that can be drawn on in the future. When a student achieves a goal, teachers, parents, coaches, or other students can confirm the achievement by the power of their responses, showing that the person is valued. This has an emotionally empowering influence. People encouraged to capitalize will remember the experiences more, keep the experiences prominent in their minds when facing future challenges, and get more pleasure from their achievements. The goal of Green Light Responding is to help people get the most benefit out of their successes by taking the time to relive them out loud.

Shelly Gable has explored the different ways that people respond to someone else's good news. She finds these responses fall into the four categories shown in the table on the next page along with typical examples of each type of response.

	Constructive	Destructive
Active	Animated and wholehearted: "That's great, tell me more!"	Invalidating or a Put Down: "You were just lucky this time." "It's not really all that good."
Passive	Low key and unenthusiastic: "Oh, that's nice."	Shifting attention to something else: "Let me tell you about when that happened to me."

Green Light Responding is both Active and Constructive and is the most effective way to help someone benefit from positive experience. It is easy to see how the responses labeled Destructive cause people to withdraw from relationships. The keeper of the nightmare response to Emily Wright's news was Active and Destructive and could have put a complete damper on her enthusiasm. People stop sharing good news with others who respond in ways that are Passive and Destructive, for example, by saying, "Yes, that happens to me, too. Let me tell you about it." When the conversation is redirected to the other person, the first person feels no validation of the good thing that happened. What's interesting from Shelly Gable's research is that Passive Constructive Responding, responding without enthusiasm and interest, is just as deflating and unhelpful as the two destructive forms of response. Often Passive Constructive Responding occurs because people fail to engage respectfully.

Green Light Responding is a relationship-building skill that people can learn by paying attention and practicing. This is true for teachers, parents, and coaches. It is also true for students who can learn to respond effectively to each other.

Mindful Moment: *Green Light Responding*

Have a conversation with another parent, teacher, or coach where you each have an opportunity to capitalize about something that went well. Spend 10 minutes in each role, so you both capitalize and respond.

After switching roles, explore the process:
- *What did it feel like to be the person who was capitalizing?*
- *What did it feel like to be the person who was responding?*
- *What did you find energizing about the experience?*
- *What did you find difficult to do?*
- *Did any of your strengths come alive in capitalizing? In responding?*
- *Did any of your strengths hinder capitalizing? Responding?*
- *What did you learn from this exercise?*

Asking Appreciative Questions

We must look for what is good in an organization before we move forward. Where the organization wants to be is based on higher moments of where they have been.
—David Cooperrider and Diana Whitney, *Appreciative Inquiry*

Besides mentoring students in Culver's *Leadership Committee for Africa*, Nancy McKinnis works with all Culver junior girls to formulate a vision for the following year when they will be senior leaders. In the past, students would get together in the dormitories and look at problems to solve. Typically, the issues revolved around the bathrooms and people taking other people's food out of the refrigerator. So, Nancy flipped the process. Instead of asking them to identify the problems they needed to fix, she asked them reflective questions that helped them appreciate what is already going well: "When have you felt best about the dorm?" or "What do we want more of?"

Nancy observed that by celebrating the best of their earlier experiences, students could better build their vision of what the dorm and its residents could be like. Within their goals and objectives were ways of behaving that took care of the situations that they might have listed as problems. In fact the students came up with similar goals to the ones adults were already thinking about. They felt ownership for the process. These discussions happened on Wednesday morning meetings before class, and instead of falling back to sleep in their chairs or looking at the clock, students were so engaged that they lost track of time and had to be told that the session needed to come to a close so they could get to their first period class.

Nancy and the girls could have used a problem-centered approach. That would probably have put the girls in defensive positions because figuring out what went wrong ultimately leads to thinking about who messed up. "Somebody has to be responsible (and I don't want it to me)." Also, thinking about needing to fix something makes people feel deep down that they are not adequate. Using an appreciative approach made it easier for the girls to see what was already going right and to use that as the basis for future action.

Shaw High School in Cleveland, a school deemed an educational emergency, used an appreciative approach in a 3-week summer camp with a group of students who then passed proficiency exams and increased self-confidence and feelings of self-worth. At Wichita State, Jackie Glasgow studied teachers at an elementary school with many students from low socio-economic circumstances. The teachers used an appreciative approach that helped them collaborate in ways that strengthened instructional practices at the school, bringing the student body to a high standard of excellence.

An appreciative approach often works best when it involves a wide range of stakeholders: parents, teachers, administrators, coaches, students, custodians and even town members who aren't normally associated with the school other than paying taxes. Asking appreciative questions can serve several purposes. It can get people to focus on the best of what is and has been. It can shift them towards imagining new possibilities instead of jumping right into fixing problems. It can also help them develop plans and sustain energy as they put the plans into action.

Don Hewitt, the late founder and producer of the TV show *60 Minutes* said that there were four essential words to developing new and engaging content for the show: "Tell me a story." Stories can be the glue of culture, conveying nuances, joys, and frustrations. We learn to appreciate a person's story and are motivated to inquire more deeply. Questions can help the people in a group share their higher moments with others and uncover the good that already exists. When the higher moments of others are heard, there is a greater opportunity to appreciate them.

An appreciative approach focuses first on asking the right questions of group members such as "What are your Strengths? "What are your higher moments?" This provides an opportunity to affirm past and present strengths, and it tends to open people to new possibilities. This leads parents, teachers, administrators, and students toward a shared strengths-based foundation that opens dialogue and further inquiry.

One approach that comes from the *Appreciative Inquiry* literature is to get people to start any major change effort by asking each other questions in 1-1 interviews. Diana Whitney suggests trying interviews with "improbable pairs" where people you don't expect to be together are paired up to ask each other questions. This could happen by pairing up a senior and a freshman, or perhaps the principal and the custodian. Here are some questions that can be used in the interview process:

One-on-One Interview Questions

How do your strengths come alive in school?

What kinds of classes or activities race your motor?

Tell me about a time when you felt most excited at school.

Where do you see yourself ten years from now?

Where do you see the school ten years from now?

Appreciative questions can also help people share ideas about how they would like to the see the organization flourish. We worked with a high school basketball team who had collective dreams of winning the state championship. After talking it through, they found they also wanted to play well as a team, be unselfish, and support each other on and off the court.

Once a community has ideas about how it wants to be, it can start associating the ideas with realistic goals, such as the ones described in Chapter Nine on Goal Setting.

Once goals have been set, it is important to establish ways to sustain progress, such as doing "pulse checks" of the group at scheduled times throughout the year.

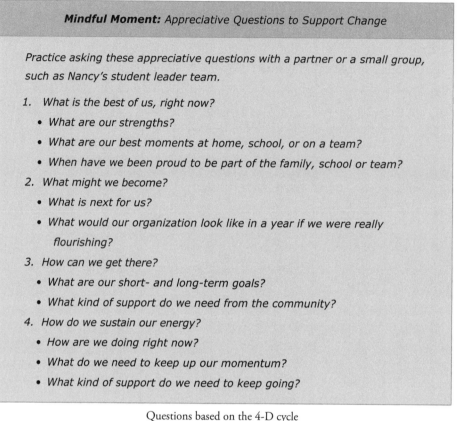

Mindful Moment: *Appreciative Questions to Support Change*

Practice asking these appreciative questions with a partner or a small group, such as Nancy's student leader team.

1. *What is the best of us, right now?*
   - *What are our strengths?*
   - *What are our best moments at home, school, or on a team?*
   - *When have we been proud to be part of the family, school or team?*
2. *What might we become?*
   - *What is next for us?*
   - *What would our organization look like in a year if we were really flourishing?*
3. *How can we get there?*
   - *What are our short- and long-term goals?*
   - *What kind of support do we need from the community?*
4. *How do we sustain our energy?*
   - *How are we doing right now?*
   - *What do we need to keep up our momentum?*
   - *What kind of support do we need to keep going?*

Questions based on the 4-D cycle
as described in Cooperrider and Whitney, *Appreciative Inquiry*, 2005.

Involving the Wider Community

Having high-quality connections within the school can be a model for behaviors needed in the wider community. High-quality connections with parents and community members can also help school members receive support and appreciation from the wider community.

We were contacted by Carl Hilling, the Superintendent of the Triton School Corporation, to facilitate an appreciative process with his administrative team. The Triton A-team consisted of members of the school committee, the elementary, and junior/senior high school principals, athletic director, transportation director, custodial-facilities director, chief financial officer, and director of technology. We started with some productive conversation about their strengths-of-action using the *Clifton StrengthsFinder* tool. In fact, two school committee members had an epiphany when they realized how one's strength of *competition* interacted with the other's *harmony* strength when dealing with hot-button issues.

One of the big dreams for the group was to upgrade the facilities. Several participants echoed concerns that realizing this goal may be difficult because it requires asking taxpayers for money, and many residents hadn't had children in the system for years. A pause came across the group, and after what seemed to be an eternity, one of the school committee members, who had been relatively quiet for most of the session, declared: "To reach this goal we need to develop better relationships with them, just like we are doing with each other today. We need to have smaller open-forums to carry on the discussion." At this moment, the head nods were going up and down, whereas before some were going side-to-side.

The A-team then paid particular attention to the process of sustaining and achieving the goals they set for themselves. One year later, we once again met with the A-team. The team was more than ready to set their sights on the following year. The group focused their dreams and goals on better coordinating interdepartmental communications, developing ways to demonstrate staff appreciation and school pride among all employees, students and parents, and upgrading facilities, to name a few. An appreciative approach is not magical, but by following the process, it provides a different pro-active angle of vision for school stakeholders to rise to the occasion by bringing out the best in each other.

This chapter centered on the importance of behaviors that lead to high-quality connections—moments that energize people and bring out the best in them. High-quality connections are possible in every exchange, no matter how brief, no matter with whom. High-quality connections can happen between teachers and other teachers, between teachers and parents, between administrators and parents, and between all of them and the students whose education is the mission of the school. High-quality connections can even occur with people in the community who support schools with their taxes but may not have much else to do with them.

All of us can learn behaviors that generate high-quality connections. We can learn to greet each other by name, respond actively and constructively to good news, and ask the appreciative questions that build the future on the best of the present.

In the Afterword, we ask you take all you have learned throughout this book and apply it to your next steps in building strengths, resilience, and relationships at home, in school, and on the athletic field.

Afterword

A Call to Action
The Challenge of Change:
From *Mindful Moments* to Best Possible Future Selves

As readers of this book, you have the potential to be pioneers in bringing *SMART Strengths* to your family and school community. We hope that you find that as exciting as we do!

The benefits of the practices described in this book can be immense. They can transform a satisfactory school into an outstanding one and they can help a failing school surpass schools that are resting on their laurels. These practices are open to any school whose teachers, coaches, and parents choose to explore them. In fact, all of us have the opportunity to be leaders when we use our strengths powers for good. Best of all, they do not require a large financial investment. It is the currency of healthy human interaction that makes *SMART Strengths* work.

This book contains many *Mindful Moments* and activities to help you explore and practice new habits of thought, speech, and behavior to make and *be* the change you desire in your school community. Achieving a more strengths-based school or school system may be challenging for adult mentors, whether they feel that their schools are faced with overwhelming needs or that they are already successful. Rob Evans, a Boston psychologist who has presented talks on school change to over 1400 schools, reminds us that to help people change, they need to understand that "change can beget conflicts. Resistance is normal and necessary, but can increase confusion." Therefore, it is important to be patient and offer generous understanding when working to create a more strengths-based community. "If it isn't broken, don't fix it!" may be the mantra of your school. However, even when things do not appear to be broken, they can become considerably better.

To assist you in making positive change happen, we invite you to reflect on three questions you may ask yourself and others who have read this book: What? So What? and Now What? What do you know differently now than you did before you read the book? What are or could be the changes taking place in your school? What will be the lasting impact of building a strengths-based school community?

What: Because of this book, you now have access to substantial Positive Psychology research-based information coupled with practical learning strategies and activities that can benefit both you and the young people you serve. These activities, grounded in *SMART Strengths*, can have a beneficial impact on both student performance outcomes and the well-being of all members of the school community.

So What: Chris Peterson, esteemed Positive Psychology researcher and University of Michigan professor, was our advisor and mentor while at UPenn MAPP. He taught us to go beyond the *what* of research findings to the *so what?* What can research do for us and for the young people with whom we live, work, and play?

We believe that young people develop through the feast of their care-givers— parents, teachers and athletic coaches, to name a few. When adult mentors intentionally form strengths-based partnerships on behalf of the young people they serve, this provides a foundation for increased resilience, achievement and well-being. In a time of increasing academic standards coupled with declining budget flexibility, now is the time to leverage what is best about each person in our communities. Positive Education works, first by benefiting teachers personally, and also by making it easier for students to engage with and persist in the work they must do to master academic material. On this foundation, and with your strength-based leadership, you can create a school culture that supports the caring, trusting relationships that distinguish excellent schools from their poor and mediocre peers, and that will be rooted in realistic optimism and resilience needed to weather change and growth.

Now what: Marianne Williamson, an internationally known lecturer and author, nudges us in her book, *A Return to Love*, to use our strengths as we make a better world for our children and ourselves. She says,

Our deepest fear is not that we are inadequate. Our deepest fear is that we are powerful beyond measure. It is our light, not our darkness that most frightens us. We ask ourselves, Who am I to be brilliant, gorgeous, talented, fabulous? Actually, who are you not to be?

There is nothing enlightened about shrinking so that other people won't feel insecure around you. We are all meant to shine, as children do.

And as we let our own light shine, we unconsciously give other people permission to do the same. As we are liberated from our own fear, our presence automatically liberates others.

We can bring the light out in ourselves, and give other people permission to do the same. We can become *social emotional leaders*, people who shape the future for the better. Louis Alloro, a leadership consultant and graduate of the University of Pennsylvania's Master of Applied Positive Psychology program, believes that social-emotional leadership rests on the idea that positive cultural change is possible, but must emerge from within primary networks, like families, schools, and teams.

In His Own Words: Louis Alloro, Louis Alloro and Associates, New York, NY

Social-Emotional Leaders believe that change is not only possible; it is inevitable, and shaped by our own designs. Social-Emotional Leaders do not have all the answers—just the questions, the vision, and some of the tools that might lead the network in a positive direction. Schools could serve as the gateway for the dissemination of the tools and knowledge coming from and into the homes they support.

By inviting others into intentional and appreciative dialogue about what it is the school, family or team needs, what it is they want, and what it is they value; character strengths, resilience and healthy relationships can be built and meaning can be constructed from within the network itself.

Social-Emotional Leaders are parents, teachers, coaches, and role models in a way that helps people within their networks become inspired and rewired. They help others find their voices, build their strengths, and realize what is possible in creating the lives we want to live. In other words, Social-Emotional Leaders help others find their better selves in accordance with what they value.

This is the call-to-action.

As you read this book you were given opportunities to capture your in-the-moment thoughts in *Mindful Moments*. Now it is time to revisit these ideas and turn those thoughts into action. Have you imagined what a strengths-based community would be like and hoped you could create one? What have you learned that you would like everyone to know?

Mindful Moment: *A Call to Action*

As you have read SMART Strengths you have had the opportunity to record your in-the-mind learning. Whether you and a friend or colleagues have read this book together or if instead you have read it solo, we hope you already have ideas about how you would apply what you have learned to benefit your school, your students, or your children.

We recommend that you get one or more others to read this book—a friend, fellow parent, a book group, a colleague, your department, or your parent-teacher association. Then perform this Mindful Moment again together and plan to support each other as you take the next step to share a strengths-based approach within the community. **We want you to put your ideas to work!**

Based on your collected Mindful Moments, list your SMART assets:

Your Strengths: *Which ones most resonate with you and will be essential for your success?* _____
_____
_____
_____
_____

Your Resilience Habits: *How will you approach challenges that will occur along the bridge to change?* _____
_____
_____
_____
_____

Your Supportive Relationships: *Who will be your personal site team?*
_____
_____
_____
_____

Your Best Possible Future:

What would it be like if everyone in your community used SMART Strengths, practiced resilience strategies, and created high-quality connections? Imagine a "Best Possible Future" for your family, team, school, and community. Spend time embellishing this narrative. Include many sensory details. Imagine what it will feel like to accomplish this future. Go beyond words and use whatever else helps you to put flesh on the future story. You can add a collage, vision board, and/or pictures that show you the change you want to make. _____

_____

_____

_____

_____

_____

_What's the first step that you can take to shape the future of your family, school, team or community for the better? What will you do?_____

_____

_____

_____

_____

_____

When will you take this step? Fill in the "Writing a Goal Plan" Mindful Moment on page 328 in Appendix B. We look forward to hearing your Strengths Stories!

_____

_____

_____

_____

_____

At the beginning of the book, we quoted Robert Quinn, author of _Building the Bridge As You Walk On It_. We reprise the quotation here and hope you are inspired to act!

When we change ourselves, we change how other people see us and respond to us.
When we change ourselves. We change the world.

Appendix A

Positive Education at Culver — A Case Study

Is it really possible to change the culture of a school in the ways described in this book, to incorporate a focus on strengths in everything that goes on? This appendix answers that question affirmatively by showing what happened at the Culver Academies between 2006 and 2010. Similar changes have occurred in other schools, including a rural public school district, Triton School Corporation in Bourbon, Indiana and Christel House Academy, an urban charter school in Indianapolis, Indiana that has many students coming from deprived backgrounds. There are many examples and stories from Culver, Triton, and Christel House Academy, Indianapolis throughout the book, but this appendix demonstrates how changes can be made, describing both the enabling conditions and the growing involvement of people throughout the school system. Changes started with school administrators and teachers and radiated out to include parents, students, alumni, and other community members.

In brief, this appendix discusses the following aspects of change, illustrating them primarily with examples from the Culver Academies.

- Enabling conditions that made creating a strengths-based culture possible.
- Incorporating a focus on strengths into the school mission.
- Performing initial staff training that generated buy-in and enthusiasm. In the process, the school developed a shared language for talking about strengths. This language facilitates communication among teachers, coaches, parents, staff, and students.
- Using appreciative and strengths-based approaches to solve cultural problems among teachers. The example given here is the need to move from departmental silos to a more collaborative culture among teachers in different departments.
- Establishing ongoing training practices to help experienced teachers lead new teachers into the strengths-based approach. This was necessary to convert the initial change into a long-lasting, self-replicating system, as opposed to a fading fad.
- Helping parents learn a strengths-based approach to learning so that they can support student learning effectively at home.
- Incorporating strengths-based learning in activities performed by students moving through the high school grades in order to reinforce student awareness of their own personal strengths.
- Involving alumni in the character formation of senior students.

Culture Change in Brief

At all three schools, we found moving toward a strengths-based culture started with a conviction at the top levels of school administration that a strengths-based culture would improve school outcomes and result in better education for students as well as a better working environment for school personnel. At the Culver Academies, Triton School Corporation, and Christel House Academy we made a variety of presentations to the faculty, gaining a core group of committed teachers where the message stuck. These teachers were curious and willing to explore the various ideas represented in *Mindful Moments* throughout this book in their classrooms. Over time, as the core group experienced positive outcomes, the message spread and other faculty started trying out the approaches, growing the size of the core group. As the beneficial outcomes became apparent, other administrators and teachers began to see the value and jump on bus.

For example, at Culver, original support for the *SMART Strengths* training came from John Buxton, Head of School. He was impressed by the messages that John Yeager brought back from the MAPP program. John's passionate belief convinced Buxton to put the ideas into practice. Support available from Dave and Sherri helped John Yeager turn the broad principles into the implementable programs described throughout this book.

In the case of Triton School Corporation, Jeremy Riffle, the elementary school principle, bought in immediately and then started soliciting faculty interest. Eventually, the principal at the Junior/Senior High School joined the process as well, as he started seeing the beneficial changes occurring in the elementary school.

In the case of Christel House Academy, the principal of the K-9 school visited Culver and was impressed by what he saw. He arranged for presentations with his faculty. Eventually the core group grew in size and a variety of enthusiastic teachers found that the practices were relatively easy to do and returned benefits far beyond the effort involved.

Do changes have to start from the top? Could a group of teachers decide to make these changes by themselves, starting at a grass roots level? That could work, although the support provided by an involved administration eased the way for teachers at these three schools.

Incorporating Strengths into the School Mission

At the Culver Academies, the mission statement of the school is an important document that guides many decisions at both the strategic planning level and the every-day operational level. The mission statement binds those involved in the school together in a common purpose and provides an opportunity for all stakeholders to declare what they think is important about the school. The existing Culver mission statement formed a fruitful foundation for a strengths-based learning environment:

Culver educates its students for leadership and responsible citizenship in society by developing and nurturing the whole individual—mind, spirit, and body— through integrated programs that emphasize the cultivation of character.

—The Culver Mission

Strengths-based learning took root naturally in this environment because it was easy to see how the principles of Positive Psychology contribute to the established shared goals of developing the whole individual and cultivating character.

Culver's mission is founded on some of the doctrines of the ancient Greek philosophers, who claimed that people knew what was right, but did not always do what was right. Learning more about strengths can help people understand the right and good and participate in the complex activity needed to build a good life. Plato suggested that people needed to develop three wills—the intellectual will (mind), the emotional will (spirit), and the physical will (body). At Culver, this understanding translates to Academic programs (Mind), Wellness/Athletic programs (Body), and formal Leadership programs (Spirit). In all three programs, an awareness of the unique strengths of each individual provides a solid foundation for developing self-control and leadership.

It is beyond the scope of this book to describe how a school system develops or renews a well-defined mission statement. What we do know is that many stakeholders in a school community participate in the creation and maintenance of the mission. Whether the mission statement already exists or needs to be developed, an important step in developing a strengths-based culture is to show how it supports the school mission and how the school mission can make it possible.

Testing the Water — Faculty and Staff Training

Once the goal was formed to bring Positive Education principles to all aspects of school life, the next step was faculty training. At Culver, twenty-two teachers volunteered for the first program, *SMART Strengths.1.* The first group completed a 3-day intensive program on building an environment that supported strengths, resilience, and high-quality connections. Since then, the training program has been extended and offered to a majority of the faculty. This program includes:

- Ways to heighten positive emotion in themselves and their students, including an understanding of the value of positive emotions
- Strategies to use their own strengths to be more optimistic, resilient, and effective as teachers
- Relationship-building approaches for building high-quality connections that maintain high levels of energy and optimism at school

Faculty and staff participants identify their own strengths by completing and interpreting the VIA-IS and the *Clifton StrengthsFinder* (CSF). This helps them be more ready to identify student strengths. They developed strategies to foster a strengths-based approach to enhance motivation, optimism, resilience, and savoring in their respective areas of responsibility (classroom, living unit, visual and performing arts, athletics, and so on). By learning about character strengths and ways to build and apply them, the teachers acknowledged, owned, and applied their own strengths, learned to value their authentic selves, and increased their effectiveness. They found this information frequently valuable in their work with groups of students in all phases of school life, as well as in their relationships with each other.

One of the positive side effects of our first faculty training was that it allowed teachers from different departments who didn't know each other very well to start conversations about what is good at the school. In fact, one teacher commented that he didn't even know that another teacher he partnered with in an exercise actually worked at the school. Another said, "I have been given license to use my strengths, and guidance to use them wisely without exaggeration . . . to attain higher goals." Many educators are all too familiar with the stereotypical teacher's room banter about what's wrong. In the workshop, they practiced becoming aware of and talking about what was already right.

After the second year of faculty training, we asked staff members throughout the school to join the faculty in the program. This has included staff supervisors and staff from the grounds, buildings, administrative services (print shop), custodial, technology services, residence directors, dormitory counselors, and health center personnel. Teachers and staff are not forced to participate, but those who see the benefits tend to nudge other teachers to get involved.

We also introduced a follow-up program, *SMART Strengths.2*. This is for teachers and staff for whom the strengths message has really stuck over the past year or two. We provide a deeper, more individualized approach for faculty and staff who are in positions to influence curriculum development, staff supervision, and leadership programs.

One outcome of the training programs is that a language of strengths has become viral at Culver, as many faculty, staff, administrators, and students share a common vocabulary for talking about strengths and a common set of skills for recognizing strengths in themselves and others. This changes the way people talk as they work their way through the day-to-day learning activities. The focus has shifted from what does not work—student weaknesses and failures—to what does work—finding the ways that each student learns how to best navigate their adolescent journey.

An Appreciative Approach to Change

SMART Strengths training had support from top administration and from classroom faculty, but it took longer before it began sticking with the academic middle managers—the academic department chairs. Few department chairs volunteered for the early rounds of training. Kathy Lintner, Culver's Dean of Faculty, and Kevin MacNeil, Culver's Academic Dean, saw this discrepancy and decided to take action to involve department chairs, believing departments would function better if they followed some of the practices conveyed in *SMART Strengths* training, especially those that help people experience high-quality connections in their interactions with each other.

Department chairs have a leadership responsibility to the teachers in their departments as well as a three-quarter teaching load. School life can be hectic in a boarding school, and the bi-weekly luncheon meetings did not always involve a high-level of energy. For the most part, the Dean of Faculty and the Academic Dean presided over the meetings, with some input from the various chairs.

One of the issues within the group was that each department—math, science, humanities, modern and classical languages, fine arts, leadership education, and wellness education—lived in their own "silos of excellence," focusing on internal department issues, without looking at what was going on in other departments.

So, when the Deans met with John and the rest of chairs to discuss a way to involve the group in the changes going on in the school, the group decided first to work on a shared goal—to become a collaborative team to build the future of Culver. To help realize this goal, the chairs would implement a strengths exploration, and then use appreciative questions to support change, as described on page 268 in Chapter Ten.

Exploring Strengths

When the chairpersons met at the end of the school year, they had read Tom Rath and Barry Conchie's book, *Strengths Based Leadership* and completed the *CliftonStrenghsFinder* inventory. Some members of the group found their individual results confirming, while others found them surprising and illuminating. By using the *SMART* Model framework (refer back to Chapter Two), the group then shared their strengths and tendered their observations of others' assets in a 360° Strengths Gallery. Each chairperson talked about how his or her strengths came alive in his or her work, and smiles came to other teachers as they acknowledged and reinforced what they heard.

John learned something very interesting about one of the department chairs. Typically, this person would remain reserved during meetings, and only occasionally offered a thought or opinion. John thought that he wasn't very interested. Only when John realized that *deliberative* was one of this chair's strengths, did he realize that this person needed to carefully and fully understand issues before responding. The teacher's behavior matched up perfectly with the *Clifton StrengthsFinder* definition of *deliberative*: "You are careful, vigilant, a private person, you know the world is unpredictable and risky." Once John realized this, he could change the way he perceived the reserved responses.

After the first session, the group was provided a handout with a matrix showing each chairperson's top strengths. The matrix now serves as a reference document during discussions. It is a reminder for each person to try to play to the strengths of each other.

Culver Department Chairs — Strengths Matrix					
Dean of Faculty	Learner	Arranger	Intellection	Input	Connectedness
Academic Dean	Strategic	Learner	Achiever	Connectedness	Intellection
Leadership	Context	Achiever	Belief	Analytical	Deliberative
Languages	Harmony	Connectedness	Relator	Arranger	Responsibility
Science	Input	Command	Learner	Ideation	Intellection
Fine Arts	Empathy	Responsibility	Developer	Maximizer	Learner

Library	Input	Woo	Adaptability	Includer	Ideation
Math	Analytical	Ideation	Deliberative	Relator	Responsibility
Wellness Ed.	Includer	Developer	Relator	Strategic	Empathy
Humanities	Harmony	Learner	Consistency	Achiever	Competition

Asking Appreciative Questions

After the *SMART Strengths* activities, there was high energy in the room that generated energy for asking appreciative questions. The chairs now asked each other about their higher moments at school during the past year, a reflection that tends to generate energy and optimism for change. The following inset shows some of the responses to the first question on page 268 in Chapter Ten, "What is the best of us right now?"

The Best of What Is

- **Humanities:** Speaking, writing, reading, globalization focus in courses, along with enhanced collegiality and cohesiveness
- **Leadership:** Collaboration with the Center for Character Excellence and the Humanities Department in the development of the *Leadership, Character and Civil War* class
- **Wellness:** Team effort and collaboration in overcoming staff attrition.
- **Math:** Ownership of "math department"—hence, energy created
- **Academic Affairs:** Christmas atmosphere drew people together; healing has begun from past losses
- **Library:** Staff getting vision of teaching in information literacy classes
- **Fine Arts:** Collegiality; Arts and Letters Hall of Fame—new inductees—students, instructors involved
- **Head of Schools (Dean of Faculty/Academic Dean):** Flexibility, focus, team effort in dealing with illnesses; Merit Scholarships: Faculty-driven process with a student focus
- **Science:** Collaborative change process in regard to Honors and Physics First

Looking at their answers together helped the group realize that they had some things in common. They then went on to the second question, "What might we become?" Some of their answers are shown in the next inset. Once again, they found some interesting commonalities, especially about collaborating and doing meaningful work.

> As a chairs group, our dreams about what we could become include being:
> - Sharing and Caring — New and different support; creativity
> - Open to more interaction time
> - Filter to Department
> - Meaningful to chairs and departments
> - Collaborating towards goals
> - Appreciative to colleagues
> - Encouraging — Building emotionally, etc. collegiality, clarity
> - Involved in collective meaningful work
> - Open to what works best
> - Willing to acknowledge individuality of faculty issues.
> - Responsible for helping each other be better department chairs
> - Responsible for the function of this group

Next the group discussed how to move toward the attributes shown in the previous inset. They established the three goals shown in the next inset and began to address the means and support needed to co-construct a plan to realize the four goals.

> - Create/Complete the new Faculty Rank and Promotion Model
> - Work as a strengths-based team in support of one another and the mission shared by the group
> - Establish a strengths-based culture (common language within all departments and levels)
> - Clarify the roles of the Department Chairs in academic policy making.

The chairs now see themselves as responsible for the delivery and sustainability of the agreed upon goals. They have developed a rapport for collaborative work through these appreciative questions and have developed the following shared mission to guide their decision-making.

> To bring out the best in Culver, the Chairs team requires the group to meet on a consistent basis, to be encouraging of each, and be collaborative towards reaching goals. This means that we play to our individual and each other's strengths and act as a filter to our respective departments.
>
> We are:
> - Ambassadors for individual departments and Culver as a whole
> - Active Sharers/Communicators of the broader community view with departments
> - Integrators (academic, student life, athletics, wellness)
> - Arbiters/Keepers of the Culver Culture
> - Promoters of Culver as a career and a calling

Over the next eighteen months, the chairs met regularly to work on the new Faculty Rank and Promotion Model. As ambassadors for the faculty, they were instrumental in consistent communication with their departments to make the new Faculty Rank and Promotion system a reality.

On-going Strengths Training in Academic Departments

With the department chairs on board, we then started working with the various academic departments (humanities, science, mathematics, modern and classical languages, fine arts, leadership education, wellness education, and academic affairs) to introduce strengths-based practices. In several departments, there were many faculty members who had already completed *SMART Strengths.1* and some *SMART Strengths.2* training. The department chairs viewed these teachers as good models for those teachers who were new to strengths work. In order to develop a process that could be replicated across the school, we ended up working primarily with the Humanities department. The Humanities department at Culver integrates the study of English and history, and has a large group of faculty. One year, with retirements and other attrition, six new teachers of various experience came to the department, so it was a good place to show how to handle turnover. One new teacher, who had six years of experience in another school, mentioned later that he was very nervous about how other teachers would see his strengths, and also was concerned how we would guestimate other teacher's strengths when participating in the 360° Strengths Gallery (refer to page 81 in Chapter Two). He was pleasantly surprised with the outcome.

It was especially challenging to educate teachers who had fixed mindsets on classroom learning, as described in Chapter Eight. The strengths-based approach to student learning represented a huge sea change in how they have typically done business. Fortunately, seeing other teachers have successes with a strengths-based approach tended to nudge them to be more open-minded. In one case, the strengths-based approach helped a teacher who had been frustrated for many years because each one of her students absorbed course material at different rates. When she saw her students as possessing unique strengths, she was able to differentiate the process of learning by teaching to their individual assets.

The Parent Strengths Initiative (PSI)

After considerable faculty and staff training, we realized that we really needed to do a better job of involving parents. We started with the parents of our incoming ninth graders. During registration in August, we asked all parents of ninth graders to review the 24 Values in Action strengths in a handout and to circle the top five strengths they believed their child possessed. We asked them about their perceptions of their child's personal characteristics and individual qualities. We also asked them, "What can you tell us so that we might know your child well? Even small details are of interest." Most parents were intrigued by this exercise. We later found that when there is a concern about a student, having parents and teachers start off the discussion with a review of the child's strengths often allows a more productive dialogue to ensue about the challenges the student faces.

Coordinated through the Humanities department, we are now engaged in providing ninth grade parents with an opportunity to guesstimate the strengths of their child and also to assess their own strengths. This extends the shared vocabulary to parents. It also helps parents play to their own strengths to support the educational process, joining teachers in modeling leadership behaviors for students. Starting from a position of strength helps build strong parent-teacher-student relationships, and creates an atmosphere conducive to constructive resolution of misunderstandings and student challenges.

The impact of these practices goes beyond outcomes in school. Parents who learn strengths-based practices can carry them out into the community, having an impact on their own relationships and achievement—at school, in the home, the office, the board room, the house of worship, the neighborhood, and so on. In fact, several parents remarked that they have completed the *Clifton StrengthsFinder* in the work environment, and were very excited that their children at Culver were having an opportunity to learn about their strengths, too.

In His Own Words, Kevin Danti, 9th Grade Humanities Teacher and Football Coach

The immediate gain from having the VIA Strengths is that we have a set list of vocabulary, a set list of strengths that helps the faculty and parents understand the student in a similar way. So the shared vocabulary automatically leads to improved communication. I could use words through email that both the parents and the student were familiar with.

In the case of my student Brian, both the father and I saw a boy on the athletic field and a boy outside the classroom that drew upon his strengths to be a success. What the father had trouble seeing was that Brian's strength of persistence was helping him in the classroom. The specific issue was in terms of a classroom assignment. Brian came up to me immediately and told me, "I don't think I can recover from this grade." That boy would never come up to me on the football field after a negative play. He felt a sense of victim mentality in the classroom that he did not experience on the football field or in other life outside that classroom. That was one immediate dialogue that Brian's father and I had. Brian has grown into an understanding that his strength of persistence doesn't automatically leave him when he enters the classroom. But there was something particular about his previous education. One teacher had run him down the year before he came to Culver saying, "You are just an athlete." To this day, Brian doesn't understand why that doesn't bother him on the football field. He feels more empowered in my classroom now.

One of the most challenging things that I have had is to empower children with a sense of ownership in their education. I believe that before children can feel empowered, they need to be motivated. The motivation can't come from within me. I can't force that on a student. They have to find what motivates them. Having a dialogue with a parent helps me understand that student outside my classroom. I get a full profile from the narrative. I get to see a snapshot of 14 years before he came to me. And that is essential, because it helps me quickly understand my student. Understanding their situation helps, and some of them have a tough situation that you have to account for before they sit in the classroom. The narrative has helped me understand that student on a more complete level.

Building on Strengths with Students

The language of strengths is important for students as well. Appendix B describes ways to use the *Mindful Moments* with students. Here we describe some of the activities carried out at Culver to help students become aware of their own strengths, be able to recognize strengths in other people, and put those strengths to work in service of their academic, leadership, and athletic goals.

Strengths Exploration Activities Across the Grades

All ninth grade students complete the VIA-Youth in their respective Humanities classes. They create a file of their top strengths to store on their respective computers. Each teacher also stores all of the student strengths file in his or her computer. New tenth and eleventh grade students also complete the VIA-Youth.

All eleventh grade students complete the *Clifton StrengthsFinder* (CSF) instrument and read Rath and Conchie's *Strengths Based Leadership*. Students become more aware of how their strengths fit into four leadership domains: Executing, Influencing, Relationship Building and Strategic.

SMART Strengths in the Curriculum

Throughout their Culver careers, students have opportunities to use their strengths in the academic curriculum, in activities, in organizations, on the athletic field, and in the dormitories. A common strengths language is threaded throughout the community. Adult mentors also provide opportunities for students to practice the behaviors that build resilience and healthy relationships described throughout this book.

While a focus on strengths shows up in varying degrees in all the academic departments, there is a particular emphasis in the Humanities, Leadership Education and Wellness Education, with additional focus in Culver's Student Life/Residential Education programs. Although co-educational in academic programs, Culver's female and male students participate in separate, but coordinated leadership systems. The Culver Academies are independent college preparatory boarding schools comprised of Culver Military Academy and Culver Girls Academy. Culver Girls Academy residential program includes a distinctive leadership program known as the CGA Prefect System. Within the warm and nurturing dorm environment, the leadership program comes to life as young women assume meaningful leadership roles. This democratic model of governing allows girls to have a voice in their dorms and campus life through a formalized committee structure. Culver Military

Academy uses the military model to educate and train young men in practical leadership. While maintaining its focus on academic, athletic, and extracurricular excellence, CMA integrates hands-on leadership with every campus endeavor.

Grade 9

Humanities. Reading *The Odyssey* helps ninth grade students understand the tension between the weakness of will and the strength of will that they encounter in their own lives. Students reflect on their own character strengths and shadow strengths and compare them to those of the major characters.

Student Life. In Culver Girls Academy (CGA) at the ninth grade level there are three components to the Residential Education program, with two central themes: *Leading Self* and *Strength of Friendship*. This program introduces students to the role of citizenship in a community and teaches them skills for making wise choices and leading in an appropriate and respectful manner. At Culver Military Academy (CMA), the focus is on followership and performance. The critical skill entails being a good team member. All ninth graders focus on being positive contributors to the community by learning to place others before self and to correct others when needed. These behaviors are the essence of good followership.

Grade 10

Humanities. Students read Shakespeare's *Othello* and John Knowles' *A Separate Peace*, among other texts, to see how characters in literature and history deal with adversity and how various explanatory styles resonate in their own lives.

Leadership Education. A course called *Character and the Application of Leadership Skills* introduces students to important elements of character and the role of virtues in applying basic leadership concepts and skills. The course weaves themes of character and virtue into discussions of self-concept, leadership traits and characteristics, goal-setting, decision-making, communications, active listening, peer counseling, assertiveness, conflict management, and problem-solving.

Student Life. In CGA, the tenth grade program takes the concept of "leading self" to the next level. Students work toward greater self-awareness, and are encouraged to act with the needs and concerns of others in mind. Lessons focus on the history, importance, and structure of the CGA prefect system, speaking to the theme, *Knowledge and Tradition*. Tenth grade students affirm their character strengths while developing the idea of collaboration. In CMA, the tenth grade focus is on helping other individuals and the entire team. Students practice the skills of following and assisting. Students learn to assess and evaluate followers and followership in situations within Culver and among their peers. They also learn the difference between being good at following orders and doing what one is told compared to acting on one's own initiative by engaging with the organization.

Wellness Education. All sophomores take a one-semester course called *Foundations of Health Behavior*. Students use this opportunity to see how their respective strengths support healthy-decision making, as well as how the shadow side of certain strengths may hinder the ability to make wise and informed decisions. Students are introduced to the *Think it Through* and *RAMP Up* resilience strategies described in Chapter Seven.

Grade 11

Humanities. Students analyze character strengths and leadership traits in figures in American history and literature, including classics such as *The Crucible, The Great Gatsby*, and *The Catcher in the Rye*.

Leadership Education. Students take a one-term class called *Ethics: Virtues and Character Education*. They practice integrating character and virtues into all facets of their daily lives. Students learn the concept of moral leadership—a balance between legitimate authority and the four cardinal virtues (wisdom, courage, moderation and justice) that form the Culver Leadership culture.

Student Life. In CGA, the 11th grade theme is *Strength and Justice*. Students implement the lessons learned in earlier years of student life/leadership education. They are granted the responsibility and honor of serving in the Prefect System. Serving as a prefect helps them learn that virtuous behavior is critical when leading others. As the juniors are empowered to lead and make a difference in the lives of others, they continue to learn through the *Leadership and Life Skills* curriculum, which covers topics such as goal setting, identifying action strengths, appreciative inquiry, dealing with crisis and conflict, and ethical decision making. They establish goals and a vision for their dorm in the upcoming year, as described in Chapter Nine. Students complete these workshops to prepare themselves for the responsibilities of senior leadership. In CMA, the junior year gives the emerging leader an opportunity to work on the skill of building teams and developing others. The focus is on *direct leadership,* meaning leadership of those with whom one has daily contact on a meaningful level. Leaders are responsible for the direction of two to five other individuals. Juniors focus on leveraging strengths within a team through analysis and asking appreciative questions.

Grade Twelve

Humanities. Two senior electives focus on character strengths, resilience, and leadership: *Mythology and Literature*; and *Leadership, Character, and the American Civil War*. Students compare their strengths with the strengths of the characters in the literature. They also focus on how characters are resilient and build or don't build positive relationships with others.

Leadership Education. In the *Servant Leadership Practicum*, all students use leadership experiences, academic learning, and personal interests to design and execute a service project that will contribute to a community of their choosing. The practicum is done either individually or within a team of students. Students then complete a web-based portfolio that illustrates the application of decision-making and problem-solving skills, and on communication, planning and reflection in all aspects of their project. In teaming projects, students are aware of and play to each other's strengths in the development and implementation of the project.

Student Life. In CGA, the residential education program culminates with the theme, *Service and Success*. Students are now prepared to lead their peers and their school. Seniors make up the governing bodies of the Prefect System. They are responsible for teaching and empowering younger students, as well as for modeling the high standards to which they hold others. The *Leadership and Life Skills* program for twelfth graders includes guest speakers and workshops addressing a variety of topics that will prepare students for transition into their next stage of life. In CMA, the critical skill for 12th grade students is both to lead and to build leaders. As they supervise others they acquire the ability to assess and evaluate both leaders and leadership in a variety of situations.

Wellness Education. All seniors take *Health Issues*, an eight-week academic course. Students acquire a deep understanding of personal, community, national, and world health issues. There is an emphasis on critical thinking and moral interpretation of health information and health behavior. Students gain a high level of understanding of the biochemical, sociological, and psychological concepts in relation to the need for happiness, the pursuit of happiness, the roots of addiction, basic desires of human nature, and the seeking of personal and social fulfillment. Students refer to strengths, positive emotions, and resilience strategies throughout the course and complete a digital portfolio of their Culver wellness experience. This includes goal setting for the future.

College Counseling. Culver seniors aspire to convey their strengths in ways that appeal to college admissions officers, who look for capable students that will bring a variety of assets to their institutions. The prospective student's story plays a large part in appealing to admissions officers. By putting a name and action to their strengths, students may better articulate their assets and what they do well. By referencing their *Values in Action Inventory* (VIA-Youth) and/or their *Clifton StrengthsFinder* results, Culver seniors have learned how to demonstrate how their strengths come alive. *The Common Application* provides seniors with a variety of essay options—significant experiences, ethical dilemmas, issues of concern, paragons, characters in literature, and life experiences. Culver seniors learn to use the elements of *SMART Strengths*—Spotting, Managing, Advocating, Relating and Training—to address different essay choices.

SMART Strengths in Athletics

Culver's sports teams foster a strengths-based approach to athletics that affects relationships between coaches and athletes and among teammates. Athletes who have developed their strengths can call on a foundation of well-formed habits in aspiring to true enjoyment, satisfaction, and excellence in sport.

Culver coaches use the *Appreciative Questions to Support Change* activity listed in Chapter Ten to help teams set guidelines and goals. Teams lay the foundations for positive relationships by sharing their strengths. Then they reflect on their higher moments in the previous season to answer the question, "What is the best of us, right now?" Players and coaches participate in the process, with small groups writing their higher moments on large pieces of newsprint taped to the wall. Then players and coaches go to each poster to read what each group wrote. There are usually a number of players with similar high moments, so the review helps form and reinforce high-quality connections. The energy in the room is usually palpable. From this point, the team is ready to talk about hopes and dreams for the upcoming season and voice what they commit to do to make their hopes materialize (Refer to Chapter Nine and Chapter Ten).

Involving Alumni

Every March, approximately 60 Culver alumni return to campus to show how they play to their strengths in their various careers. All twelfth grade students attend symposia and meet in small groups with alumni mentors to discuss leadership dilemmas in the workplace. The alumni and students discuss and compare their strengths, both VIA and CSF and then talk about how their strengths inform their decisions. Seniors have a wonderful opportunity to listen to ways that various alumni exhibit strengths, resilience, and the ability to form positive relationships.

Conclusion

This appendix shows that incorporating *SMART Strengths* can affect all aspects of life in a school and can take advantage of the strengths of all stakeholders—not just administrators, teachers, and students, but also parents and alumni. The *SMART Strengths* program at Culver Academies started with a committed Head of School, gained momentum through a core set of teachers, and then spread to more teachers, department heads, and staff across the school. Teachers learned new skills and vocabulary that helped them bring out the best in students and talk effectively with parents, even when dealing with significant challenges. Teachers who bought into the approach early became mentors for other teachers so that the approaches became self-sustaining without requiring constant renewal by outside consultants. The ideas of strengths, resilience, and high-quality connections were incorporated in the curriculum and had an impact on athletic programs. The programs described in this appendix emerged from the talents and strengths of many people working together to support a shared mission that included bringing out the strengths of students in all aspects of life.

Appendix B

Strengths, Resilience, and Relationship Activities for Youth

We feel strongly that as a parent, teacher, or coach you need to both practice and model strengths, resilience, and relationship skills in your own life. Not only will this benefit you as an adult, it really is the only way you will be prepared to guide youth through the principles presented in *SMART Strengths*.

In this section of the book, we have collected the *Activities* and *Mindful Moments* from *SMART Strengths*, provided additional activities, and presented them for use with youth. You will notice that some of the activities are scripted like lesson plans. These scripts were contributed by colleagues working in education who also have completed a MAPP degree. For each activity, it will help you to think through the following:

Hopes and Goals (Objectives): What do you hope to accomplish? If you are a teacher, you might match your objectives to your school's curriculum frameworks. If you are a parent, you might have important values around which you base your family management. If you are a coach, your team has both individual and group hopes and goals.

- **Materials:** What materials will you need to collect before you begin? Being prepared will help you and students stay focused on the activity.
- **Procedure:** What steps will you take and in what order? The activities here are scripted in ways that have been used successfully. Try them alone before presenting them to the class or try them as presented before modifying.
- **Check for learning:** How will you know that the hopes and goals have been met? What will be the clues to your success? How do these clues support your SMART Strengths?

We have included suggested grade levels with each activity should you want to adapt it for use with students. Keep in mind that any activity can be made age appropriate for students by being mindful of their needs for scaffolding, background knowledge, and concreteness. You know your students best!

We have organized this section into three categories:
- Activities for Learning, Building and Using SMART Strengths
- Activities for Supporting Resilience and Achieving Goals
- Activities for Building Relationships and Appreciating the Good

Contents Appendix B

Activities for Learning, Building and Using Your *SMART* Strengths

Activities for Supporting Resilience and Achieving Goals

Activities for Building Relationships and Appreciating the Good

Activities for Learning, Building and Using Your *SMART* Strengths

Taking the VIA-Youth (5th grade and up)

- To access the VIA-Youth you can use the account you made in Chapter One when you took the adult version of the VIA at www.authentichappiness.com. Those under 18 years old cannot register themselves.
- Log in and scroll to the part of the website which lets you register a child for the VIA-Youth.
- There are 198 questions. It may be helpful to read the questions aloud to 5th and 6th grades classes who are taking the VIA in a group setting. Reading them while students answer should take about 30 minutes. Do not help students answer the questions or hint at what you think an answer might be. Just as when you took the test, each student responds for himself or herself.
- Be sure to scroll to the bottom of the page that has the top five strengths and click on the button to access all 24 strengths.
- You may want to print or save a document with each student's strengths. The results for each student are stored on the website.

Strengths Families
Knowing and Using Your Strengths (5th grade and up)

What are your strengths? What do they look like in action?

_____

_____

_____

How often and under what circumstances do you get to do activities that engage your strengths? _____

_____

_____

How can you increase opportunities to use and develop these strengths in everyday life and work? _____

_____

_____

What are your most powerful strengths combinations? How can you tell?

_____

_____

_____

How can you use these strengths teams more often? _____

_____

_____

What are your best supporting strengths? How and when do you use them?

_____

_____

_____

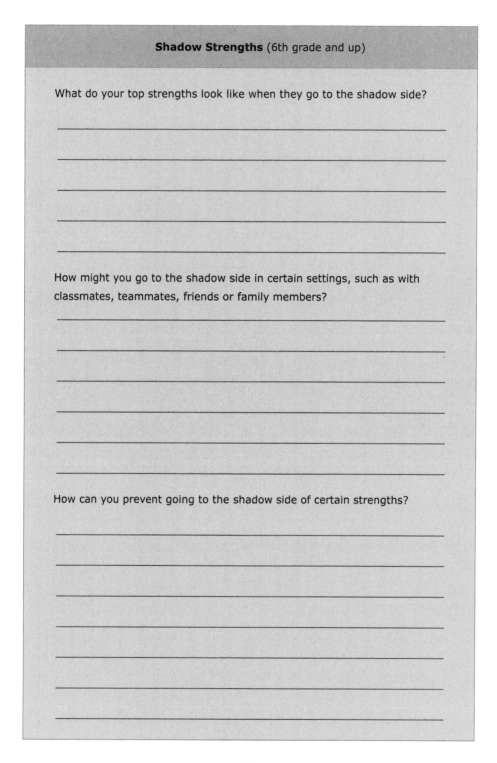

Shadow Strengths (6th grade and up)

What do your top strengths look like when they go to the shadow side?

_____

_____

_____

_____

_____

How might you go to the shadow side in certain settings, such as with classmates, teammates, friends or family members?

_____

_____

_____

_____

_____

How can you prevent going to the shadow side of certain strengths?

_____

_____

_____

_____

_____

_____

_____

Strengths Buttons (7th grade and up)

When our Strengths Buttons are pushed, the shadow side of another strength can leak out. Which of your strengths may pair like this?

_____

_____

_____

_____

Provide some examples of when other people push your strengths buttons.

_____

_____

_____

_____

What is it that others say or do that provokes a negative thought in you?

_____

_____

_____

_____

Now that you know what pushes your strengths buttons, how can you use other strengths to buffer your responses?

_____

_____

_____

_____

Strengths Matching (7th grade and up)

Compare your strengths with another person you know well. Are they similar? Do they differ? _____

_____

_____

_____

_____

_____

_____

How do you use your strengths for good when you both interact? _____

_____

_____

_____

_____

In a bigger group, such as a family, team, class or friends, how can strengths matching help to substitute for strengths that are not well represented at the top of the VIA list? _____

_____

_____

_____

_____

_____

Grades K-5 Strengths Activities
Dana Vellios, Guidance Counselor,
Glenwood Elementary School, Media, Pennsylvania

The following is a developmental guidance counselor's lesson plan for each grade level in relation to strengths. It outlines an overall objective of the lessons, as well as a building block plan for building upon each lesson from year-to-year.

Grade Level SMART Lessons

Kindergarten

Objective: To have students understand the definition of strengths and name one thing they are good at.

Materials: One Thing I Am Good At worksheet; a copy of the children's book *Today I Feel Silly* by Jamie Lee Curtis and Laura Cornell.

Procedure: Read the book *Today I Feel Silly* to students. A good idea is to stop and define words in the book that are character strengths, such a bravery and honesty. At the completion of the book, explain how the child was using her strengths or things about her that were very good and she did well as a person. Next, hand each student a worksheet about things they are good at. Instruct the students to draw at least one thing they are good at doing.

Check for learning: Check to make sure each student understands that the word strength means something they are good at. You can use pictures to show a representation of a strength.

Take back to classroom: Have the teacher hang each student's worksheet outside the classroom for him or her to see. Send the worksheet home with students with the instruction to discuss with parents.

First Grade

Objective: To have students be able to name activities and parts of themselves that are strengths. During first grade is when you can really begin to use strengths language.

Materials: 3 pieces of paper, hole punch, binding materials, markers and crayons.

Procedure: Have each student create a book of 3 things that are their strengths. Review with students that a strength is something they are good at or are proud of about themselves. Some examples can be: 'I am a hard worker' or 'I am brave.' Reinforce that these are strengths. Let children write down their strength and draw a picture, if wanted. Bind the books and have each child read their book aloud during a follow-up session as soon as possible.

First Grade (continued)

Check for learning: During the read-aloud portion of the project, have students state why they chose each strength. Ensure that students understand the link between strengths and what they are good at.

Take back to classroom: Have the books bound together. Either send home the books or post them in the room or hallway for Open House or Back to School Night.

Second Grade

Objective: To have students be able to let others know what strengths they see in a peer and share them aloud.

Materials: Paper for each child as a rough copy, writing utensils, and good copy construction paper.

Procedure: Before students begin, post the 24 VIA strengths and discuss their meaning. Tell students they should try to use the signature strength words for this activity if possible. Assign each child another student in the class through random assignment. Each student must then pick three strengths (or things that person is good at) and write them on construction paper with illustrations. These should be worked on privately and then handed in for binding. A second session can be used for presenting each booklet to the class so everyone can see what each child thought others' strengths were.

Check for learning: Each child should be able to notice and say something that others are good at.

Take back to classroom: The activity, including the presentation, should be done with the teacher present, so that they are aware of students' work as well as the signature strengths language.

Third Grade

Objective: To have students understand the meanings of the different signature strengths.

Materials: Access to computers, dictionaries, construction paper, writing utensils.

Procedure: Assign each student one of the 24 VIA strengths. They are to research what the word means and be able to give one example about how one could show that strength. Each student should write their word, the definition, and example on the construction paper to further the expression of the strength they

Third Grade (continued)

were assigned. Have each student present their word and post their construction paper with the definition and example up for viewing as each student tells about their word. Follow with the checking for learning below. If you do not have enough students to complete each word, then have student who finish quickly do second word or complete them yourself for presenting.

Check for learning: Before students leave, have them say one strength from the defined list that they think they exhibit.

Take back to classroom: Hang the construction paper strength definitions in the third grade hallway for students to continue to view in their everyday setting.

Fourth Grade

Objective: To have students comprehend the different meanings of the strengths and discuss what strengths fit them best.

Materials: Brief Strength Survey

Procedure: Have students take a brief strengths survey. This can be created by taking definitions of each strength and putting them into a kid friendly way for students to check off whether they think this is a strength of theirs. This project is more used as a tool to help them continue to learn the vocabulary of the 24 strengths, as well as build validity for when the student actually takes the VIA strengths survey for children in 5th grade. Review terms and have students share the strengths that fit them best. Ask questions such as why do we all have different strengths? How can a classroom with people having different strengths be a good thing?

Check for learning: Check to ensure each student comprehends vocabulary and concepts by popcorn questioning explanations for each strength.

Take back to classroom: Have teacher also take the brief strengths survey and share their strengths so they feel connected with the material. Encourage the regular classroom teacher to employ strengths discussion during literature assignments to analyze characters and plots.

Fifth Grade. Two sessions

Objective: To have students understand their Signature Strengths and how to use their strengths in new ways.

Materials: Computers for each student and the VIA-Youth, available at www.authentichappiness.com. A book to read if students finish early is optional.

Procedure: Assign each student a VIA code under your log-in name on authentichappiness.com. You can log-in multiple students at one time to take the VIA or have them all create their own log-ins and passwords, using your discretion. Before having students begin the VIA it will be useful to review how a Likert Scale is used, as that is the scoring of the VIA. One useful strategy is to have the regular education teacher review the Likert Scale method during math class with the students.

Invite students to ask questions about any test questions that are unclear to them. However, students should to try to take the test on their own, the best they can. Teachers or other students should not help students by prompting or giving examples that might sway the students' own response. Appropriate accommodations can be made for students with disabilities, such as reading the test questions aloud and possible responses in a separate setting.

Check for learning: A follow-up session will be needed to review student's strengths with them. Assign an activity about using their strengths in a new way or how to conquer lesser strengths by utilizing your strengths. This can be done quietly in a journal reflection by students while you meet with other students individually. Try to organize small groups of students with common strengths to make the process faster if possible. The goal for each student is to know something they can do with their strengths.

Take back to classroom: Using software such as Microsoft PowerPoint, each 5th grade student can create a slide of their strengths with illustrations. Laminate and hang each child's strengths in the 5th grade hallways for all to see and take note of.

Mental Models of Strengths (Kindergarten to 5th Grade)

Defining a strength, writing it in a sentence, and sketching a drawing of it can help form a bridge for understanding what a strength looks like and how it comes alive in the student's life.

Name of the Strength _____

Definition of the Strength _____

_____

_____

_____

_____

Write about the Strength in a sentence _____

_____

_____

_____

_____

_____

_____

Activity: (continued)

Make a sketch/drawing of what tshe strength looks like.

Example: Teamwork

- Teamwork — team work
- Working together in a group to finish something
- We used teamwork to complete the social studies project.

The Strengths Bio (9th grade and up)

This can be adapted for lower grades, as the VIA-Youth is designed for students in grades 5-12. The *Clifton Strengths Finder* inventory is used with high school students.

Ed Kelley has students in his 10th Grade Humanities class use the *Clifton Strengths Finder* to develop an autobiography as seen through the student's strengths. Here is Ed's model that he shares with the class.

Favorite Character Strength and Why	**Woo!** I am immediately drawn to others. I am committed to producing and providing as much as I can for others— this is my mantra. I want others to feel welcome and comfortable.

Character Strength Most Used	Communication
	I can't walk by someone without saying hello. I tell my students they should do the same. I enjoy seeing others smile when I ask them how they are doing. I'm compelled to reach out to others by simply saying *hello*.
Are there any shadows?	I get frustrated when other people are negative. I am an overly positive person who expects others to see the good in all they do. When others complain, I get judgmental. I need to be more empathetic and possibly try to understand why others may not be so positive all the time.
How Have My Strengths Helped Me?	I wouldn't be at Culver if it wasn't for my ability to win others over. I am committed to a life of service and Culver saw that in me when I interviewed. They were kind enough to give me the job of a lifetime. I owe much to the institution that has afforded me so much in the short term. They let me practice what I love doing most—working with others!

In My Element: A Video Photostory (5th grade and up)
A resource for staff and students
Dan Haesler & Ray Francis, Emanuel School,
Sydney, New South Wales, Australia

Sir Ken Robinson defines the *Element* as the place where your natural talents (strengths) and passions meet. To be in your element is to be in a state of flow.

This activity allows the students to explore their *Element* by identifying their strengths (VIA, *Clifton StrengthsFinder*, or own perceived strengths) and identifying their passions or affinities.

By using commercially available software, (eg. Microsoft Movie Maker, Photostory, or Apple's iMovie) students create a short presentation that demonstrates their strengths and passions and how they interrelate. This presents a number of cross curricular teaching opportunities. Presentations can then be viewed in class for peer discussion or reflection based on the needs of your class. Importantly, this video can be stored on a database so teaching staff can access them and see the pupil as a child first, student second. By knowing what makes a child thrive, teachers can endeavor to engage even the most distant student.

This is also a very interesting activity to run for teaching staff on a training day or over the course of a semester. Knowing what makes your colleagues thrive can be very enlightening and can lead to more positive relationships.

The 360° Feedback Gallery (5th grade and up)

These activities provide a graphic understanding about how other students see each other. Based on reviewing the 24 strengths of the VIA, have students choose what they believe to be another student's signature strengths.

- With large newsprint, have each student write their name on the top of a sheet.
- Tape each sheet to the wall and have the student stand next their corresponding sheet.
- Give each student a marker.
- Going either clockwise or counterclockwise, have each student rotate to the next sheet and write down the strengths they observe in each corresponding student.
- If there are multiple endorsements for a certain strength, then the student will place a check-mark next to the strength.
- After completing this portion of the activity, have the students circle around one of the completed sheets. The teacher asks the students to provide one or two examples of how they see this strength come alive in the chosen student.
- Then the chosen student will share how their VIA strengths match up with what his or her peers perceive as strengths.
- Rotate to each student in the class.

The 360° Feedback Strength Cloud (5th grade and up)

- Here is an additional way of accessing the 360° approach that can be used to represent the top strengths of individuals or the entire group. Go to www.wordle.net to create "Strength Clouds."

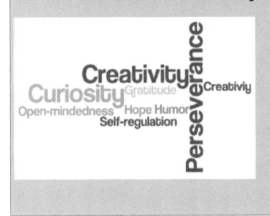

  - Students and teachers can individually type in their endorsement of strengths.

  - In the sample graphic, Creativity, Curiosity and Perseverance are multiply endorsed within the group, so they have a stronger emphasis in the cloud.

Positive Introduction: Me at My Best Part 2 (7th Grade and up)

- Choose a partner. Decide who will share first.
- You will each have 3-5 minutes to share with this partner. Keep your story to this time frame. Tell your "Me at My Best" story straight through: a beginning wil set the scene, the middle will expand and add details for the listener, and the end will wrap things up.
- Your partner will *listen for the strengths you used* during this best moment and *tell you what she or he heard*.
- You will return the favor.

What did you most admire in your partner's story? What strengths were evident? _____

_____

How did you tell your partner this, if you did? _____

_____

_____

What surprises were there, if any, in what you learned about your partner?

_____

_____

How did the storyteller feel about having their strengths highlighted?

_____

_____

How did the listener feel about the storyteller? _____

_____

Strengths Mapping (7th grade and up)

What are the strengths of your fellow students? _____

_____

_____

_____

How can you help bring out the best in them? _____

_____

_____

_____

What strengths do you have in abundance? How can you foresee

using these? _____

_____

_____

What strengths might you need to borrow for more effectiveness? Do you
know where to find these in your school? _____

_____

_____

_____

Strengths in Literature and History (7th grade and up)

This activity can be modified for younger grades by addressing only the first and last bullet points.

- After reading a passage, compare your strengths with those of a character or person in the book. _____

  _____

  _____

- Do the character or person's strengths resonate with yours? If not, why not? _____

  _____

  _____

- Using the SMART Strengths model, respond to the following questions:
    1. What are the shadow sides of the character or person's strengths?

    _____

    _____

    2. How does the character or person manage their team of strengths?

    _____

    _____

    3. How does the character or person advocate for their strengths?

    _____

    _____

    4. How does the character or person relate their strengths with others? What presses his or her strength's buttons? _____

    _____

    _____

    5. Is the character or person able to bring out the best in others?

    _____

    _____

Creating a SMART Future Story (5th grade and up)

- What is something you really enjoy and would love to do more of?

  _____

  _____

  _____

- What are you doing to help this happen? How do your strengths help?

  _____

  _____

- Can you use your strengths in new ways so that you can enjoy this thing more often? _____

  _____

- What else do you need? Who can help you? _____

  _____

  _____

- Who is somebody you look up to? What is it that you admire about this person? _____

  _____

  _____

  _____

- What are his or strengths? What do they do well? _____

  _____

  _____

  _____

  _____

- What are some things in this person that you also see in yourself?

  _____

  _____

  _____

My Coach's Stengths (9th grade and up)

What strengths does my coach have that work to help him or her fulfill the four core traits of being a sucessful coach? How do these strengths help me play my best? How might certain coaching strengths challenge me?

Purpose and Vision _____

_____

Strength _____

An example of this strength in action. _____

_____

_____

Skills and Competence _____

Strength _____

An example of this strength in action. _____

_____

_____

Relationships _____

Strength _____

An example of this strength in action. _____

_____

_____

Character Habits — Another strength that shows my coach has positive character. _____

_____

Play SMART (9th grade and up)

Spotting. How do my top strengths come alive when I play sports?

_____

_____

_____

Managing. How do I use my strengths to manage my own play? What strengths possibly go to the shadow side?_____

_____

_____

_____

Advocating. How do I best appeal to the strengths of my fellow players and coaches? _____

_____

_____

Relating. What parent, player, or official behavior presses my strengths buttons? What other strengths of mine can I use to lessen the intensity of the button pushing? _____

_____

_____

_____

Training. What can I do to help my fellow players focus more on their strengths?_____

_____

_____

Hardiness (11th grade and up)

How do your strengths support the three hardiness domains? Write down your strengths that influence each domain.

These strengths help me adapt to challenges: _____

_____

_____

_____

_____

_____

_____

These strengths reinforce my commitment and dedication: _____

_____

_____

_____

_____

_____

These strengths help me understand what I can and can't control:

_____

_____

_____

_____

_____

3XG Learn to Savor (7th grade and up)

Remember how you learned how to shift your focus to good things that have happened in your life? Sometimes this is called a "gratitude journal," especially if you are collecting good things that happened and for which you are grateful. We call it 3XG: Three times good. You can use the same format for savoring.

1. Start by...
   What happened? _____

   _____

   What was good about it? _____

   _____

   What do you want to remember about it? _____

   _____

2) Then decide what type of savoring will tap into your strengths most. Record your high point memories in a way which will allow you to revisit them.

   Basking_____

   _____

   Marveling _____

   _____

   Luxuriating _____

   _____

   Thanksgiving _____

   _____

Group Savoring for Class, Family, Team or Friends (7th grade and up)

Choose a variety of events that your class, family, team or friends have experienced. What strengths do and your group associate with the good moments? Do some strengths match up better with some savoring styles? You can use the following chart to help record the experience.

Savoring Domain	Event	Associated Strengths
Marveling	Our entire class participated in the sevice learning project to collect can goods for those in need.	Gratitude and Citizenship/Teamwork
Luxuriating		
Thanksgiving		
Basking		
Marveling		
Luxuriating		
Thanksgiving		
Basking		
Marveling		
Luxuriating		
Thanksgiving		
Basking		

Using SMART Stengths for Managing Well-Being (7th grade and up)

What strengths do you use to help self-regulate health behaviors?

*Sleep*_____

_____

_____

_____

_____

Nutrition _____

_____

_____

_____

*Physical Activitiy*_____

_____

_____

_____

Stress _____

_____

_____

_____

What would it be like if each of these areas of your life were in balance?

_____

_____

_____

Activities for Supporting Resilience and Achieving Goals

The Negative Emotions Litmus Test (5th grade and up)

Think of several situations when you tend to express the following negative emotions. When is it helpful for you and others? When is it harmful for you and others? (You do not have to fill in all the columns. Fortunately, there are not many positive uses of disgust.)

	It's helpful when...	It's harmful when...
Fear		
Anger		
Disgust		
Shame		
Guilt		
Sadness		

The Positive Emotions Litmus Test (5th grade an up)

Think of several situations when you tend to express the following positive emotions. When is it helpful for you and others? When is it harmful for you and others? (You do not have to fill in all the columns. Fortunately, there are not many negative uses of joy and gratitude.)

	It's helpful when...	*It's harmful when...*
Joy		
Interest		
Contentment		
Gratitude		
Elevation		
Love		

Positivity in School, at Home, and on the Athletic Field (9th grade and up)

This 3-part activity is a way for you to evaluate positivity ratios. So you can see why some groups may flourish, and others flounder when it comes to relationships and performance.

Pre-reflection

- Think of a regular group activity that you participate in with others. Think of the members of the group—be it friends, family, classmates or teammates.
- In the time the group spent assembling, participating in the activity, and then departing, estimate the ratio of positive statements to negative statements during this group activity. Positive statements are those you would rate as likely to result in positive thoughts and emotions in those who heard the statement. Negative statements would be likely to lead to negative thoughts and emotions.

Interaction Charting

- Keep an interaction chart of all your activities for a week and evaluate for positivity and negativity. After each interaction during the week, put a plus or minus sign by the name of the person with whom you had the interaction. A plus indicates an interaction that you found energizing or otherwise positive. A negative indicates a de-energizing, negative interaction. At the end of the week, calculate the positivity ratio for your interactions with each individual.

Post-reflection

- Are any of these relationships at or above the 3:1 positivity ratio? 5:1?
- Are there any relationships you would like to "Warm up?" Pay particular attention to relationships where a little warming might move the relationship to or above the 3:1 ratio. If so, try warming up that relationship for a few weeks, then reassess.
- Are there any changes you can make so you spend less time in low-positivity relationships and more time in high-positivity relationships?

Knowing When You are In the Zone — What is Your IZOF?
(9th grade and up)

At home, in school, or on the athletic field, when have you found yourself in the IZOF? You'll know because your talents met your challenges, you emerged from the zone having lost track of time, and you would go back to that time if you could. _____

_____

_____

_____

What was your optimal arousal level? Were you in the low, medium, or high range IZOF, and how could you tell? What factors contributed to getting you into that optimal state? _____

_____

_____

_____

What were the factors that helped you stay in the IZOF? _____

_____

_____

_____

Would your IZOF level of arousal level work for you in another situation? Answer the questions for a different domain to discover the answer (e.g., the athletic field, an arts performance, or the classroom). _____

_____

_____

_____

Combining Thinking It Through and RAMP Up (7th grade and up)

We have learned that resilience takes practice and that using these tools as a team will pay dividends. Now it's your turn to put these tools together.

Think It Through

First, think of a recent time when things did not go your way. It may have been at work, at home, or with friends. Were you . . .

- Sad
- Embarrassed
- Angry or frustrated
- Guilty or ashamed
- Afraid or anxious
- Disgusted

What happened?

List just the facts, and try not to analyze.

Who? _____

What? _____

When? _____

Where? _____

Think (List your thoughts or beliefs as the event happened.) _____

_____

_____

Feel (What emotions went with those thoughts or beliefs?) _____

_____

_____

Do (What did you do?) _____

_____

_____

RAMP Up

Reject and Rethink:

Look for evidence that would cause you to reject and rethink your first thought. *What have you missed?* _____

_____

_____

_____

Alternatives:

Generate other ways of explaining the event. *Can you think of causes with shorter duration, narrower scope, and that leave you more in control?* _____

_____

_____

_____

Minimize:

Create some wiggle room. If you cannot reject or develop an alternative, *can you at least narrow the duration and scope of the cause in your first thought?*_____

_____

_____

_____

Plan:

Sometimes our thoughts are more about "what next" than "why." When challenging "what next" thoughts, a plan to achieve better outcomes can help. *What steps can prevent the worst and make the best more likely?* _____

_____

_____

_____

_____

Your Mindset — Fixed or Growth? (7th grade and up)

1. Make a list of your top five high moments of the last month. For each, tell why the event happened. For instance, if you write, "Our team won the championship," you might add, "We have an outstanding coach," or "The other team was no match for our power," or "This team was meant to win."

_____

_____

_____

_____

_____

_____

2. Evaluate what you have written by thinking about each event this way: Have you explained the "why" of the event in a Fixed or a Growth mindset way? Is your "why" thought permanent and pervasive? What would make it possible for your event to be repeated?

_____

_____

_____

_____

_____

_____

_____

Adjust Your Effort (9th grade and up)

When you connect the dots between your efforts and your achievement, it is more obvious what works.

What do you do to be competent and to replicate your good work?

_____

_____

_____

_____

How would you help a classmate, teammate, friend or family member replicate their good work? _____

_____

_____

_____

_____

Below are some ways to get started. See Joseph T. Hallinan, author of *Why We Make Mistakes: How We Look Without Seeing, Forget Things in Seconds, and Are All Pretty Sure We Are Way Above Average.*

Here are three important ways he suggests that we can adjust our metacognitive skill and self-appraisal:

- Keep a written record of hits, misses, and never-attempted items to prevent us from an after-the-fact view through rose-colored lenses.
- Value being happy, because happier people make quicker decisions both more accurately and with less back-and-forth
- Know how strengths may cloud your vision, making you think you are more virtuous, and thus higher achieving, than you really are.

Writing a Goal Plan (9th grade and up)	
Means...	**Stimulate Growth Through These Nutrients**
Specific and Written: The goal needs to identify exactly what will be accomplished and may need to be broken down into very tiny, sequential steps on the way to something big.	**Challenging:** Easy goals don't feel worth it, and sometimes a person needs something big to capture their imagination and focus. You may need to work backwards from the big picture to the incremental steps needed.
What is a goal you want to accomplish?	Why is this goal challenging for you?
Measurable: If it cannot be measured, there's no way of knowing if a goal has been accomplished.	**Provide Meaningful Feedback:** Regular and incremental review feedback ideally comes from both an objective source, e.g. a stopwatch, measuring tape, video, or rubric, as well as your personal site team of one or more people to whom you are accountable.
How will you know that this goal has been achieved?	How will you receive meaningful feedback, both objectively and from your personal "site team"?
Approach versus avoidance: Goals are something to accomplish rather than avoid, e.g.: take steps to get a good grade rather than avoid a bad one; win a game rather than avoid losing one.	**Intrinsically valuable**: The person doing the work wants to achieve the goal—not just doing it for someone else, like a parent, teacher, or coach, or to avoid making that person angry, sad, etc.

Is your goal stated in a way that shows it is something you are attracted to and which will involve you?	Who are you doing this for? Is your goal something that will make you feel more . . . Skilled? Independent? Connected? Happy?
Leveraged: Take advantage of and contribute to other goals.	**Nonconflicting**: Won't harm accomplishment of other goals or be in opposition to your values.
What are other goals you have that are related to this one? How will achieving this goal specifically contribute to other goals?	Cross-check (and maybe check with your personal site team to be sure your goals are a good fit for each other and your values. Are they? How do you know?
Use your Strengths: S-M-A-R-T	**Engaging**: Using strengths in the service of attaining goals puts you into flow state where you build well-being resources.
List up to five of the strengths you feel most aligned with how you will use them in the service of attaining your goals. *Think: Spotting, Managing, Advocating, Relating and Training your strengths.*	*Anticipate your success! What will it be like when you achieve your goal? Write your imagined future:*

Goal Setting Work Sheet (6th grade and up)

Derrick Carpenter, MAPP

Founder of VIVE Training — physical and psychological wellness training.

The purpose of this goal setting worksheet is to help students redirect their focus from outcome goals to process goals. The worksheet includes five steps that should be facilitated by an adult.

In Step 1, the student is asked to consider a goal. If the student doesn't have a clear goal, the following questions can help get the wheels turning: *What is something you could work towards that would make you really happy? What would you like to do over the next 3 months? Tell me about something you would like to get better at. What is something you want and can get it you try?*

In Step 2, the student is asked to list behaviors they can take to achieve their goal. The major emphasis here should be on shifting focus inward and helping the student name strategies they can use to work towards their goal. Students should be encouraged to think about the process of achieving their goal and to name the things they can do or practice in service of their goal.

In Step 3, the student is asked to visualize himself carrying out the strategies named in Step 2. Research shows that visualizing the strategies needed to accomplish a goal is more effective than visualizing the outcome in increasing commitment to goal strategies and at facilitating goal achievement1. By visualizing these strategies as well as potential obstacles, the student can begin to see them as realistic and can prepare for putting these strategies into action.

In Step 4, the student is asked to frame the strategies as new goals by specifying when and how often the strategies will be completed. These process goals should be specific and measurable so that a student could easily evaluate whether or not the process goal has been met. These process goals should become the focus of the student's goal-oriented actions.

In Step 5, the student is asked to list outcomes of the goal beyond the goal itself. These outcomes should clarify the student's motivation for the goal. The student should be encouraged to list outcomes in the first person that express their intrinsic motivation for the goal (*I will feel proud* rather than *My parents will be happy*).

By focusing on the processes rather than the outcome, students can better understand the value of developing mastery as they work towards goal. If students are encouraged to evaluate their success in relation to their process goals (*I will study math 30 minutes every night*) rather than their outcome goals (*I want an A in math*), they have greater control of their outcomes and may be more likely to develop greater motivation for pursuing goal-oriented strategies for future goals.

Here is an example of a completed worksheet: (student portion, 6th grade and up)

1. *To set the school record in free throws for a season.*

2. *Practice my free throw form. Be less nervous on the line during games. Get tips from the coach.*

3. I am practicing free throws in the school gym just after basketball team practice at about 4pm. I am with my teammate, Chris, and I feel happy, focused, and confident. We might have to convince the custodians to let us stay after practice.

4. Practice free throws 20 min every day after team practice. Take a deep breath each time I'm on the line before shooting. Talk with the coach before practice on Saturday for advice.

5. My name will be on the records plaque. I will have developed discipline. I will feel proud.

Pham, L. B. & Taylor, S. E. (1999). From thought to action: Effects of process- versus outcome-based mental simulations on performance. Personality and Social Psychology Bulletin, 25(2), 250-260.

Activities for Building Relationships and Appreciating the Good

The ROCC of Trust (7th grade and up)

Think about the following questions in terms of your relationships at school with teachers, fellow students, parents, or coaches.

1. Are you reliable? Can people depend on you to deliver on your promises?
   - What could you do to increase your reliability?

   _____

   _____

   _____

2. Are you open? Do you provide people with the information they need to understand what's happening? If you are every unable to deliver (and that happens to all of us sometimes), were you open about why?
   - What could you do to increase your openness?

   _____

   _____

   _____

3. Are you competent? Can other people depend on what you produce?
   - What could you do to increase your competence?

   _____

   _____

   _____

4. Are you compassionate? Do people feel you will treat them with consideration and respect if they are open with you?
   - What could you do to increase your demonstration of compassion for others?

   _____

   _____

   _____

Green Light Responding (7th Grade and Up)

Have a conversation with a friend, classmate or teammate where you each have an opportunity to capitalize about something that went well. Spend 10 minutes in each role, so you both capitalize and respond.

After switching roles, explore the process:

- What did it feel like to be the person who was capitalizing?

  _____

  _____

- What did it feel like to be the person who was responding?

  _____

  _____

- What did you find energizing about the experience?

  _____

  _____

- What did you find difficult to do?

  _____

  _____

- Did any of your strengths come alive in capitalizing? In responding?

  _____

  _____

- Did any of your strengths hinder capitalizing? Responding?

  _____

  _____

- What did you learn from this exercise?

  _____

  _____

Intergenerational Joyful Blessings Day (All grades)
Elaine O'Brien, MAPP, International Dance-Exercise/Health trainer,
consultant and speaker

Many schools have a family day or parents weekend event where students are encouraged to bring family members to share in what's great about being part of their school community. The actual event may be called by different names. This is an example of a positive psychology-infused approach to such an occasion.

Joyful Blessings Day is an experiential way to build gratitude and appreciation in the framework of intergenerational reconnection. It recaptures gratitude and nurtures communication in a safe and empowering way by kindling awareness, curiosity, and memory. The goal is to build reciprocal understanding, as well as increase gratitude literacy.

Family members are joined by students in an intergenerational dance or exercise workout followed by lunch. During the meal, the students chat with family members. The Joyful Blessing Day model follows a plan that allows for movement, a meal, and the the additional goal of raising gratitude levels and fostering positive conversations across generations.

Joyful Blessings Days: Directions

1. Select music inspired by gratitude for the dance/exercise/movement portion. Here are some suggestions that have been popular with different generations:

- *You Are The Sunshine Of My Life* Stevie Wonder
- *I Just Called To Say I Love You* Stevie Wonder
- *I'll Be There* Jackson 5
- *I'm Sticking With You* Velvet Underground
- *Joy To The World* 3 Dog Night
- *Just the Way You Are* Bruno Mars
- *Cherish* The Association
- *Your Song* Elton John
- *What the World Needs Now is Love Sweet Love* Jackie DeShannon
- *Thanks For The Memories* Bob Hope
- *Wouldn't It Be Nice?* Beach Boys
- *All I Want Is You* Barry Louis Polisar
- *Come To Me* Mary J. Blige

2. Begin lunch with a blessing (adapted from the Native American prayer on page 196 of *Thanks!* by Robert Emmons)

"We give thanks for the resources that made this food possible; we give thanks for the earth that produced it, and we thank all those who labored to bring it to us. May the wholesomeness of the food before us bring out the wholeness within and among us."

3. Introduce the idea of and the four types of savoring: basking, marveling, thanksgiving, and luxuriating, which all promote positive emotions in the present. Encourage light discussion of ways to better savor the mealtime.

4. Encourage students and adults to ask each other questions to generate moments of insight or wonder. Here are some suggested questions:
- What have you been most grateful for earlier in your life?
- What makes you happy?
- What are you most grateful today? Can you help somebody else have a similar experience?
- What is a high point moment today? How can you create more of these moments?

Have the students and adults engage in dyads, or small groups, to commune, and actively listen to each other's responses. The intention of the questions and stories is pointed toward fostering gratitude and consideration. The viewpoints and experience of the adults can help school students reframe to a different time and way of thinking and being, and vice versa.

The questions are inspired to cultivate curiosity and bring to mind treasured moments. There are no wrong answers here. Jot down thoughts to foster perspective and sharing on sticky notes. Post them in the front hallway of the main entrance to the school. Create a home activity to take the joy home.

5. At the conclusion of the Joyful Blessing Day, conduct a debriefing with a contemplative parable of gratitude.

An example is about an Asian woman named Haikun. Every morning Haikun walked a mile to the spring to gather a bucket of water for her family. At the end of the day, she would walk back to the spring and return any leftover water to the spring. The hope of this message would be to instill a reminder of our gratitude to nature.

Conclude the Joyful Blessings Day program with the Breath of Thanks exercise from the book *Thanks!* This exercise reminds us that gratitude starts with the basics. During the exercise, ask people to bring attention to breathing, noticing how breath flows in and out, in and out. For 5-8 breaths, ask them to say the words "thank you" silently. This gift of breath reminds us how lucky we are to be alive.

Case Western Reserve's David Cooperrider has used intergenerational interviews through the appreciative inquiry process (See Chapter 10) to create curiosity and wonder. Positive changes in the interviewer and interviewee occurred and intergenerational sensitivity was raised. In addition, the students doing the interviews excelled in school, especially in math and science.

The Joyful Blessings Day model has the potential to create a world of thanks, the vision of a good society, and a better today.

Random Acts of Kindness — What's in it for me? (7th grade and up)
From Dan Haesler & Ray Francis,
Emanuel School, Sydney, New South Wales, Australia

"Why should I be nice to people? They aren't nice to me..." This is a common response from adolescents when we try and engage them in the notion of being kind.

Researchers will tell us that because of the adolescent brain, the teaching of such concepts need to demonstrate: "What's in it for me?"

The following activity has been shown in a variety of settings to do just that.

Each member of the class is assigned a random "Secret Buddy." Over the course of a number of weeks each person should perform one or two acts of kindness for their "Buddy" per week.

Each week the group is surveyed anonymously as to how happy they were with the act of kindness they received (if indeed they identified it) as well as how happy they felt after performing an act of kindness.

Depending on your class you can add more questions relating to how their mental well-being was affected by either giving or receiving the act of kindness.

Typically over the course of 3 weeks or more, students report that performing acts of kindness makes them happier than receiving. Furthermore, students will often report that feeling happy improves their mental well-being, so they can extrapolate that further by saying that being kind to other people is actually good for their health... and that's what's in it for me.

Included below are the findings from our 2010 activity with fifty 15 and 16 year olds over a three-week period. They rated their responses on a scale of 1-10, with 1 = "Not at all" and 10 = "Ecstatic."

- 64% rated their happiness scale at 6+ when receiving an Act of Kindness.
- 80% rated their happiness scale at 6+ when performing an Act of Kindness.
- Only 4% said that receiving an Act of Kindness made them happier than performing one.
- 76% said that the more thought/effort they put into performing an Act of Kindness, the happier they felt because of it.
- 94% said they happier they felt, the better (in terms of mental well-being) they felt.
- 72% said because of doing the "Secret Buddy Activity" they can now see how doing Acts of Kindness for others actually improves their mental well-being.
- 50% said because of the "Secret Buddy Activity" they are now more like-ly to volunteer or do charity work, with a further 38% either undecided or would have done voluntary work anyway. Only 12% said that the Activity had definitely not inspired them to do any voluntary or charity work.

www.danhaesler.com

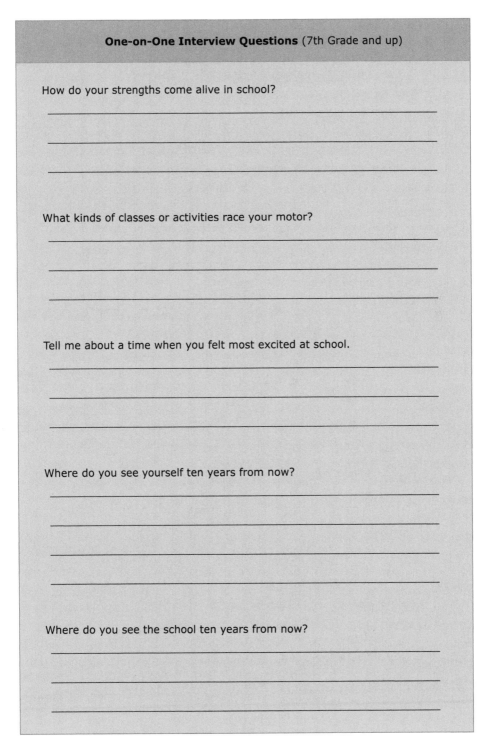

One-on-One Interview Questions (7th Grade and up)

How do your strengths come alive in school?

_____

_____

_____

What kinds of classes or activities race your motor?

_____

_____

_____

Tell me about a time when you felt most excited at school.

_____

_____

_____

Where do you see yourself ten years from now?

_____

_____

_____

_____

Where do you see the school ten years from now?

_____

_____

_____

Appreciative Questions to Support Change (11th grade and up)

Practice asking these appreciative questions with a partner or a small group.

1. What is the best of us, right now?
   - What are our strengths? _____

     _____

   - What are our best moments at home, school, or on a team?

     _____

   - When have we been proud to be part of the family, school or team?

     _____

2. What might we become?
   - What is next for us? _____

     _____

   - What would our organization look like in a year if we were really
     flourishing? _____

3. How can we get there?
   - What are our short- and long-term goals? _____

     _____

   - What kind of support do we need from the community? _____

     _____

4. How do we sustain our energy?
   - How are we doing right now? _____

     _____

   - What do we need to keep up our momentum? _____

     _____

   - What kind of support do we need to keep going? _____

     _____

Questions based on the 4-D cycle
as described in Cooperrider and Whitney, *Appreciative Inquiry, 2005.*

A Call to Action (11th grade through adult)

Based on your collected Mindful Moments, list your SMART assets:

Your Strengths: Which ones most resonate with you and will be essential for your success?

_____

_____

_____

_____

_____

_____

Your Resilience Habits: How will you approach challenges that will occur along the bridge to change?

_____

_____

_____

_____

_____

Your Supportive Relationships: Who will be your personal site team?

_____

_____

_____

_____

_____

_____

Your Best Possible Future:

What would it be like if everyone in your community used SMART Strengths, practiced resilience strategies, and created high-quality connections? Imagine a "Best Possible Future" for your family, team, school, and community. Spend time embellishing this narrative. Include many sensory details. Imagine what it will feel like to accomplish this future. Go beyond words and use whatever else helps you to put flesh on the future story. You can add a collage, vision board, and/or pictures that show the change want to make.

_____

_____

_____

_____

_____

What's the first step that you can take to shape the future of your family, school, team or community for the better? What will you do?

_____

_____

_____

_____

When will you take this step? Fill in the "Writing a Goal Plan" Mindful Moment on page 328. We look forward to hearing your Strengths Stories!

_____

_____

_____

_____

_____

Notes

Introduction

xviii. Sandra Schneider, a professor of psychology at the University of Southern Florida has done some interesting work on realistic optimism. See Schneider, S. (2001). "In Search of Realistic Optimism: Meaning, Knowledge, and Warm Fuzziness," *American Psychologist*. 56, 3, 250-26.

xx. Sherri and Dave researched teachers in a large, non-urban school system who completed one or more positive psychology questionnaires assessing strengths of character; happiness; orientation toward pleasure, engagement, and meaning as three different paths to happiness; explanatory style; orientation toward teaching as a job, a career, or a calling; and job satisfaction. Results from the sampled teachers were compared with those obtained from an Internet sample of 2,538 teachers on four of the same instruments. See Fisher, S.W. and Shearon, D.N. (2006). *Building a Foundation for Positive Psychology in Schools*. www.sas.upenn.edu/lps/graduate/mapp/capstone/2006.

xxi. Martin Seligman and Mihalyi Csikszentmihalyi provide the history of studying the positive functioning of people. See Seligman, M. E. P. and Csikszentmihalyi, M. (2000). "Positive Psychology: An Introduction," *American Psychologist*, 55, 5-14.

xxi. Seligman calls on his many years of research to show how optimism influences overall happiness. See Seligman, M.E.P. *Learned Optimism*. NY: Vintage, 2006.

xxi. Explanatory style is about how people respond to specific events in their lives. There are two types of explanatory styles: positive and negative. See Gillham, J., Shatté, A., Reivich, K., and Seligman, M. (2001). "Optimism, Pessimism, and Explanatory Style," In E. Chang (Ed.), *Optimism & Pessimism: Implications for Theory, Research, and Practice*. Washington, DC: American Psychological Association, 53-75.

xxi. Karen Reivich and Andrew Shatte provide a strong basis for and strategies to better understand explanatory styles. See Reivich, K. and Shatté, A. *The Resilience Factor: 7 Keys to Finding Your Inner Strength and Overcoming Life's Hurdles*. New York: Broadway Books, 2003. Also, Senia Maymin and Kathryn Britton are editors of a book that shows a variety of approaches to resilience. Sherri and Dave are contributors to this collection. S. Maymin and K. Britton (Eds.), *Resilience: How to Navigate Life's Curves*. Positive Psychology News Daily, 2009.

xxii. Terrence Deal and Kent Peterson expand on the "keepers of the nightmare." See Deal, T.E. and Peterson, Kent. D. *Shaping School Culture: The Heart of Leadership*. San Francisco: Jossey-Bass, 1999.

xxii. Martin Seligman expands on "rising to the occasion." See Seligman, M.E.P. *Authentic Happiness: Using the New Positive Psychology to Realize Your Potential for Lasting Fulfillment*. New York: Free Press NY, 2002.

xxiii. After working with each other in the MAPP program, John, Sherri and Dave formed *Flourishing Schools*, a consulting and coaching group integrating best practices in education with cutting edge Positive Psychology research. We help schools flourish by focusing on identifying, broadening, and building the unique strengths of the school, faculty, parents and students to create positive environments where school communities flourish. www.flourishingschools.org.

xxiv. Jane Dutton, from the Ross School of Business at the University of Michigan, lays out the foundational components of building high quality connections in organizations. See Dutton, J.E. *Energize Your Workplace: How to Build and Sustain High-Quality Connections at Work*. San Francisco: Jossey-Bass, 2003.

xxvi. Nel Noddings, a former math teacher and professor emeritus at Stanford University, is a well-respected author on the philosophy of education. See Noddings, N. *Happiness and Education*. Cambridge, UK: Cambridge University Press, 2005.

Chapter One

29. Nansook Park and Chris Peterson, psychologists at the University of Michigan, are pioneering researchers in the study of character strengths. See Park, N., and Peterson, C. (2006). "Character Strengths and Happiness Among Young Children: Content Analysis of Parental Descriptions," *Journal of Happiness Studies, 7*, 323-341.

33. Aristotle's Nichomachean Ethics serves as a foundation for building strengths. See Aristotle. *The Nichomachean Ethics*. J.A.K. Thompson, H. Tredennick, and J. Barnes. New York: Penguin, 2004.

35. Steven Tigner, a professor of philosophy and professor of education at Boston University, teaches in BU's Core Curriculum, a program within both the College of Liberal Arts and in the School of Education.

35. Roy Baumeister is a major researcher in the area of self-regulation. See R.F. Baumeister, and K.D. Vohs (Eds.) *Handbook of Self-Regulation: Research, Theory, and Application. Edition 1*. New York. Guilford Publications, Inc., 2007.

36. Chris Peterson and Martin Seligman researched the world's philosophies and faith traditions in the development of the VIA Classification of Strengths. See Peterson, C. and Seligman, M.E.P. *Character Strengths and Virtues: A Handbook and Classification*. Oxford: Oxford University Press, 2004. Also, see Park, N., Peterson, C., and Seligman, M. E. P. (2004). "Strengths of Character and Well-Being," *Journal of Social and Clinical Psychology*, Vol. 23, No. 5, pp. 603-619.

38. Nansook Park and Chris Peterson collaborated to develop the Values In Action-Youth inventory. See Park, N. and Peterson, C. (2006). "Moral Competence and Character Strengths Among Adolescents: The Development and Validation of the Values in Action Inventory of Strengths for Youth." *Journal of Adolescence, 29, 891-905*. Also, see Park, N.

and Peterson, C. (2005). "The Values in Action Inventory of Character Strengths for Youth," In K. A. Moore and L. H. Lippman (Eds.), *What Do Children Need to Flourish? Conceptualizing and Measuring Indicators of Positive Development.* New York: Springer.

39. Tom Rath provides a practical understanding of the 34 CSF talent themes and strategies for action. See Rath, T. *StrengthsFinder 2.0.* New York: Gallup Press, 2007.

39. The late Philip Stone, Harvard psychologist and Gallup Organization Senior Scientist compared results of the Clifton Strengths Finder (CSF), Myers-Briggs Type Indicator (MBTI) and Values in Action Inventory (VIA). He found that there is a good degree of consistency among the CSF and VIA. We use this when considering strengths from the CSF and VIA. "Comparing Results of Clifton StrengthsFinder (CSF), Myers-Briggs, and Values in Action (VIA)," Presented at the Fourth International Positive Psychology Conference, Washington, DC, October 2005.

44. Chris Peterson defines tonic versus phasic strengths. See Peterson, C. *A Primer in Positive Psychology.* Oxford: Oxford University Press, 2006.

47. Robert Emmons discusses the research and practical applications of gratitude. See Emmons, R. A. *Thanks! How the New Science of Gratitude Can Make You Happier.* New York: Houghton Mifflin, 2007.

48. Bill Gates, the founder of Microsoft, is one of the more influential people in the world. As a philanthropist, he founded the Bill and Melinda Gates Foundation, an endowment that focuses on global health and learning. Steve Jobs, co-founder of Apple Computer, is one of the world's greatest innovators of computer technology.

53. In Peterson's graph, the strengths that are further away from the middle of the grid are less common among youth and adults. For example, authenticity is more common in adults while zest is more common in youth. See Peterson, C. *A Primer in Positive Psychology.* Oxford: Oxford University Press, 2006.

54. The *Clifton StrengthsFinder* test's definition of the strength of "strategic" is "You sort through the clutter and find the best route; you see patterns where others see complexity." See Rath, T. *StrengthsFinder 2.0.* New York: Gallup Press, 2007.

56. The Culver mission statement and principles can be viewed at www.culver.org.

57. The formal Culver research focused on character strengths being an indicator of increased academic achievement, leadership and health. See Yeager, J. (2006) *Character Strengths and Well-Being Among Adolescents,* 2006. www.sas.upenn.edu/lps/graduate/mapp/capstone/2006.

Chapter 2

59. William Arthur Ward, the author of *Fountains of Faith,* was a prolific and inspirational writer.

60. The No Child Left Behind Act of 2001 focuses on standards-based education reform.

Standards and goals are set by individual states. This act has implications for federal funding for schools. www2.ed.gov/policy/elsec/leg/esea02/107-110.pdf.

60. Peter Scales and his colleagues at the *Search Institute* compiled an empirical list of developmental assets among young people. They studied middle and high school students to find the influence of seven "thriving" indicators on gender, grades, and levels of youth: 1) school success, 2) leadership, 3) helping others, 4) maintenance of physical health, 5) delay of gratification, 6) valuing diversity, and 7) overcoming adversity. Three areas: school success, leadership, and wellness – maintenance of physical health – warrant further examination. See Scales, P.C., Benson, P.L., Leffert, N. and Blyth, D.A. (2000). "Contribution of Developmental Assets to the Prediction of Thriving Among Adolescents," *Applied Developmental Science,* 4 (1) 27-46.

60. Bill Milliken, co-founder of *Communities in Schools,* has been a staunch advocate for supporting marginalized youth. See Milliken, B. *The Last Dropout: Stop the Epidemic.* Hay House, 2007.

60. The notion of the servant leader is "first to serve, not to lead." See Greenleaf, R.K. *Servant Leadership – A Journey into the Nature of Legitimate Power and Greatness.* Mahwah NJ: The Paulist Press, 1991.

61. Nel Noddings uses the term "motivational displacement." Motivational displacement occurs when the level of a person's caring is influenced by the needs of the person that he or she is caring for. Motivational displacement is supplemented with "engrossment" where the caring person has a deep understanding of the person cared for.

61. Noddings distinguishes the difference between natural and ethical caring in that natural caring is something that the person caring wants to do, instead of something they must do. See Noddings, Nel. *Caring: A Feminine Approach to Ethics and Moral Education.* Berkeley: University of California Press, 1984.

62. Nansook Park and her colleagues provide compelling evidence that there is a positive relationship between academic success and certain character strengths. See Park, N., Peterson, C. and Seligman, M. E. P. (2004). "Strengths of Character and Well-Being," *Journal of Social and Clinical Psychology,* 23, 603-619. Also, see Park, N. (2004). "Character Strengths and Positive Youth Development," *The Annals of the American Academy of Political and Social Science,* 591, 40-54.

63. Angela Duckworth and Martin Seligman's paper is a very powerful examination of the power of Grit. See Duckworth, A.L. and Seligman, M.E.P. (2005). "Self-Discipline Outdoes IQ in Predicting Academic Performance of Adolescents," *Psychological Science, 16 (12)* 939-944. Also, Emiliya Zhivotovskaya, the founder of *Flourish, Inc,* makes nice connections between grit and mindsets. See Zhivotovskaya, E. *Got Grit? Start with Mindset.* Positive Psychology News Daily, February 21, 2009. positivepsychologynews.com/news/emiliya-zhivotovskaya/200902211582.

63. There is significant research that shows prosocial behavior is a predictor of academic achievement. See Carprara, G.V., Barbanelli, C., Patorelli, C., Bandura, A. and Zimbardo, P.G. "Prosocial Foundations of Children's Academic Achievement," *Psychological Science, 11*, 302-306. Also, Scales and his colleagues claim that "young people who care deeply about how they do in school have accepted the challenge to confront increasingly difficult subject matter as they move through their school experience." See Scales, P.C., Benson, P.L., Leffert, N. and Blyth, D.A. (2000). "Contribution of Developmental Assets to the Prediction of Thriving Among Adolescents," *Applied Developmental Science*, 4(1) 27-46.

63. There has been significant research conducted through the Positive Psychology Project at Strath Haven High School in the Wallingford-Swarthmore, PA, School district.

66. Park and Peterson discuss the reliability and validity of the *Values in Action —Youth* assessment. See Park, N. and Peterson, C. (2006). "Moral Competence and Character Strengths Among Adolescents: The Development and Validation of the Values In Action Inventory of Strengths for Youth," *Journal of Adolescence*, 29 (6) 891-909.

75. Jane Gillham and Karen Reivich are major investigators co-directors of the Penn Resiliency Project. See Brunwasser, S. M., Gillham, J. E., and Kim, E.S. (2009). "A Meta-Analytic Review of the Penn Resiliency Program's Effect on Depressive Symptoms," *Journal of Consulting and Clinical Psychology*, 77, 1042-1054.

75. Ted Sizer opened a window to teachers' notions about education. See Sizer, T. *Horace's School: Redesigning the American High School*. New York: Houghton Mifflin, 2002.

77. In 1930, philanthropist Edward Harkness, a graduate of St. Paul's School, NH, provided a gift the Phillips Exeter Academy. Schools use the Harkness table to allow and encourage students to think for themselves as they develop discussion and logic skills.

90. Roger Goddard had done significant research with teachers on the influence of collective efficacy. See Goddard, R.D., LoGerfo, L. and Hoy, W.K. (2004). "High School Accountability: The Role of Perceived Collective Efficacy," *Educational Policy*. 18 (3) 403-425.

Chapter Three

105. Walter Mischel's "marshmallow experiments" in the late 1960's and early 1970's focused on delayed gratification of young children by measuring impulse control. Children were told that they could eat one marshmallow immediately or the child could wait and eat the treat when the teacher returned in a couple of minutes. If she waited for the teacher, the child could then have two marshmallows. Longitudinal research with the original participants showed that delay of gratification in pre-schoolers predicted SAT scores and academic success. See Mischel, W., Shoda, Y. and Rodriguez, M. L. (1989). "Delay of Gratification in Children," *Science*, 244 (4907), 933-938.

105. The findings in Angela Duckworth's research on Grit are so robust that we are compelled to mention the reference one more time. See Duckworth, A.L. and Seligman, M.E.P.

(2005). "Self-Discipline Outdoes IQ in Predicting Academic Performance of Adolescents," *Psychological Science*, 16 (12), 939-944.

106. Nansook Park, Chris Peterson and Martin Seligman found that eastern cultures have a higher incidence of self-control than in the United States. See Park, N., Peterson, C. and Seligman, M.E.P. (2006). "Character Strengths in Fifty Four Nations and Fifty US States," *The Journal of Positive Psychology*, 1:118–129.

107. We reprise Roy Baumeister's work in self-regulation. See R.F. Baumeister and K.D. Vohs (Eds.) *Handbook of Self-Regulation: Research, Theory, and Application. Edition 1.* New York: Guilford Publications, Inc., 2007.

107. Albert Bandura has made significant contributions to the study of social learning theory and self-efficacy. See Bandura, A. *Self-efficacy.* In V. S. Ramachaudran (Ed.), *Encyclopedia of Human Behavior* 4, 71-81. New York: Academic Press, 1994. (Reprinted in H. Friedman (Ed.), *Encyclopedia of Mental Health.* San Diego: Academic Press, 1998).

108. Richard Ryan and Edward Deci are pioneers in the psychological theory of self-determination. See Deci, E. L., & Ryan, R. M. *Intrinsic Motivation and Self-determination in Human Behavior.* New York: Plenum, 2005. Also, see Deci and Ryan share more on self-determination. See Deci, E. L. and Ryan, R. M. (2000). "The "What" and "Why" of Goal Pursuits: Human Needs and the Self-determination of Behavior," *Psychological Inquiry, 11,* 227-268. And Ryan, R. M., & Deci, E. L. (2000). "Self-determination Theory and the Facilitation of Intrinsic Motivation, Social Development, and Well-being," *American Psychologist, 55,* 68-78.

111. Philip Cowan and Carolyn Pape Cowan remind us of the importance of parents being partners in the development of their children. See Cowan, C.P. and Cowan, P.A. *When Partners Become Parents: The Big Life Change for Couples.* Mahwah, NJ: Lawrence Erlbaum Associates, 2000.

Chapter Four

118. John Wooden's principles can be found in Wooden, J. and Jamison, S. Wooden: *A Lifetime of Observations and Reflections on and off the Court.* Chicago: Contemporary Books, 1997.

121. Tom Lickona and Matt Davidson are leading character educators and authors of *Smart and Good Schools: The Smart & Good Schools Initiative* (K-12), a project of the *Center for the 4th and 5th Rs* and the *Institute for Excellence & Ethics* (IEE) which focuses on research, development and training. www.cortland.edu/character/sg_initiative.asp

121. Ed Diener is a pioneer in the study of psychological well-being. See Diener, E. and Biswas-Diener, R. *Happiness: Unlocking the Mysteries of Psychological Wealth.* Malden, MA: Blackwell, 2008.

130. Once again, Robert Greenleaf's notion of servant leadership is examined. See Greenleaf,

R.K. *Servant Leadership – A Journey into the Nature of Legitimate Power and Greatness.* Mahwah NJ: The Paulist Press, 1991.

130. Sam Osherson demonstrates the power of mentoring young people. See Osherson, S. (1999). "The Art of Mentoring," *Independent School Health Association Newsletter.*

135. Drew Hyland demonstrates the influence of sports participation on well-being. See Hyland, D. (1985). "Opponents, Contestants, and Competitors: The Dialectic of Sport," *Journal of the Philosophy of Sport.* 11, 63-70.

135. The *Sport Experience Questionnaire* is an unvalidated survey for coaches and players. See Yeager, J., Buxton, J., Baltzell, A. and Bzdell, W. *Character and Coaching: Building Virtue in Athletic Programs.* Port Chester, NY: Dude Publishing, 2001.

Chapter Five

143. John Corlett, from the University of Winnipeg, frames the Red Queen Effect in reference to sports participation. See Corlett, J. *Proceedings of the Fourteenth Annual Conference on Counseling Athletes,* Springfield College, 1998.

143. Michael Eysenck has popularized the term "hedonic treadmill," which is a metaphor for the tendency for people to return to an earlier established level of well-being after a positive or negative event. For example, increased wealth may provide a temporary surge in happiness, but there will be a return to a set-point of well-being, and to reach a higher level of happiness it will be necessary to hop back on the treadmill. See Brickman, P. and Campbell, D.T. (1971). "Hedonic Relativism and Planning the Good Society." In M.H. Apley (Ed.), *Adaptation Level Theory: A Symposium,* New York: Academic Press, 287–302.

144. Barry Schwartz offers sage advice on some of the negative consequences of having too many choices. See Schwartz, B. *The Paradox of Choice: Why More is Less.* New York: Harper Collins, 2004.

150. Michael Cohn and Barbara Fredrickson show how meditation can benefit overall well-being. See Cohn, M.A. and Fredrickson, B.L. (2010). "In Search of Durable Positive Psychological Interventions: Predictors and Consequences of Long-term Positive Behavior Change," *The Journal of Positive Psychology,* 5 (5) 355 – 366. Also, see Fredrickson, B.L., Cohn, M.A., Coffey, K.A., Pek, J. and Finkel, S.M. (2008). "Open Hearts Build Lives: Positive Emotions, Induced through Loving-kindness Meditation, Build Consequential Personal Resources," *Journal of Personality and Social Psychology,* 95 (5), 1045–1062.

151. Suzanne Kobasa and Salvatore Maddi's investigations confirm the influence of the hardy personality on well-being. See Maddi, S. R. (2006). "Hardiness: The Courage to Grow from Stresses," *The Journal of Positive Psychology,* 1(3), 160-168.

154. Steven Berglas provides great insights about how there can be lingering disappointment after achieving success in a life event. See Berglas, S. *The Success Syndrome: Hitting Bottom When You Reach the Top.* New York: Plenum Press, 1986, and Berglas, S. *Reclaiming*

The Fire: How Successful People Overcome Burnout. New York: Random House, 2001.

154. Fred Bryant analyzes the components of savoring. See Bryant, F.B. (1989). "A Four-Factor Model of Perceived Control: Avoiding, Coping, Obtaining, and Savoring,*" Journal of Personality, 57(4),* 773-797, and Bryant, F. and Verhoff, J. *Savoring: A New Model of Positive Experience.* Mahwah, New Jersey: Lawrence Erlbaum Associates, 2007.

155. We reprise Robert Emmons contributions to the study of gratitude. See Emmons, R. *Thanks! How the New Science of Gratitude Can Make You Happier.* Boston: Houghton Mifflin, 2007.

159. James Gangwisch and his colleagues found that adolescents with earlier sleep times were less likely to be depressed. Gangwisch, J.E., Babiss, L.A. Malaspina, D., Turner, J.B., Zammit, G.K., and Posner, K. (2010). "Earlier Parental Set Bedtimes as a Protective Factor Against Depression and Suicidal Ideation," *Sleep.* 33 (1), 97-106.

159. Mary Carskadon has compiled compelling evidence on sleep rhythms and sleep/wake patterns in young people. See Carskadon, M.A., Acebo, C. and Jenni, O.G. (2004). "Regulation of Adolescent Sleep: Implications for Behavior." In R. E. Dahl and L.P. Spear (Eds). "Adolescent Brain Development: Vulnerabilities and Opportunities." *Annals of the New York Academy of* Sciences, 1021, 276-291.

159. Barbara Strauch provides instructive insights on adolescent sleep patterns. See Strauch, B. *The Primal Teen: What the New Discoveries about the Teenage Brain Tell Us about Our* Kids. New York: Anchor Books, 2003.

162. Isaac and Ora Prilleltensky, from the University of Miami, provide compelling evidence about the power of relationships and well-being. See Prilleltensky, I. and Prilleltensky, O. *Promoting Well-Being: Linking Personal, Organizational, and Community Change.* Hoboken, NJ: Wiley, 2006.

Chapter Six

166. Jill Bolte Taylor provides a professional and personal understanding of the influence of neural connections and emotions. See Taylor, J. B. *My Stroke of Insight: A Brain Scientist's Personal Journey.* New York: Plume, 2009.

167. Barbara Fredrickson's research on the power of positive emotions is ground breaking. Fredrickson, B. L. *Positivity.* New York: Crown, 2009.

168. Marcial Losada has done much work in the area of team performance. He has focused on the connectivity of business teams and the positivity/negativity ratios of interactions within those teams. See Losada, M. (1999). "The Complex Dynamics of High Performance Teams," *Mathematical and Computer Modelling,* 30 (9-10), 179-192. Also, see Losada, M. and Heaphy, E. (2004). "The Role of Positivity and Connectivity in the Performance of Business Teams: A Nonlinear Dynamics Model," *American Behavioral Scientist,* 47 (6), 740-765.

169. Barbara Fredrickson collaborated with Marcial Losada to predict ratios of positive

and negative affect in individuals and teams. See Fredrickson, B. L. and Losada, M. (2005). "Positive Affect and the Complex Dynamics of Human Flourishing," *American Psychologist*, 60 (7) 678-686.

170. Robert Wright offers a powerful view of win-win situations in business, political and other environments. See Wright R. *Nonzero*. New York: Vintage, 2001.

171. Gary Strauss, from the University of Nevada, and Daniel Allen, from the University of Maryland School of Medicine, have studied the influence of positive and negative emotions on attention. Negative emotions interfered with attention when there was "high time pressure." However, when there was less time pressure, positive emotions interfered with attention. See Strauss, G. and Allen, D. (2009). "Positive and Negative Emotions Uniquely Capture Attention," *Applied Neuropsychology*, 16 (2) 144-149.

171. Brett Q. Ford, May Tamir, and their colleagues at Boston College studied emotion and visual attention. An angry person may approach something more aggressively while a person working from a positive emotion may approach it in a more gracious and welcoming way. To get the same results, some people need to pay close attention to an object when they are under the influence of a negative emotion. See Tamir, M., Ford, B.Q., Brunye, T.T., Shirer, W.R., Mahoney, C.R. and Taylor, H.A. (2010). "Keeping Your Eyes on the Prize: Anger and Visual Attention to Threats and Rewards," *Psychological Science*. 21 (8) 1098-1105.

171. Chris Peterson's declaration that "other people matter" reinforces an important factor in developing healthy emotions. See Peterson, C. *A Primer in Positive Psychology*. Oxford: Oxford University Press, 2006.

171. Roger Goddard demonstrates in his research how the healthy collaboration of teachers can yield positive results in schools. See Goddard, R.D., LoGerfo, L. and Hoy, W.K. (2004). "High School Accountability: The Role of Perceived Collective Efficacy," *Educational Policy*, *18*(3) 403-425.

173. Todd Kashdan presents some very interesting research with respect to emotional health. He studied how students who can name their emotions and differentiate among them are less inclined to self medicate by overdrinking. See Kashdan, T. B., Ferssizidis, P., Collins, R. L. and Muraven, M. (2010). "Emotion Differentiation as Resilience Against Excessive Alcohol Use: An Ecological Momentary Assessment in Underage Social Drinkers," *Psychological Science*, 21, 1341-1347.

176. Psychologist Jonathan Haidt introduced us to the "rider and the elephant" metaphor in his book, The Happiness Hypothesis. See Haidt, J. *The Happiness Hypothesis: Finding Ancient Truth on Modern Wisdom*. New York: Basic Books, 2006. Also, see Heath, C. and Heath, D. *Switch: How to Change Things When Change is Hard*. New York: Broadway Books, 2010. The authors masterfully apply Haidt's metaphor to change, especially at an institutional level.

177. Jim Taylor and Mark Jones explain how certain emotions influence athletic perfor-

mance. See Taylor, J. and Jones, M. "Emotions." In J. Taylor and G.W. Wilson (Eds.), *Applying Sports Psychology*. Champaign, IL: Human Kinetics, 2005.

179. For a greater understanding of "flow," see Csikszentmihalyi, M. *Flow: The Psychology of Optimal Experience*. New York: Harper-Perennial, 2008.

180. Yuri Hanin of the Research Institute for Olympic Sports in Finland, shows how people may fit into different zones of functioning based on their optimum performance and arousal relationships. Hanin, Y. "Individual Zones of Performance Relationships in Sport." In *Emotions in Sport*. Champaign, IL: Human Kinetics, 2000.

Chapter Seven

187. Martin E.P. Seligman and his co-researchers have studied the concept of explanatory style and its impact on emotions, expectations, and performance. See Seligman, M. E. P. *Learned Optimism*. New York: Knopf, 1991.

187. The skills-based approach to resilience in this chapter is heavily influenced by the work of Karen Reivich, Andrew Shatté, Jane Gillham and others, especially in almost two decades of work with the Penn Resilience Program, a skills-training program for middle school students. Their work is currently being applied extensively in the United Kingdom and Australia. The adult version of that program is also currently being delivered by the United States Army as part of Comprehensive Soldier Fitness. See Reivich, K. and Shatté, A. (2002). *The Resilience Factor: 7 Essential Skills for Overcoming Life's Inevitable Obstacles*. New York: Broadway Books, 2002. See also, Reivich, K. Seligman, M., and McBride, S. (2011). "Master Resilience Training in the U.S. Army," *American Psychologist*, 66(1) 25-3.

187. Dr. Robert Brooks, a psychologist on the faculty of Harvard Medical School, has lectured nationally and internationally on resilience in young people. See Brooks, R. and Goldstein, S. *Raising a Self-disciplined Child: Help Your Child Become More Responsible, Confident, and Resilient*. New York: McGraw-Hill, 2009.

188. Tim Judge and Charlice Hurst studied income levels of pessimists and optimists. See Judge, T. A. and Hurst, C. (2007). "Capitalizing On One's Advantages: Role of Core Self-evaluations," *Journal of Applied Psychology, 92*(5) 1212-1227.

188. The National Longitudinal Study of Youth began in 1979 with 12,686 participants between the ages of 14-22 years old. Students who had low core self-evaluations and higher GPAs earned less money at age 50. Admittedly, annual income is not the sole or even the best measure of the good life, but the impact of positive habits of cognition, emotion, behavior and relatedness seems clear. See *The National Longitudinal Surveys NLSY79 Users Guide*. Ohio State University: Center for Human Resource Research, 1997.

188. Suzanne Segerstrom's research supports the positive health effects of optimistic behavior. See Segerstrom, S.C. (2007). "Optimism and resources: Effects on Each Other and on Health Over Ten Years," *Journal of Research in Personality*, 41(4), 772-786. Also, see

Segerstrom, S.C. *Breaking Murphy's Law: How Optimists Get What They Want From Life and Pessimists Can Too*. New York: Guilford Press, 2006.

197. Daniel Goleman, an internationally recognized psychologist, focuses on brain science and intelligence. See Goleman, D. *Emotional Intelligence: Why It Can Matter More Than IQ*. New York: Bantam Dell, 2006.

208. Julie Hall and Frank Fincham convincingly show how self-forgiveness is an important step in sustaining well-being. See Hall, J.H. and Fincham, F.D. (2005). "Self-Forgiveness: The Stepchild of Forgiveness Research," *Journal of Social and Clinical Psychology*, 24, (5) 621-637. Also, see Hall, J.H. and Fincham, F.D. (2008). "The Temporal Course of Self-Forgiveness," *Journal of Social and Clinical Psychology*, 27 (2) 174-202. And McCullough, M. M. (2001). "Forgiveness: Who Does It and How Do They Do It?" *Current Directions in Psychological Science*." 10 (6) 194-197.

Chapter Eight

212. Carol Dweck's work is a must read for parents, teachers and coaches. See Dweck, C.S. *Mindset: The New Psychology of Success*. New York: Random House, 2006.

217. Tojo Thatchenkery and Carol Metzker demonstrate how teachers can provide an environment for students that promotes success while discovering their talents and strengths. See Thatchenkerry, T. and Metzker, C. *Appreciative Intelligence: Seeing the Mighty Oak in the Acorn*. San Francisco: Berrett-Koehler, 2006.

217. Ernest Shackleton's amazing voyage and return has been written about by a variety of authors. For one perspective, see Lansing, A. *Endurance: Shackleton's Incredible Voyage*. New York: Carroll and Graf, 2002.

218. A leader in the field of deliberate practice, K. Anders Ericsson presents his research in this article and book. See Ericsson, K. A. "The Influence of Experience and Deliberate Practice on the Development of Superior Expert Performance." In K. A. Ericsson, N. Charness, P. Feltovich, and R. R. Hoffman, R. R. (Eds.), *Cambridge Handbook of Expertise and Expert Performance*. Cambridge, UK: Cambridge University Press, 2006.

219. Malcolm Gladwell's *The Physical Genius* appeared in *The New Yorker* magazine, August 2, 1999, pp. 57-65. Also, Gladwell suggests that people make split second decisions much of the time. See Gladwell, M. *Blink: The Power of Thinking Without Thinking*. New York: Little, Brown and Company, 2005. In addition, his book *Outliers*, is an interesting read. See Gladwell, M. *Outliers: The Story of Success*. NY: Little, Brown and Company.

220. Carol Dweck calls upon her research on mindsets of both boys and girls. See Dweck, C.S. *Self-theories: Their Role in Motivation, Personality, and Development (Essays in Social Psychology)*. Philadelphia, PA: Taylor Francis Psychology Press, 2000.

222. Justin Kruger and David Dunning offer further evidence of how people can miscalibrate perceptions of their level of competence in an area. See Kruger, J. and Dunning, D.

(1999). "Unskilled and Unaware of It: How Difficulties in Recognizing One's Own Incompetence Lead to Inflated Self-assessments," *Psychology*, 1, 30-46.

228. Dr. Robert Brooks, a psychologist on the faculty of Harvard Medical School, has lectured nationally and internationally on resilience in young people. See Brooks, R. and Goldstein, S. *Raising a Self-disciplined Child: Help Your Child Become More Responsible, Confident, and Resilient.* New York: McGraw-Hill, 2009.

Chapter Nine

230. Liisa Ogburn is the Program Director of the Hine Documentary Fellows Program for the Center for Documentary Studies at Duke University.

230. Ambiguity tolerance is the ability for people to react and respond well to uncertain situations. For example, some people may be more open to experience that does not have a lot of structure. See Wilkinson, D. *The Ambiguity Advantage: What Great Leaders Are Great At.* London: Palgrave Macmillan, 2006. Also, see Tegano, D.W., Groves, M.M. and Catron, C.E. (1999). "Early Childhood Teachers' Playfulness and Ambiguity Tolerance: Essential Elements of Encouraging Creative Potential of Children," Journal of Early Childhood Teacher Education, 20(3), 291 – 300; and DeRoma, V.M., Martin, K.M., and Kessler, M.L. (2003). "The Relationship Between Tolerance for Ambiguity and Need for Course Structure," *Journal of Instructional Psychology*, 30 (2), 104-109.

232. Caroline Adams Miller, our MAPP classmate and an inspiration for us in our writing, provides fascinating and practical research-based perspectives on goal setting in her book. See Miller, C.A. and Frisch, M.B. *Creating Your Best Life: The Ultimate Life List Guide.* New York: Sterling, 2009.

234. Gary Locke and Edwin Latham have done pioneering goal setting research with organizations. See Latham, G. in "Motivate Employee Performance through Goal Setting." In E.A. Locke, (Ed.), *Handbook of Principles of Organizational Behavior.* Malden, MA: Blackwell, 2000. Also, Locke, E.A. and Latham, G.P. *A Theory of Goal Setting and Task Performance.* Englewood Cliffs, NJ: Prentice Hall, 1990.

234. Shane Lopez and his colleagues address the concepts of waypower and willpower. See Lopez, S.J., Snyder, C.R.,. Magyar-Moe, J.L., Edwards, L.M., Teramoto Pedrotti, J., Janowski, K., Turner, J.L. and Pressgrove, C. "Strategies for Accentuating Hope." In P. A. Linley and S. Joseph (Eds.), *Positive Psychology in Practice.* Hoboken, NJ: Wiley and Sons, 2005. Also, see Snyder, C.R., Rand, K.L., and Sigmon, D.R. "Hope Theory: A Member of the Positive Psychology Family." In C.R. Snyder and S.J. Lopez (Eds.), *Handbook of Positive Psychology.* Oxford: Oxford University Press, 2005.

240. Ken Bain's work on the "promising syllabus," based on his research of the best college teachers, can be transformative at all levels of teaching. See Bain, K. *What the Best College Teachers Do.* Cambridge, MA: Harvard University Press, 2004.

243. John Murray, CEO of Advanced Path Academies, leads the development of non-traditional students with practical solutions to lessen the drop-out crisis.

243. Through United States Lacrosse, the national governing body of the sport, we surveyed players, coaches, officials and parents associated with interscholastic programs. 83% of those involved in female programs, and 77% in male programs believed that "setting goals" was essential to overall enjoyment and success in the game. See Yeager, J. *Our Game: The Character and Culture of Lacrosse*. Port Chester, NY: Dude/National Professional Resources, 2006.

245. Amy Baltzell is the Coordinator of the Sport Psychology specialization and a faculty member of the counseling program at Boston University. She is a contributing author to the books *Whose Game Is It, Anyway? A Guide to Helping Your Child Get the Most From Sports, Organized By Age and Stage.* (2006); and *Character and Coaching: Building Virtue in Athletic Programs* (2001). Also, she is a co-author of the chapter "Arousal and Performance" in the *Handbook of Sport Psychology* (2001).

245. Once again, we reprise Grit. See Duckworth, A.L. and Seligman, M.E.P. (2005). "Self-Discipline Outdoes IQ in Predicting Academic Performance of Adolescents," *Psychological Science*, 16 (12), 939-944.

248. Laura King emphasizes the power of the imagination in goal setting. See King, L.A. (2001). "The Health Benefits of Writing about Life Goals," *Personality and Social Psychology Bulletin.* 27 (7) 798-807.

249. Ruby Payne's positive influence in schools is palpable. She provides a clear lens for educators to see the dynamics of poverty, and at the same time, work with students to develop a best "future story." Payne, R.K. *A Framework for Understanding Poverty*. Highlands, TX: aha! Process, Inc., 2005.

Chapter Ten

252. Jane Dutton, from the Ross School of Business at the University of Michigan, lays out the foundational components of building high quality connections in organizations. See Dutton, J.E. *Energize Your Workplace: How to Build and Sustain High-Quality Connections at Work.* San Francisco: Jossey-Bass, 2003.

258. Aneil and Karen Mishra's ROCC model of trust offers a practical rubric for parents, teachers and coaches. They suggest that a teacher can be reliable without being competent, and vice versa. See Mishra, A. and Mishra, K. *Trust is Everything: Become the Leader Others Will Follow.* Available at www.lulu.com, 2008.

260. Rolheiser, C. and Anderson, S. "Practices in Teacher Education and Cooperative Learning at the University of Toronto." In E. G. Cohen, C. M. Brody and M. Sapon-Shevin (Eds.), Teaching Cooperative Learning: The Challenge for Teacher Education (pp. 27-44). The State University of New York Press, 2004.

263. Shelly Gable, from the University of California, Santa Cruz, focuses her work on social interaction and close relationships. See Gable, S. L., Gonzaga, G., and Strachman, A. (2006). "Will You Be There For Me When Things Go Right? Social Support for Positive Events," *Journal of Personality and Social Psychology*, 91 (5), 904-917; and Gable, S. L., and Reis, H. T. (2010). "Good News! Capitalizing on Positive Events in an Interpersonal Context." In M. Zanna (Ed.). *Advances in Experimental Social Psychology*, 42, (pp. 198-257) New York: Elsevier Press, 2010.

265. David Cooperrider and Diana Whitney are pioneers of Appreciative Inquiry. See Cooperrider, D. and Whitney, D. *Appreciative Inquiry: A Positive Revolution in Change.* San Francisco, CA: Berrett-Koehler, 2005.

267. Diana Whitney and Amanda Trosten-Bloom fine tune the concept of asking the right appreciative questions in organizations. See Whitney, D. and Trosten-Bloom, A. *Appreciative Leadership: Focus on What Works to Drive Winning Performance and Build a Thriving Organization.* New York: McGraw-Hill, 2010.

Afterword

270. Robert Evans is a widely-traveled consultant for schools and organizations. He is the author of *Seven Secrets of The Savvy School Leader.* San Francisco: Jossey Bass, 2010; *The Human Side of School Change.* San Francisco: Jossey Bass, 1996; and *Family Matters: How Schools Can Cope with The Crisis in Childrearing.* San Francisco: Jossey Bass, 2004.

271. Marianne Williamson's quote is commonly, yet inaccurately attributed to Nelson Mandela. See *A Return to Love: Reflections on the Principles of "A Course in Miracles."* New York: Harper-Collins, 1992.

274. Once again, Laura King emphasizes the power of the imagination in creating your "Best Possible Future Self." See King, L.A. (2001). "The Health Benefits of Writing about Life Goals," *Personality and Social Psychology Bulletin*, 27 (7) 798-807.

274. Robert E. Quinn is a co-founder of the Center for Positive Organizational Scholarship at the University of Michigan Ross School of Business. He is the author of *Building the Bridge As You Walk On It: A Guide for Leading Change.* San Francisco: Jossey-Bass, 2010.

Resources

On Our Shelves: Positive Psychology Research-based Books

Ben-Shahar, Tal. *Happier: Learn the Secrets to Daily Joy and Lasting Fulfillment.* New York: McGraw Hill, 2007.

Ben-Shahar, Tal. *Even Happier: A Gratitude Journal for Daily Joy and Lasting Fulfillment,* McGraw-Hill Professional, 2010.

Brooks, Robert and Sam Goldstein. *Raising a Self-disciplined Child: Help Your Child Become More Responsible, Confident, and Resilient.* New York: McGraw-Hill, 2009.

Brooks, Robert and Sam Goldstein. *Raising Resilient Children: Fostering Strength, Hope, and Optimism in Your Child.* New York: McGraw-Hill, 2002.

Buckingham, Marcus and Donald O. Clifton. *Now, Discover Your Strengths.* New York: Free Press, 2001.

Cooperrider, David L. and Diana Whitney. *Appreciative Inquiry: A Positive Revolution in Change.* San Francisco: Berret-Koehler, 2005.

Csikszentmihalyi, Mihaly. *Flow: The Psychology of Optimal Experience (P.S.).* New York: Harper Perennial, 2008.

Diener, Ed and Robert Biswas-Diener. *Happiness: Unlocking the Mysteries of Psychological Wealth.* Malden MA: Blackwell, 2008.

Dweck, Carol. *Mindset: The New Psychology of Success.* New York: Random House, 2006.

Emmons, Robert A. *Thanks! How Practicing Gratitude Can Make You Happier.* New York: Houghton Mifflin, 2007.

Fredrickson, Barbara. *Positivity.* New York: Crown, 2009.

Gladwell, Malcolm. *Blink: The Power of Thinking Without Thinking.* New York: Little, Brown, 2005.

Greenleaf, Robert K. *The Servant-Leader Within: A Transformative Path.* Mahwah, NJ: Paulist Press, 2003.

Haidt, Jonathan. *The Happiness Hypothesis: Finding Ancient Truth in Modern Wisdom.* New York: Basic Books, 2006.

Kashdan, Todd. *Curious? Discover the Missing Ingredient to a Fulfilling Life.* New York: Morrow, 2009.

Linley, Alex, Willars, Janet, and Robert Biswas-Diener. *The Strengths Book: Be Confident, Be Successful, and Enjoy Better Relationships By Realising the Best of You.* Coventry, UK: CAPP Press, 2010. (This book uses a new strengths tool, the "Realise2" Model of Strengths.)

Lyubomirsky, Sonja. *The How of Happiness: A Scientific Approach to Getting the Life You Want* New York: Penguin, 2007.

Miller, Caroline Adams and Frisch, Michael B. *Creating Your Best Life: The Ultimate Life List Guide.* New York: Sterling Publishing, 2009.

Niemiec, Ryan and Wedding, Danny. *Positive Psychology at the Movies: Using Films to Build Virtues and Character Strengths.* Cambridge MA: Hogrefe Publishing, 2008.

Noddings, Nell. *Happiness and Education.* New York: Cambridge University Press, 2003.

Peterson, Christopher. *A Primer in Positive Psychology.* New York: Oxford Press, 2006.

Pollay, David J. *The Law of the Garbage Truck: How to Respond to People Who Dump on You, and How to Stop Dumping on Others.* New York: Sterling Publishing, 2010.

Quinn, Robert. *Building the Bridge as You Walk on It: A Guide for Leading Change.* Jossey-Bass: San Francisco, 2004.

Quinn, Ryan and Quinn, Robert. *Lift: Becoming a Positive Force in Any Situation.* San Francisco: Berrett-Koehler, 2009.

Rath, Tom and Barry Conchie. *Strengths Based Leadership: Great Leaders, Teams, and Why People Follow.* New York: Gallup Press, 2008.

Rath, Tom. *Strengths Finder 2.0.* New York: Gallup Press, 2007.

Reivich, Karen and Andrew Shatté. *The Resilience Factor: 7 Essential Skills for Overcoming Life's Inevitable Obstacles.* New York: Broadway Books, 2002.

Schwartz, Barry. *The Paradox of Choice: Why More is Less.* New York: Harper Perennial, 2004.

Seligman, Martin E.P. *Flourish: A Visionary New Understanding of Happiness and Well-being.* New York: Free Press.

Seligman, Martin E.P. *Authentic Happiness: Using the New Positive Psychology to Realize Your Potential for Lasting Fulfillment.* New York: Free Press, 2002.

Seligman, M.E.P. *Learned Optimism: How to Change Your Mind and Your Life.* New York: Pocket Books, 1998.

Seligman, M.E.P., Reivich, K., Jaycox, L., & Gillham, J. *The Optimistic Child.* Boston: Houghton Mifflin, 1995.

Thaler, Richard H. and Cass R. Sunstein. *Nudge: Improving Decisions About Health, Wealth, and Happiness.* New Haven: Yale University Press, 2008.

On-Line

Flourishing Schools
www.flourishingschools.org
John Yeager, Sherri Fisher, Dave Shearon, Louis Alloro
UPenn MAPP trained educators use a systems approach to positive education in schools, applying empirical findings of Positive Psychology to all aspects of teaching and learning. Speaking, workshops, program development, coaching.

Authentic Happiness

www.authentichappiness.com

Free positive psychology assessments when you participate in (anonymous) research. VIA Strengths Inventory, the GRIT Test, many more available here.

Positive Psychology News

www.positivepsychologynews.com

Articles by world leaders in Applied Positive Psychology (The authors of *SMART Strengths* have published over 120 positive psychology-based articles here on a broad variety of topics with applications to strengths, resilience, relationships and education.)

Culver Academies

www.culver.org

Outstanding independent college preparatory boarding schools comprised of Culver Military Academy and Culver Girls Academy.

Louis Alloro and Associates

www.louisalloro.com

A network of change agents helping individuals and organizations kick it up a notch through Positive Psychology, the Science of Success, Well-Being, and Flourishing.

International Positive Psychology Association

www.ippanetwork.org

Promotes the science and practice of positive psychology; facilitates communication and collaboration among researchers and practitioners around the world.

Positive Psychology Center, UPenn

www.ppc.sas.upenn.edu

Promotes research, training, education, and the dissemination of Positive Psychology. Extensive information, resources, and links

Values in Action Institute

www.viacharacter.org

Ryan M. Niemiec, Psy. D., Psychologist and Educational Director

The VIA Institute on Character (once called the "Values in Action" Institute) is a non-profit, positive psychology organization in Cincinnati, Ohio. It was created in 2000 by Dr. Neal Mayerson, following extensive collaboration with Dr. Martin Seligman, founder of "positive psychology," and a number of top scientists. With the generous support of the Manuel D. and Rhoda Mayerson Foundation, the VIA Institute created the VIA Classification of character strengths and virtues and the VIA Survey, the psychometric tool that measures the 24 character strengths. The VIA Institute aggregates and disseminates the latest research and practices around character strengths.

Centre for Applied Positive Psychology

www.cappeu.com

Strengths-based consultancy focuses on research and application of positive psychology in organizations. Developer of the Realise2 strengths model.

Dr. Robert Brooks

www.drrobertbrooks.com

Dr. Robert Brooks, a psychologist on the faculty of Harvard Medical School, has lectured nationally and internationally to audiences of parents, educators, mental health professionals and business people about topics pertaining to motivation, resilience, school climate, family relationships, the qualities of effective leaders, and balancing our personal and professional lives. He is the author or co-author of 14 books including The Self-Esteem Teacher; Raising Resilient Children; Raising a Self-Disciplined Child; The Power of Resilience: Achieving Balance, Confidence and Personal Strength in Your Life; and Handbook of Resilience in Children. His lectures and writings reflect the strength-based approach that he applies in his work.

Christine Duvivier

www.christineduvivier.com

Christine is a positive change leader/speaker/mentor. She shows how to unleash the hidden talents in every young adult. Christine challenges the notion that if you are not a top performer, you are not positioned for future success and there is something wrong with you. She leads positive change in three areas: in communities, in business and in families. Christine's vision is one where our education model develops students' innate abilities, instead of chasing grades and standardized learning, a model in which every student is viewed as gifted.

Weaver Center

www.weavercenter.org

R.A. Weaver: Strengths focused Clinical Neuropsychologist

Derrick Carpenter

www.vivetraining.com

Coaches individuals and corporate clients on creating high-engagement lifestyles through physical   and psychological wellness.

The Gallup Organization

www.gallup.com and www.strengthsfinder.com

Publisher of StrengthsFinder 2.0., Strengths Based Leadership and the Clifton StrengthsFinder assessment. Consultancy, research, strategic advisory, and training services

Appreciative Inquiry Commons

http://appreciativeinquiry.case.edu

Extensive tools and research for creating strengths-based positive organizational change.

Acknowledgments

This book, which has been cultivated over time, is the result of a web of dialogue we have had with many people, including scholars, practitioners, parents, teachers, coaches and students. We are grateful for the support of Caroline Adams Miller, our MAPP classmate, whose belief in the project gave us the motivation to move forward. She introduced us to her agent, Ivor Whitson. Ivor has been a constant support for us. With his vast experience as an agent and publisher, Ivor has expertly navigated us through the writing and editorial process. His belief in the project nudged us to make the book a reality. Ronnie Whitson's creative and painstaking editorial work on the final manuscript made it come alive. We appreciate her exceptional work on the book's cover design and graphics. We are grateful to Rochelle Melander for her support in book coaching and development editing, especially during our dark nights of the soul, when there were more frustrations than elations with the manuscript. And we thank Kathryn Britton, another of our classmates in the MAPP program, for her deliberate content editing, making sure our assumptions were backed up with scholarly research.

Thanks also to those who made the MAPP program possible, starting with Martin Seligman, and especially James Pawelski and Debbie Swick. Our MAPP classmates, and those who have gone through after us, have helped confirm the real-world workability of what we studied by their amazing accomplishments. We are grateful to a group of our MAPP classmates who contributed to the book: Louis Alloro, Chrstine Duvivier, Gabe Paoletti, Dana Vellios, Derrick Carpenter, Elaine O'Brien, Dave Bonner, Eleanor Chin, and Sean Doyle. And, of course, we thank the MAPP faculty and guest scholars, including Ed Diener, Barry Schwartz, Bill Robertson, Jon Haidt, Jane Gillham, David Cooperrider, Karen Reivich, Nansoon Park, Mark Linkins, and Jane Dutton with a special thanks to Chris Peterson, who introduced us to the world of strengths.

We are grateful to many people at Culver for their support with the project, especially John Buxton, head of school at the Culver Academies, for his unwavering support of bringing a strengths-based approach to Culver, and to the senior administrative staff — Kathy Lintner, Kevin MacNeil and Josh Pretzer and to the Culver Positive Education site-team — Nancy McKinnis, Angie Fulton, Ed Kelley, and Kevin Danti. Tom Duckett, Gary Christlieb, John Buggeln, Sonny Adkins, Emily Ryman, Laura Weaser, Kelly Jordan, Dan Cowell and Dan Davidge have all been instructive in their support for the SMART Strengths model. Mike Hogan, Chet Marshall and Steve Sturman from Culver's Development Department have been instrumental in creating a marketing plan and mining Alumni relationships to support the book project. And thanks to Alan Loehr and Mary Beth Ryan from Culver's Alumni Department for getting the SMART Strengths word out and setting up Culver Clubs events as part of the national book tour. Thanks to Culver's Communications department for marketing the project — Bill Hargraves, Gary Mills, Doug Haberland,

Lensie Howell, Jan Garrison, and Trent Miles. For Technology support, we thank Larry Emmons, Mark Sayer, Lew Kopp, Matt White, and Bryan Falk. Thanks to Kim Frazier, Tammy Durbin, Jenny Reid, and Jade Hoesel in Culver's administrative services department, for reproducing the many earlier drafts of the book. We are also grateful to Phoebe Hall, Meghan Grieves, and Clint Zumer, Culver students who have made a commitment to living a strengths-based life.

We are thankful for our wonderful collaboration with the Triton School Corporation — Carl Hilling, Jeremy Riffle, Josh Van Houten, Christine Cook, Bob Ross, Mike Chobanov, and Mason McIntyre. And we are also grateful for our collaboration with Christel House International and Christel House Academy, Indianapolis — Christel DeHaan, Carey Dancke, Brad Sever, Faiza Serang and Jill McKinney.

Thanks to Neal Mayerson and Ryan Niemiec at the VIA Institute for Character and Tom Rath and Erik Nielsen at the Gallup Organization. We thank Helene Hanson at National Professional Resources, INC. for her generous permission to use excerpts from *Character and Coaching*, and *The Character and Culture of Lacrosse*. We are grateful for permissions from Mihaly Csikszentmihalyi and Yuri Hanin to use the respective "Flow Channel" and "Individual Zones of Optimal Functioning" graphs.

Liisa Ogburn, graciously provided us with photos of hope from the TY Joyner elementary school poster. We are also very appreciative of the wonderful art work from John Fenley and Jill Paolini. A special thanks to Ashleigh Brilliant for use of his insightful "pot-shots."

Thanks to scholars and practitioners Nel Noddings, Steven Tigner and Edwin Delattre, Ken Bain, Amy Baltzell, Buck Weaver, and Todd Kashdan. We appreciate the instructive contributions from a variety of parents, teachers and coaches: Joan Young, Kevin Hicks, John Pirani, Casey Jackson, Kate Dresher, Dee Stephan, Alan McCoy, Dom Starsia, Mark Harris, and Dan Haesler.

We also appreciate the support of Senia Maymin and Kathryn Britton, the co-editors of the *Positive Psychology News Daily*. All three of us write for the online publication, PositivePsychologyNews.com (PPND). Some of the ideas in this book were originally published as articles on PPND, where people commented on them and asked questions. To find the authors' articles and the discussions that ensued, check out the following Web sites. If you have questions, please post them in the comment space associated with the article.

- John Yeager: http://positivepsychologynews.com/news/john-yeager
- Sherri Fisher: http://positivepsychologynews.com/news/sherri-fisher
- Dave Shearon: http://positivepsychologynews.com/news/dave-shearon

John: Thanks to Robert Brooks, after whom I modeled my work ethic for the project after. And to my wife Laura and daughter Megan, who have been ever so patient over the past five years in the growth of Positive Education at Culver and the development of the book; and to the Culver students I have been associated with since 2000.

Sherri: Thanks to Isaac for his wisdom, love, and belief in me; Meg and Iain for providing fertile ground for sowing strengths; Beth, parent extraordinaire, for personifying the virtues of patience and love; Kristen, David, Ari, Greg, Jill, Lexi, Maria, Jake and thousands of other students for teaching me about strengths, resilience, and relationships before there was a positive psychology to put science to experience; Nancy for always being in the right place; and Culver Academies for so generously sharing its resources, personnel, and support.

Dave: My lovely and patient wife, Teresa, deserves a special thanks. It takes a special person to keep loving someone who's gone through as many re-creations of his life as I have. I also thank my two sons, Tyler and Patrick, who have shown wonderful grace and composure as Dad has worked his way through much thinking and talking about schools, education, and learning. Bill Robertson, who not only challenged us to think about positive psychology in organizations and leadership, also opened the door for me to some of my earliest work in the field of education as part of the Superintendents Study Councils of the Graduate School of Education at Penn. I also want to acknowledge the debt I owe Harris Sokoloff and Ashley Del Bianco who run the Superintendents Study Councils. Finally, I want to acknowledge the role that my friend Tom Ward has played in shaping my views and approach to education. I met Tom, an assistant principal in Metro Nashville Public Schools in the summer of 1979 and we've been friends and colleagues in a variety of endeavors ever since, including his work now with Vanderbilt University's Principals Leadership Academy of Nashville (PLAN).

We would like to acknowledge each other. We've worked together since MAPP and have found ways to blend our strengths even when our shared strengths have sometimes pulled us in slightly different directions. Without John's fairness, Sherri's kindness, and Dave's ideation, this book would not have happened.

Index